THE
TECHNOLOGY
REVOLUTION

The Not-For-Dummies Guide to the Impact, Perils, and Promise of the Internet

J. R. Okin

Ironbound Press
Winter Harbor, Maine

First Ironbound Press edition, 2005

Ironbound Press books may be purchased for educational, business, or sales promotional use. For information, please write: Special Markets Department, Ironbound Press, P.O. Box 250, Winter Harbor, ME 04693-0250

Cover image, *The Blue Marble: Earth's City Lights*, courtesy of NASA's Visible Earth, located at: http://visibleearth.nasa.gov/

Ironbound Press Web Site: http://www.IronboundPress.com
Ironbound Press email inquiries: info@IronboundPress.com

Printed and bound in the United States of America.
Printed on acid-free paper.

Library of Congress Control Number: 2005925937

ISBN 0-9763857-2-4 (cloth)
ISBN 0-9763857-1-6 (paper)

10 8 6 4 2 ∗ 1 3 5 7 9

To my brothers,
        Peter and Rick,
for always being there.

Other books available from Ironbound Press by J. R. Okin:

- The Internet Revolution: The Not-For-Dummies Guide to the History, Technology, and Use of the Internet

- The Information Revolution: The Not-For-Dummies Guide to the History, Technology, and Use of the World Wide Web

Foreword

Prior to the commercialization and privatization of the Internet in the early 1990s, the subject of technology, not unlike its use, was something that engaged and concerned a very small number of individuals and a relatively small number of businesses. Today, we are inundated with technology, and technology-based businesses can be found across the globe. Computers are in our homes, businesses, schools, libraries, and corner coffee shops, and many of us carry these devices with us wherever we go or rely on smaller networked devices, like cellular phones and personal digital assistants (PDAs), to keep us connected and reachable at all times. The businesses that manufacture these devices or provide related services and support range in size from startups that employ a couple of people to multi-national corporations that employ tens of thousands of people. The proliferation of these businesses and the proliferation of the high-tech devices that we use and see around us every day are a sign of the times. We are living in the midst of a technology revolution, and for better or worse it has only just begun.

How many of us have taken the time to consider what this revolution may mean for us, our children, our communities, and society in general? Using email and chat, listening to remote radio stations and downloading music, reading the news, sports scores, and comics on a Web portal, playing games with friends in virtual worlds, and buying products online are simple and innocuous activities, and millions of us routinely and eagerly engage in one or more of these activities on a regular, even daily basis. The technology of computers, computer networking, and the Internet empowers us through an ever-growing selection of new and engaging communication capabilities, a wealth of information resources far larger and more diverse than anything else ever created, and an entirely new way in which to interact with others, share information, form communities, and participate in the world around us. But this same technology has many other capabilities, too. These other capabilities are empowering to individuals and organizations that exploit them for their own purposes, and they do so at our expense and typically without our knowledge or consent.

Weighing the promise against the perils of the Internet's technology is no easy task. But our growing use of and reliance on the Internet in both our personal and professional lives demands that we gain some awareness of the risks inherent in its use. Failure to do so will only serve to further erode control over our privacy, put more of our information at risk, make our computers that much less secure, and put our children in greater danger of being exposed to unsuitable and inappropriate images, information, and people. Our reliance on the Internet and its technology also demands that we recognize its promise. We need to take the time to consider what these new capabilities mean to us as individuals and to an entire world of individuals interconnected by this technology.

As I wrote in the forewords to *The Internet Revolution* and *The Information Revolution*, my experiences with the Internet (and the Web) — as an ordinary user, as a systems engineer and developer, and as a dot com manager — and my fascination with the impact of the Internet and its technology inspired me to write a book about the Internet. My goal was to combine the story of the Internet's creation and development with an explanation of its technology that anyone could understand and an exploration of the Internet's impact on our lives, jobs, and community and social structures. After two years of research and writing, I created a book that presented all of these subjects and that was divided into three nearly equal parts.

I decided to publish each of the three parts as a separate book. This volume, which focuses on the impact of the Internet's and the Web's technology, is the third in the series. The first book, which focuses on the history and technology of the Internet, is entitled *The Internet Revolution*. The second book, which focuses on the history and technology of the Web, is entitled *The Information Revolution*.

In this book I examine several of the key consequences resulting from our remarkably fast and eager integration of the Internet and its technology into our lives. I present an overview of what was behind the dot com boom and bust (or bubble) that began in the late 1990s and ended in 2001. I describe the history and technology of Java and explain its role in the evolution of the Internet. I examine how information access on the Internet is impacting our privacy and how we may be able reclaim some control over our privacy and our personal correspondence. I explore why security is considered key to the Internet's future and the role that *trust* will play in delivery security. I explain how the Internet created the *digital divide*, describe what this divide looks like, and examine what it means. I also explore how the Internet is responsible for building new types of community structures, why these structures are so popular and empowering, and what they mean with respect to how we choose to interact with others and participate in the world around us. Finally, I explain why the Internet is so much more than the sum of its parts and why it is the revolution of our times.

I believe that each of the three books in the series can be read and understood (and, hopefully, enjoyed) independently of the other two. Together, the three books present a broad and thorough depiction of the revolution of our times, that began as a remarkable technological innovation but became — because of us — a force that has changed and is changing the way we work, play, ask questions, find answers, buy and sell products, communicate, and interact with others.

J. R. Okin
October, 2005

Acknowledgments

Writing is a solitary and sometimes lonely pursuit. But producing a book is a collective effort that owes its completion to many different types of contributions from a large number of individuals.

To my family, who, over the last three years, expressed support, urged me on, sheepishly asked how I was doing, and eventually were kind enough to stop inquiring about the book, I convey my thanks (for all of the above). More specifically, to my father, to Peter, Lisa, Daniel, and Stephen, to Rick, Thea, Sara, Emily, and Megan, thank you all for your patience and for the gentle nudges conveyed in words said, and left unsaid, to finish up the book and move on. I must convey a special thanks to Toni DeAngelis, whose nudges resemble kicks and whose words of encouragement often come in the form of marching orders, but whose caring and love are nonetheless transparent and are always overwhelming.

To my extended family in Maine, I owe a separate measure of thanks. The questions, kind words, and encouragement I received from Mary and Greg Domareki, their children, Sarah, Catherine, John, Greg, Luke, and Bridget, Sarah's husband, Mike Kazmierczak, and their son, Michael, and Greg's wife, Erin, and the rest of their large and loving family helped me in no uncertain terms to stay the course and find my way to the completion of this project.

To my friends, who answered questions, provided solicited (and unsolicited) advice, checked in on me, and reminded me again and again that there was an audience for the book, I am forever grateful. I owe thanks to Carol Schur, who was kind enough to read an early draft of the book and provide valuable feedback, to Ann Hagerman, who was always generous with her suggestions and opinions, to Barry Orr, who called and emailed and was never in short supply of humor or kind words, to Helene Armitage, who offered support, suggestions, and encouragement when I first started out, and, off an on, throughout the course of the project, and to Ellen Dreyer, who provided much needed information about the inner workings of the world of publishing along with some gentle words of encouragement.

Acknowledgments

To my editor and good friend, Bob Lippman, who never tired in his efforts to correct my mistakes, to question my arguments and conclusions, and to identify material that needed further explanation or that demanded simplification, I am in your debt. I could not have asked for a more skillful or thorough editing of the book; and, thanks to you, I now have a new appreciation for the meaning of the phrase, brutal honesty. I am grateful that you found the time to take on this project and I very much appreciate your commitment to seeing the work through to its conclusion. Whatever value or use this book may find, it was greatly enhanced by the time, effort, and skill you put into editing its contents.

Finally, to Mary, who kept me from giving up, who held my hand, who cajoled me, and who never wavered in believing in me, words are inadequate to express how I feel. I will have to work hard to find a way to repay you. But I will find a way.

Contents

Contents

Contents

Contents

The Technology Revolution

Ideas

Revolutions are the by-products of new ideas. New ideas in the fields of physics, theology, philosophy, politics, agriculture, sociology, and engineering incited revolutions that have transformed how we conceive of our place in the universe, how we regard our place in society, how we travel from location to location, how we grow food, how we manufacture goods, how we educate ourselves, how we communicate with others, how we wage war, and how we maintain the peace. Ideas that bring about revolutions are typically characterized as ones whose time has come. Ironically, it can take many years for a new idea to become sufficiently accepted and popularized before being recognized as one whose time has come.

Today's most widespread and far-reaching revolution is a technology revolution. Technology, in one form or another, has been around for a long time, and the word's definition has grown and its meaning to us has changed over the years. The word technology comes from the Greek word *technologia*, which is defined as the systematic treatment of an art. Common use of the word today includes the categorization of products, services, and methodologies into high technology (high tech), low technology (low tech), and no technology (no tech). When most of us interact with or talk about technology today, it's of the high-tech variety, which involves the use or production of computers or other sophisticated electronic devices. It is our use of these devices that is responsible for today's technology revolution.

Today's technology revolution, however, would have never happened were it not for the creation of the Internet. The Internet, which was a by-product of the technology race that followed the launching of the world's first satellite, Sputnik I, by the Soviet Union, provided the necessary catalyst — in the form of a computer network — to transform these high-tech devices from isolated productivity tools into communication nodes on the new electronic frontier called cyberspace. The technology revolution of the Internet derives from the simple and fundamental idea that computers and other electronic devices should be able to communicate with one another, share resources, and share information. And because the Internet is a global network, the technology revolution it incited is a global revolution.

The Internet's technology revolution is being delivered to us on computerized devices that can be commonly found in our homes and places of work, in our local libraries, schools, and community centers, in our cars, alongside highways, and at city intersections, and in our pockets, knapsacks, briefcases, and handbags. These devices take the form of microprocessor chips that are now integral to many of the products we buy, including such things as toys, appliances, and automobiles. They are, however, more immediately recognizable in the form of laptop and desktop personal computers, cellular telephones and personal digital assistants, and a wide variety of other networked computer devices that send, receive, and store information. These devices — and the Internet that interconnects them — are transforming how we communicate, how we share resources and information, how we work, how we play, how we educate ourselves and our children, how we form communities, and how we live our lives.

Impact, Perils, and Promise

The impact of the Internet is evident all around us. References to the Internet in the form of Internet addresses — like the devices we use to connect to the Internet — are difficult to avoid. Less obvious, but more profound changes can be discerned in the impact of the Internet's technology on our behavior, desires, and expectations. The Internet's impact can also be found in such things as the handling (and mishandling) of our personal information, the creation of new business enterprises known as dot coms, and the emergence of a new type of social division — named the digital divide — that distinguishes those who use the technology from those who do not.

The perils of using the Internet, like references to the Internet, are also difficult to avoid. These perils take many forms, such as the frequent security threats of computer viruses, worms, and trojan horses, the limited ability to protect information from theft and abuse, and exposure to undesirable and offensive information. Every individual and organization that uses the Internet is a potential target. These perils affect children and adults, novice and experienced users. They damage computer systems, destroy information, invade our privacy, and cost all of us a lot of money to remove, recover from, and defend against.

The promise of the Internet, unlike its perils, is different things to different people. How we use the Internet and the interest we take in its technology varies considerably from one individual to the next. The same is true of our expectations of what the technology can offer us and the extent of its impact on our lives. The promise of the Internet to any one individual will be affected by that individual's age, place of residence, employment, understanding of the technology, physical abilities or disabilities, and any number of other factors. For example, the availability of Internet access will mean something very different to someone with a physical disability that prohibits that person from leaving home than it will to someone capable of traveling to work, visiting a grocery story, and attending a meeting in person. The Internet's promise can be found in its amazing potential to empower the individual, which is why it will always be different things to different people.

This book explores the impact of the Internet's technology revolution, and it examines some of the perils introduced by our widespread acceptance of the Internet's technology and the promise that this technology holds for our future. The purpose of this book is not to provide comprehensive coverage of subjects related to our use of the Internet. Instead, its purpose is to introduce several select subjects that are most responsible for shaping the composition of today's Internet and, accordingly, may have the greatest bearing on how the Internet will change in the near future.

This book presents how the Internet's technology is being used and abused, where this technology may be heading, and what every Internet user should understand about what this technology can and cannot do. It is hoped that this book will prompt users of the Internet to pause and think about how they are using the technology in light of the risks to the privacy and security of their information. Another hope is that it will foster an appreciation for what this new technology is capable of creating for each of us and for the world in which we live.

Internet Privacy: Protected or Abandoned?

1

Privacy

Most of us don't think about our privacy while we are connected to the Internet. After all, the act of sitting at a desk in our home or in an office while staring into a computer screen is, more often than not, a solitary and private activity. Moreover, when you consider how we hide our identities behind screen names, user names, and email addresses, it is easy to understand why we feel safe, secure, and hidden from view. But no matter how hard we try to remain anonymous or to mask our identity, every time we venture onto the Internet we reveal some information about ourselves and we leave bread crumbs behind, revealing the path back to our location, without our being aware of it.

With respect to privacy — and associated issues like copyright protection and even free speech — it's clear that the Internet and its technology has outpaced both the law and the development of any behavioral expectations or ethical standards. How can we expect to keep our personal information under our control and private when the very definition of what constitutes our personal information is neither clear nor complete. The new technology has created new ways to collect, store, and share information about us; and, in the process, it has also created new types of personal information to collect. But who draws the line to separate private information from public information? Who determines, and how do they determine, what information belongs to us and what information belongs to them (e.g., Web site owners, Internet advertisers, and affiliate management organizations)? Who has the right to collect our personal information in the first place, and who gave them that right?

Even if we were able to get all of these questions answered to our satisfaction, we have to consider that the Internet is global. Every country has different laws and manifests different social expectations with respect to an individual's right to privacy and to the oftentimes related right of free speech. National borders are difficult to discern on the Internet, but they are always there, given that every computer, whether personal or part of a business, is connected to a local network inside one country or another. Today, the networks that interconnect to form the Internet neither recognize nor erect any standardized checkpoints along these borders that are designed to serve and protect the individual and his or her right to privacy. Instead, the Internet information guards that do exist, and which examine and control the flow of information between countries, serve the interests of the local governments, with no regard for the individual, his or her information, or any stated or implied privacy rights.

Some people put their trust in the law. No doubt we will see more and more laws, some comprehensive in nature, others targeted to specific technologies or specific actions, that will attempt to define what constitutes our personal information, what we can reasonably expect regarding the handling of that information, how we can retain control over it, and how adherence to the law will be enforced. Many laws already exist, but, so far, they raise more questions than they answer. Moreover, at best they exhibit an ignorance of the technology they are attempting to legislate or constrain, and at worst a blatant disregard for how that technology functions. More significantly, there seem to be as many laws trying to secure or defend the state's right to access and collect our personal information (under the assertion — or guise — of better protecting us) as there are laws trying to protect our right to privacy. The convergence of the legal system, the technology of the Internet, the interests of the state, and the interests of the individual is, simply put, a new frontier.

Other people put their trust in the technology. For them, the best means to retain control of our personal information and guard against its collection, use, and abuse by others is through the technology itself. Data encryption is one path that is being actively pursued. It promises to secure our data by rendering it unreadable and by protecting its contents behind an impenetrable lock; we control the key to that lock and hand it out only to those individuals and organizations we trust. However, secure data encryption will not appeal to law enforcement agencies and the government. They view our personal information and our right to privacy from a perspective unlike ours and unlike that of commercial organizations on the Internet. They view our behavior on the Internet, the information resources we access, and the information we communicate as if it were, or might be, connected to some criminal activity or terrorist act. For them, the privacy of the individual is of secondary importance compared to the security of the state, and the Internet carries a wealth of information that should be at their disposal. Data encryption and other comparable technologies that are capable of protecting our personal information pose a threat to their unconstrained use of that information, unless they were able to secure some sort of master key.

The following sections examine how privacy issues relate to specific activities (e.g., email or Internet shopping) and how technology can work both for and against us in our effort to retain control over our private lives. They also explore some of the different perspectives on privacy, such as those of business and the government, and some general issues related to Internet technology and privacy. The final section deals with the the abuse of the Internet to obliterate the notion of privacy, quickly, furiously, and irrevocably. An incident related to former U.S. president Bill Clinton provides a perfect example of such abuse.

Privacy and Internet Communication

You have just returned to your desk after a heated conversation with your boss. He said some things you didn't want to hear; and you said some things you had only ever said before in your daydreams. To calm yourself down, you decide to write an email to your sister. You let off some steam by describing what happened, using a few choice expletives that you somehow managed not to say directly to your boss. You send the email off and start to relax. You feel better, and you get back to work.

However, if you understood how easy (and how common) it is for emails to be read by people other than their intended recipients, you might never again send such a message. While it is true that, generally speaking, your emails will leave your computer and go coursing through the Internet to their intended destination without being copied, intercepted, or diverted, you should not count on this. If anything, you should recognize that the opposite is possible; anyone with the knowledge and opportunity (i.e., access to one of the computer systems involved with sending, forwarding, or receiving the message) may be reading your emails. Moreover, they can do so without your ever knowing that they have.

The technology makes the process of intercepting and copying email messages terribly easy. Not only that, there are tools specifically designed to help businesses configure their systems for just such a purpose. For example, businesses can choose to copy and archive all incoming and outgoing email, making it simple to later search messages for certain types of content or to more generally monitor business activities. They can also choose to target specific individuals, so that the message you just sent to your sister gets automatically copied to your boss at the same time (without your knowledge or consent). Additionally, any email can be intercepted at any point along its journey through the Internet. It might just be copied for storage and snooping. It could just as easily be altered and then allowed to continue on its way. The technology makes these things possible, and its use in this manner is rising.

An incident that occurred with email transmitted by the Web portal site Yahoo! illustrates the ease with which email content can be changed. Security concerns related to viruses and other malicious programs carried by email prompted Yahoo! to install content filtering that automatically and silently (i.e., without notification) changed certain words in email composed and sent on its service. Yahoo! was later forced to acknowledge that the word *eval* was being changed to *review* and the word *mocha* was being changed to *espresso*. The two words (i.e., eval and mocha) are keywords in the Javascript programming language that are known to have been used on occasion in the creation of malicious programs. There are, however, better ways to prevent such abuses, ways that do not involve changing email messages without their senders' knowledge. What this simple, rather innocuous incident demonstrates is how easily the technology can be employed to violate our privacy. We are, in many respects, at the mercy of what the technology allows, despite any implied, stated, or perceived understanding regarding our right to privacy. The technology can also be employed to protect our personal information. But, in the end, what the technology makes possible, people will find a way to use (and abuse), and we must keep this in mind as we use the Internet, especially when we feel compelled to send an email describing our boss in unflattering language or, more generally, to communicate any thoughts or feelings that might be best kept private.

This example also raises questions about which words will be targeted next and why, and who is responsible when a filter (such as the one used by Yahoo!) or other intervening program alters the meaning of an email message and unexpected and undesirable consequences ensue? Imagine emailing a cover letter along with your resume in response to a job posting and having some intervening program mangle one or more words, making it look like you haven't even taken the time to proofread your letter. It is highly unlikely you would ever discover that your application had been immediately rejected for this reason. But if you did find out what happened, could you hold Yahoo! or some other Internet service provider accountable? Do you have any rights, stated or implied, with respect to the privacy and security of your personal information? Do these rights include knowing what service providers are doing to and with your personal information? If you knew, for instance, that your email might be changed by Yahoo!'s filters, you might well choose to take your business elsewhere, to a business that protected your privacy rather than casually sacrificing it for some small measure of additional security.

The privacy statements found on most Web sites and that are routinely included as small-print pamphlets accompanying our credit card statements, banking statements, and bills are the corporate response to the growing number of questions and ambiguities regarding your right to privacy and the handling of your personal information. Privacy statements detail how a company treats your information. Your employment contract probably includes or references a privacy document that defines the company's policy and practices regarding information stored or transmitted on its computers and network. If you have Internet access from your home, your ISP likely has a similar document that defines its policy and any protections afforded to you with respect to the information you send and receive across its computers and network.

But privacy statements can only speak to intent and agreed-upon behavior. They cannot change how the technology works or reduce the inherent vulnerability of the information contained in your email. They also cannot speak to what happens to your message once it leaves their domain, as it eventually must. Moreover, numerous lawsuits have proven that email sent or received at work becomes the property of the business. In effect, this means that you cannot expect that email sent or received at work will be treated as private. Do not be lulled by the technology into thinking otherwise. There is absolutely no way for you to know who else may be reading the messages you receive at work, and the same is true for those you send. Even messages you receive and immediately delete may not be truly deleted; many organizations archive all incoming email. They may contain your words and the subject matter may be very personal, but it is their equipment and their network. In the near future, with the general adoption of encryption technology, options to protect the privacy of your personal information (even in the workplace) may become available. But no technology is tamperproof.

Incidentally, if for some reason you really must send and receive personal email while at work (as most of us must), register for one of the free, Web-based email services and use that account for your personal exchanges. Because the service is Web-based, no email messages will be transmitted across the computers in your business environment; you view their content through a Web browser, but the email files and the email traffic remains on the Web service's computer systems. The Web pages could still be cached locally (i.e., stored on the computers at work), but overall it is a safer, smarter approach to retaining some privacy while at work.

Unsolicited Email

Related to the issue of email privacy is the unsolicited, junk mail — known as spam — that we all receive. Unsolicited, mass emailings cost the sender next to nothing to produce and distribute. But they consume a considerable amount of bandwidth on the Internet and clutter the email boxes of millions of recipients. Moreover, while most mass emailings promote legitimate business interests, a sizable and growing number instead promote fraudulent business practices. Unfortunately, the problem of spam is related to the controversy surrounding the question of how to keep the Internet free, unrestricted, and unregulated and still make it possible to effect positive change and prohibit abusive and outright illegal behavior, a controversy that is still far from being resolved. Will legislation be adopted — within individual companies or internationally — that will limit, control, tax, or even prohibit specific activities on the Internet, such as spam? Who will make the determination about which activities are acceptable and which are not? Who will draw the digital lines in the ether of the network? There are as yet no answers to these questions.

From the perspective of the technology, once your email address is "out there," it will eventually fall into the hands of either those who are directly involved in distributing unsolicited email messages or those who create email lists and resell them. It's difficult, perhaps even impossible, to keep your email address utterly private. On the other hand, email programs now include features that can be configured to filter or reject unsolicited emails. These features can evaluate the sender's address against a list of known addresses and search for specific words or phrases in the message's body or subject line to determine whether or not to delete an email automatically or move it immediately from the inbox and into another folder. But nothing will work 100% of the time. Whatever you do, do not fall for the ploy used by many spammers (i.e., organizations that create and distribute spam) in which they include a link in their message that you can click on to remove yourself from their mailing list. Clicking on that link will only serve to confirm to the spammer that you exist and that you use the email address to which the mail has been sent.

Internet Chatting

Email is not the only form of Internet communication that suffers from privacy violations. Nor is it alone in raising many unanswered questions regarding the privacy policies and practices of service providers on the Internet. Internet chat, like email, was not engineered with privacy considerations (or any requirements regarding privacy) in mind; and, like our use of email, our use of chat — especially in one of its most popular forms as a one-on-one communication tool — presents a false sense of security regarding the privacy of the thoughts and feeling we express. The messages that quickly scroll by in a chat room window may seem fleeting and lacking in permanence, but they are not; and they may be intended only for the other person or persons present in the chat room, but they are accessible to others.

All chat exchanges can be configured to record their events (i.e., the comings and goings of participants and all the messages exchanged). The events are stored in log files on one or more chat servers. While there may or may not be a straight, solid line connecting you to a certain conversation and to a certain screen name used in that conversation, the technology does link the specific identities used in chat conversations to specific IP addresses, for example, the IP address of your computer. Your screen name may conceal your identity from others, but it will not conceal it from the technology. The screen names you use, the chat rooms you visit, even the newsgroups you frequent, are recorded on the computers you use at home and at the office. Your privacy with respect to your communication over the Internet is more imagined than real.

Privacy and the World Wide Web

When you examine the Web from the perspective of your privacy the use, reuse, and abuse of your personal information quickly take on broader and potentially far more damaging implications. The Web diminishes our ability to maintain our privacy in two ways. The first involves the information we readily volunteer. For example, the name and address we type into a Web form when buying a book or purchasing an airline ticket online is information that we relinquish control over once we submit the form. The Web server accepting the information may (and should) be using a secure protocol (e.g., HTTPS) to protect the security of that information while it is being transmitted from your computer to theirs. Once received, however, the Web server stores your personal information on its computer, inserts it into a database for storage with the same type of information collected from other individuals, and copies it to other computers as needed. You no longer control who else may see the information or how it may be shared. Computers, the Web, and the Internet were engineered for the purpose of sharing information. Once we (or others) put some information onto the Internet, there is no means to take it back, as the section below on President Clinton and the Starr Report clearly demonstrates. It is alarming how much of our personal information — volunteered by us or by others — is available over the Web. Do a search on yourself or someone you are familiar with; you may be surprised by what you discover.

The second way in which the Web diminishes control over our privacy involves the information we unwittingly relinquish as we routinely surf the Web and use its resources to locate information, buy products, and interact with others. This information is a by-product of our use of the Web; it is also a commodity that is collected, studied, sold, and resold, comprising information about our behavior, likes, and dislikes. It results from any number of different activities, among them viewing a Web page, clicking on a banner advertisement, and reading a Web-based email message. We have virtually no control over the collection of such information. Yet its collection and subsequent use constitute clear and gross invasions of our right to privacy. The only reason (that makes sense) that this collection of our personal information is tolerated is that few people realize it is happening and still fewer people have considered its long-term consequences. The legal system has yet to produce any legislation to limit or prevent the unauthorized and covert collection of our information. Nor has any technology emerged that will make us the ultimate arbiter regarding the safekeeping of our personal information by sensing any attempts to collect information about us, alerting us, and allowing us to make a conscious and informed decision whether to release the requested information or deny its release.

Using the Web requires you to relinquish some control over your privacy. Your best defense may be your awareness of this fact. Whether you charge the purchase of a book in person at a bookstore, or over the phone, or through a Web site, you are providing the same basic personal information to the bookseller. What does it matter if that information is provided through the swiping of your credit card, your statements over the phone, or the boxes and buttons on a Web form. Regardless of how it is provided, the information ends up in a database on one of the bookseller's computers.

Once merchants obtain such information, you have no choice but to rely on the policies — stated or otherwise — and the procedures they have in place to protect your personal information. A new type of business venture on the Web consists of organizations that inspect a company's Web site and information infrastructure to validate its practices against some type of industry standard for the protection of personal information. Merchants, and other types of Web businesses, that submit themselves to this type of third-party examination may then be eligible to display a seal of approval with respect to their trustworthiness and the safeguards they have employed to protect an individual's right to privacy. These seals, combined with ratings by individuals, should better enable us to discern which merchants care as much about our privacy as we do. The only other way you can hope to retain control over your privacy in the area of commerce is to pay for everything in person and in cash (and carry the merchandise home yourself).

Many Web sites expend a lot of time and resources trying to convince you to become a member. Depending on the type of site — a Web portal, an informational site, a merchant or Web mall — it will dazzle you with all sorts of free services, price savings, coupons, and other incentives, all to entice you to fill out a form and join. Although they don't normally advertise this, these sites are, in effect, offering you a trade. They are swapping services for your personal information, which they may then choose to resell, or to include as part of the demographic information they supply to advertisers or use for any number of other purposes. The only information you enter that can be easily verified is your email address, leaving you free to falsify other information. But your email address alone is worth some money on the Web. Moreover, each time you elect to join a site, you lose a little more control over your personal information and your privacy. This is something you should consider the next time you are asked to fill out a membership form. If you're not convinced that your personal information is a highly prized and frequently traded commodity on the Web, enter some information incorrectly on a Web form (e.g., misspell your first name), and then wait to see what information comes your way with that same error.

There is also a tradeoff with respect to your privacy in using many of the information services found on the Web. Web portals, for instance, often include simple and attractive tools for tracking stock portfolios, paying bills, and building personal calendars to track all the various events in your life. These Web services rely on storing this personal information on their computers. So, when you enter information about the 250 shares of IBM you bought at $50 per share, or the check for $100 to your aroma therapy counselor, or party information for your son's birthday in July, this information goes into some company's database. What more may be done with that information, and who else may be accessing it, is impossible to say. Is the information accessible by employees in that company? At the very least, the database specialists must have access to it. Is the information being resold? Is it being pooled with information from others for more general, aggregate-based demographic purposes? Just because you must pass through some semblance of security by presenting a login and password, don't assume that your information is private and secure.

When it comes to the personal information you volunteer, remain guarded about the type of information you provide and, if possible, make sure you recognize the organization to which you are supplying the information. It's one thing to fill out a survey regarding your favorite food. It's another thing altogether to enter potentially more damaging information, like your phone or social security number. Even companies with the best intentions can't absolutely guarantee the privacy of this information. Our digital, networked information age couples greater access to information with greater vulnerability of information to theft and abuse.

You may be willing to accept the privacy tradeoffs with respect to the information you volunteer. But how do you feel about the personal information that is taken from you without your knowledge or consent? The information collected by Web sites, affiliate management organizations, and others through banner advertisements, Web beacons (or Web bugs), spyware utilities, and other means constitutes what most people would consider the greatest invasion of their privacy. Some of this information is innocent enough and assists Web site owners in understanding the traffic patterns on their sites in order to provide better service or prevent or remedy problems. But a large and growing percentage of this information is of no benefit to you, and what is most worrisome is the potential abuse of such information, especially when it's collected into large databases for data mining operations.

Data mining operations will use our personal information in ways that most of us cannot imagine and far beyond its typical application today in creating junk mail campaigns, targeting advertising to audiences predisposed to the product or service being marketed, or tailoring Web site material to each of its visitors. Insurance companies could theoretically tap into such data warehouses to help make a determination about awarding or denying you coverage. You might, for instance, purchase medication for high blood pressure on the Web for your mother; but that information is now linked to you and could, without your ever being aware of it, be taken into consideration when you apply for health or life insurance, or even for employment.

A solution to protecting the privacy of individuals as they use the Web is going to be difficult to find and perhaps impossible to implement and enforce. It's easy to understand how such privacy issues arose, given the nature and history of the technology. The Web was built on the sharing of information, rapidly, freely, and with few limitations. But as usage of the Web grew, and information contained in log files accumulated, it didn't take long for some to see this captured information as a resource in and of itself. As features were added to the Web to expand its potential, particularly with respect to commercial applications, the Web's capacity for tracking information expanded as well. Cookies surreptitiously found their way onto our computers to compensate for the stateless nature of the Web's fundamental protocol, HTTP (i.e., HTTP's inability to record any connections between the pages viewed by a user's visit to a Web site). Our clicks from page to page could now be viewed as a stream of clicks that told a story about our surfing behavior. Meanwhile, hidden Web beacons captured more information about our movements across the Web, further refining this picture of our behavior. The data was there, growing ever larger. Exploiting this data, at the expense of our privacy, was only a matter of time and effort.

It seems unlikely that there's any way to stop this train or to put it into reverse. The debate now centers on what can be done to control its impact. Some think that legislation will fix the problem; but it's already a little late in coming and any legislation is going to be difficult to enforce. Nevertheless, a few laws have already been introduced and are making some progress, especially where children are concerned. For instance, several companies that collected personal information from minors without their parent's consent were recently fined for violating the Children's Online Privacy Protection Act (COPPA). Others think self-regulation by the industry will solve the problem. Stronger privacy policies combined with watchdog organizations should help reduce the overall risk. But only time will tell.

Privacy Policies

The first few years of the Web might be considered its wild, wild West period. Legislation and monitoring were non-existent. There were few, if any, oversight organizations. Everyone essentially made up their own rules as the technology and business opportunities evolved. Eventually, privacy issues started to surface and their continued discussion and debate brought about privacy policy statements consisting of a few paragraphs to a few pages of information describing a company's concern and respect for your privacy. At first these statements appeared only on larger, better known Web sites. But over time they became commonplace. Now, nearly every Web site has a link on their homepage, or on every page, to their privacy policy.

If you're still unsure about whether or not your privacy should be a concern while you navigate the Web, visit one of the major portal sites like Yahoo!, Netscape, or Microsoft, and read through their privacy policy information. The majority of this information is less about your privacy than it is about how they collect information from you and about you, what information they collect, how they store this information, how they use it, and who they share it with. The policy statements are all about how they treat your personal information, and they make only passing mention of your privacy. In many respects, the notion of privacy actually seems alien to these policy statements. Read one for yourself.

Privacy policies are great for the legal system; they define what a business is doing with your information. Theoretically, the business can be held accountable if they violate their own policies or those set out in existing legislation. But, realistically, such policies don't help you much. How many have you read? Are you going to read the privacy policy of every Web site you visit? How do you read about their policies *before* you visit their site, so that you can make a determination before your personal information is collected? What happens when they change their policies, as they often do? Privacy policies are certainly a step in the right direction, but they represent a small step at best.

Privacy Preferences

Not surprisingly, the World Wide Web Consortium (W3C) and Tim Berners-Lee (the inventor of the Web) look to technology for at least part of the solution to the issue of online privacy. They are actively developing something called P3P, the Platform for Privacy Preferences Project. P3P is an intriguing specification that describes technology that will allow you to specify your own privacy settings, effectively controlling the information you are willing to share, and allowing this information and a Web site's privacy policy to be automatically exchanged and negotiated. This would theoretically turn a Web site's privacy policy into something more tangible and allow for a free exchange of personal information at a level dictated by you.

The idea of turning privacy statements and the issue of privacy into something more generally quantifiable is in itself an inventive concept that promises to bring more measurable control into the whole area of privacy. It introduces privacy to the domain of the computer, taking many aspects of privacy and the collection of personal information out of the shadows and placing them in the light of day. Its acceptance and integration across the Web would introduce a level of accountability that is currently lacking. It would also foster the creation of new tools that could transform privacy on the Web from something we reluctantly relinquish into a something that could be measured for improved and safer browsing.

Computer Records, the Internet, and You

There seems to be no end to the number of Web sites solely in the business of performing background checks. For fees that range from $20 to well over $100 these businesses will search a wide variety of databases looking for records connected to you, a potential employee, a tenant, your child's nanny, perhaps your daughter's fiancé, or your father's perky (or not so perky) new girlfriend. They can check for a criminal history, financial troubles or general credit information, property ownership, civil judgments, and more. There was never a shortage of publicly available information recorded and stored by our local, state, and federal governments. But the Internet has eliminated many of the boundaries, difficulties, time constraints, and costs related to accessing those records.

There are many benefits to simplifying access to such information, just as there are many legitimate reasons for paying for such services. Perhaps you just want to track down an old high school friend. Or you want to see if the contractor you are about to hire to remodel your house has any judgments against him for shoddy workmanship or incomplete jobs. Or you might want to conduct a search on yourself, to see exactly what information exists and to verify its contents. The information you can access is empowering. It can enable you to make better, safer decisions. You don't have to trust as much in what you are told. Now you have a way to double check information in order to protect yourself, your family, your business. But what if the information you receive has mistaken one person for another, or it's out of date, or it contains errors. You would be able to catch these mistakes with your own information, but not with anyone else's.

Then factor in the whole notion of privacy with respect to these records and their new, online access. The nature of public records being open and available to the public is one thing; and it's something that hasn't effectively changed. But computers and the Internet have transformed the relevance and potential abuse of this information by greatly simplifying its availability. We no longer need to walk into a town's hall of records to request and locate information. Now we only need to fill out a form on the Web from across town, across the state, across the country, or from the far side of the globe. There is currently no notion of access to information being too easy, and what this might mean to all of us. No doubt there are people who will abuse this access, using this public information against an individual for personal or professional gain. Others might gather this information in an attempt to steal someone else's identity. Then there's always the government to consider. Their intentions are not always above reproach. Neither is their information error free. Mistakes will be made; records will be wrong.

Maybe a combination of technology and new laws will address and rectify the problem. What if, for instance, we were notified whenever a search was done on our information and we were automatically sent a copy of the search results? From the standpoint of the technology, this would be relatively simple. We could then more easily dispute, and hopefully resolve, errors. We could also then retain some sense of control over information that is, after all, essentially ours. Sometimes even a simple change such as this can help restore control to a situation that has the potential for misuse and serious damage.

Privacy in the Office

The advances in computers, networks, and more generally in the wired world of electronic devices, have given new meaning and scope to the place of surveillance in our daily lives. Nowhere is this more apparent than at the office. We understandably lower our expectations regarding privacy when we enter any business environment, but you should know that monitoring employee behavior at many corporations has been steadily rising. The following are typical areas for which surveillance is routinely performed.

- Monitoring Internet connections, including Web sites accessed and Internet chatting.

- Storing and examining email messages, sent and received.

- Recording and examining telephone conversations, including voice mail.

- Examining telephone logs to determine how telephone access is being used.

- Copying and examining computer files.

- Examining computer log files to determine how computer access is being used.

- Video recording of offices and common areas.

We can't expect the kind of privacy we enjoy at home to be available in a public or business environment. But it seems that the enabling of so many different types of surveillance brought about by the advances in technology, along with technology's increased integration into our lives, has taken us to the other extreme. Limited privacy has become, or is closely bordering on, zero privacy; and any semblance of trust has been denigrated to the point that we are considered guilty while we wait on log files and other records to manifest our innocence, if in fact they can.

It's unpleasant to consider that the very technology that promises to empower us with rich, new information resources and simpler, faster, more effective ways to communicate, and that enables us to share our ideas and dreams, might be the same technology used to indict and imprison us, to restrict our movements and control our behavior, or simply to make us paranoid. The technology to build the Big Brother of Orwell's "1984" is with us now; and it's seeping more and more into our personal and professional lives. The greatest dangers with the collection of all this information rest with the simple and obvious perils connected to its interpretation. It's not difficult to falsify records, providing malicious individuals yet another means to harm others. It's not difficult to misread information, mistake one person's identity for another, erroneously connecting one innocuous event with another innocuous event and in turn recognizing some evidence of wrongful behavior that just doesn't exist. But the information is there, waiting.

The Government and Our Privacy

The fight is on, there's no doubt about it. In the U.S., Canada, the European Union, and elsewhere throughout the world, governments are actively and heatedly debating the growing concern over the individual's right to privacy, the ever growing number of data records collected by business and our governments, the inherent vulnerability of that information, the technologies and businesses that provide access, and the law. Fortunately, there are clear and numerous examples of government agencies and individuals promoting laws to protect the privacy of the citizenry, much as the business community is advocating and promoting its own privacy measures. Meanwhile, others seek to exploit the technology in the name of better government, safer communities, and necessary anti-terrorism efforts. A few of the more prominent examples are provided below.

Information Awareness and the U.S. Citizen

The Total Information Awareness Initiative (TIA) under President Bush promotes the use of data mining technology for the express purpose of electronically tracking and monitoring the lives of Americans. The TIA expects access to credit card records, as well as records related to health and travel expenses, Internet access log files and book loans from public libraries, and much more, in an effort to build better tools for anti-terrorism activities. The stated goal of the TIA is the creation of "revolutionary technology for ultra-large all-source information repositories" in order to build a "virtual, centralized, grand database." Their expectation is to recognize the "information signature" of individuals in order to track potential terrorists and criminals. But you have to track everyone in order to find who you're looking for.

The organization, incidentally, was formed under DARPA, the agency that brought us the Internet.

Civil rights organizations and others argue that the potential for abuse of such information far outweighs the possible gains. Meanwhile, some members of Congress are voicing their own concerns. One effort to reign in control on the TIA is the Data Mining Moratorium Act introduced by Senator Feingold. It proposes to limit the use of such technology without concrete protections for civil liberties. Others, including computer scientists and information technology specialists within and outside the government, are questioning the technical feasibility of the TIA.

In January, 2003 the U.S. Senate requested unanimously for development of the TIA to be suspended until privacy concerns could be adequately addressed. It's highly unlikely that this will be the end of the story. The controversy, even inside the corridors of the government, clearly illustrates the importance of the issue and the widely divergent perspectives relating to it.[1]

Electronic Surveillance in the European Union

In March, 2003 thirty-eight members of the European Parliament signed an open letter to the European Council declaring their opposition to data gathering and retention proposals, not unlike those sought by the TIA, relating to citizens of the European Union. These EU guidelines were designed to expand the electronic surveillance of its citizens by mandating that telephone and Internet companies retain their data records in storage for at least twelve to twenty-four months. Collected information would include phone calls, credit card statements, emails, Internet usage, and more. Law enforcement agencies would then have access to these records for any number of unspecified uses.

A similar effort in the United Kingdom by Members of Parliament and members of the House of Lords sought the elimination of data retention legislation there. Their reasons include excessive costs, lack of industry support, basic concerns regarding the practicality of retaining such large amounts of data, and fears that the whole effort may be fundamentally unlawful from the perspective of individual rights and privacy.[2]

These efforts reinforce the global nature of this controversy. They give rise to the following basic questions: who will control all the various types of information collected about us; for what purposes will this information be employed; and under what conditions, and with what measure of accountability, will this information be used?

Microsoft Technology and the Rights of Individuals

Microsoft's .NET Passport technology, which gathers and retains personal information that can be automatically shared among conforming Web sites, ran afoul of privacy advocates in the European Commission. A Passport account allows individuals to record their personal information with Microsoft so that they don't have to repeatedly enter this information on each Web site they visit. This information typically includes name, address, phone numbers, credit card information, and login information. Concern was voiced over inadequate explanations on how the technology worked and inherent difficulties in terminating an account. General security concerns were also raised about this sort of technology, in which a single source, or a single company, records, maintains, and shares so much personal information.

Accordingly, Microsoft was forced to make radical changes to the technology. These changes, however, only apply to Web users identifying themselves as residing in the European Union. One change meant that the specifics of the Passport system will be explained more fully to those users. Another change enables users to acquire more control over the type and amount of personal data collected and stored by Microsoft. With respect to Passport accounts in the U.S., Microsoft agreed to comply with a request from the Federal Trade Commission to allow another company to perform security audits of the system.[3]

In this instance, it's a matter of how technology designed to reduce the redundant requests for personal information became a source for the vulnerability of that private information. The government can, as shown here, legislate changes after problems arise. But it's clear that even technology from the largest corporations, created with the best intentions, are still not up to the task of protecting our privacy to the degree that most of us would consider acceptable.

Private Data That Walks

A different sort of privacy issue involved the loss and subsequent recovery of a hard drive in Canada that contained the confidential information of some one million people. The drive went missing from ISM Canada, a national computer and data management company that provides services to Canadian government agencies as well as commercial organizations. Information on the drive included sensitive government employee data, data on client accounts for a mutual fund, and tax records for more than 40,000 businesses in Manitoba. Fortunately, this was not apparently a case of someone stealing the hard drive for the data it contained, since they discovered that the original data had been overwritten by other programs when they recovered the drive. However, a class action suit was filed on the day the drive was recovered on behalf of the people whose records were on the drive.[4]

This event illustrates the very basic vulnerability of such massive amounts of private information. Sometimes all it takes is the physical removal of a small piece of hardware, something the size of an address book, to put the privacy of hundreds of thousands of people in jeopardy.

Privacy Versus Copyright Infringement and Beyond

In January 2003, a U.S. Federal court ruled on a privacy issue between the Recording Industry Association of America (RIAA), a trade group for some of the best known recording labels in music, and Verizon, a large telecommunications company that provides Internet access. Verizon refused to identify one of its Internet subscribers that the RIAA accused of illegally offering more than 600 songs for download through that individual's computer. The judge ruled that the subpoenas issued to obtain the identity were enforceable under the Digital Millennium Copyright Act (DMCA) that protects intellectual property rights. But Verizon has appealed the decision.

Privacy rights groups, along with Verizon, are concerned with the larger privacy issue that's at stake: who is able to request information about anonymous Web users and for what purposes. The DMCA does not require a judge's order to issue such a subpoena, establishing a significantly lower standard of proof to force the release of such personal and confidential information. In another such instance, AOL Time Warner acquired this same sort of information from a different ISP in order to identify someone they thought was infringing on one of their copyrights. This resulted in their sending a warning letter to a young girl whose computer contained a file named "Harry Potter." Her file was apparently a book report for a school assignment.[5]

These incidents present yet more evidence of how seemingly innocuous information about our use of the Internet and the Web can be made available to others without our knowledge or consent, and can be used against us. They raise serious questions about policing the Internet, especially given the clear existence of illegal and wrongful behavior and activities that occur each and every day on the Internet. But who will do this policing, how will they conduct their surveillance, and at what and whose expense?

Privacy Issues in the News

The following list is a sample of news stories on privacy issues dating from March, 2003. The sheer number and remarkable variety of these incidents (then and today) make clear the seriousness of the problem in protecting the privacy of our information.

- The online records for more than 55,000 students and faculty were stolen from insecure database servers at the University of Texas at Austin.

- Monster.com, a large job placement site, warned its members that fake job listings were being used to steal personal information from unsuspecting applicants.

- The process of stealing free access to a network, and even the Internet, by locating wireless networking signals and tapping into the open frequency is becoming so popular it now has a name. It's called *war chalking*, in reference to chalk marks left behind on a street corner where open wireless access has been located. These wireless intruders are not only stealing access, they are potentially stealing files and other information left exposed on the wireless network.

- According to a survey by the American Management Association, more than 75% of large corporations in the U.S. monitor, record, and analyze employee communications and other job-related, electronic activities. This is double the rate of just six years earlier.

- Mrs. Fields, a Utah-based cookie maker, terminated its popular online cookie club for kids after complaints about how it collected information from under-age applicants to the club.

- Google.com, a major search engine site, was accused of using its free Google Toolbar to track more information than most users were aware of about the types of searches an individual performs, to the extreme of being able to retain a list of every site a person visits.

- The American Civil Liberties Union (ACLU), an activist group concerned with promoting better privacy, inadvertently exposed a large list of individuals' names and email addresses when it emailed one of its newsletters. Such information is normally kept hidden and protected. (This is a good example of how the technology can work against and confound even those people with the best intentions.)

- Online florist, FTD.com, confirmed that a security hole allowed customer billing records with names, addresses, and phone numbers to be accessed by any number of individuals through its Web site.

■ A patch was released for version 7.0 of the Opera Web browser that fixed several severe security flaws, including one that allowed Web sites to read files and gather usernames and passwords from a user's PC.

President Clinton and the Starr Report

On September 10th, 1998, Independent Counsel Kenneth Starr finally issued his report on U.S. President William Clinton, concluding his four year exploration into the President's Whitewater land deals with an explicit account of the President's relationship with Monica Lewinsky and the alleged efforts to cover up this relationship. As required by the Independent Counsel Law, the report was delivered to the House of Representatives, which voted, within twenty-four hours, to release all 445 pages of the main document to the public. One of the ways they chose to release the document was through the Internet.

Putting aside the questionable politics behind the report's creation and release, and putting aside the questionable behavior described in the report, what you're left with are the ramifications of the report's release. Word spread quickly across the Internet about the accessibility of the report. Bandwidth was quickly exceeded as Web servers that housed the report struggled to keep up with requests. Surveys conducted at the time indicated that some 20 million people went online to access the report within the first two to three days of its release. Few people, however, were interested in reading the entire report. The majority only wanted to locate and read the details regarding the ten sexual encounters, descriptions that under any other circumstances most people, including those honorable members of the House of Representatives, would consider pornographic.

The report's release on the Internet, therefore, raises two fundamental questions. Does the technology of the Internet demand that we change, and perhaps even relinquish, our expectations for privacy? How can we protect our children from accessing unsuitable material when such material may easily be found even on government sites? The issue of information access and the fact that everything isn't for everyone is discussed in another chapter. That issue at least may be solvable. What the Starr Report and its release illustrates, however, is that the issue of privacy in our Internet-driven information age may be a lost cause.

The global, decentralized, open nature of the Internet dictates that once information is made available, once it's published on the Internet, it may be impossible to ever fully protect. The situation is no different than that of a scientific discovery. Once that new knowledge exists, once the bottle is open and that genie is let out, there's no way to reverse or undo the effect. It's there forever. Unlike previous publication environments where you could stop the presses, recall books, or at the very least greatly limit their reach and exposure, information on the Internet can travel at the speed of light; and the technology doesn't simply display information, it functions by copying data from location to location to location. We don't travel the Internet, information does. In a matter of hours the Starr Report, or at least pieces of it, went from residing on a few government Web servers to taking up space on hundreds of thousands of computers all across the globe. You can't undo that kind of effect, even though many House members who voted for the report's release regretted their decision only twenty-four hours later.

The fact that Clinton was a public figure and should, according to an earlier U.S. President, Thomas Jefferson, therefore consider himself "public property," is sufficient justification to many for removing any privacy considerations in releasing the Starr Report and other information regarding the more private side of Clinton's life. This precedent doesn't bode well for other public figures, especially current and future politicians. But the more significant question is what does it mean for us. If no aspect of the life of one of the world's most powerful individuals can be considered private, or be kept private, what hope can we have for privacy now that the technology exists for anyone and everyone to broadcast and access any and all types of information?

It appears that the very definition of privacy has been slowly but surely eroded just as the technology to free information from the confines of paper and locked file cabinets has evolved into today's digital revolution and the global information space of the World Wide Web. This has obvious implications, as in the world of politics, but it's the subtle implications that are only now being recognized and scrutinized. Consider the medical information stored by your physician or the financial records stored by your bank. Technology has changed the way all that very private information is recorded and maintained. That data now resides on computers, which immediately makes such information more accessible to more people. Add these computers onto a network, as most already have and the others eventually will, and access to your information grows exponentially.

Sure, there are security measures in place to offer some protection against unwanted access and abuse. But thinking about security is not the same as considering your privacy. Who is consulting you about your particular wants and needs for the privacy of your information? Who is making decisions about the release and sharing of your information? Have you ever filled out a form with your doctor or your bank about the types of information they collect, and who can and who cannot have access? Will we ever be presented with such choices? Moreover, if we are, who will enforce them, and how? It's your information. But the question remains: is it yours to control?

Internet Security: To Trust or Not To Trust

2

Security

Security on the Internet — and discourse on the subject — arrived late. Deficiencies in security became harder and harder to avoid as more people started to use the Internet and as more information started to travel across its network of computers. The minimal (and, in places, marginal) security protections that existed on the Internet (for both people and their information) came under increasing scrutiny as the Internet evolved from an academic playground into a commercial marketplace. Slowly, but surely, it became apparent to those in the business of providing Internet products and services, as well as to more and more everyday users of the Internet, that these protections were far from adequate.

The news media routinely reports on security threats and violations that take place on the Internet. The most common stories describe the latest incident of an Internet-borne virus infecting millions of computers across the globe. Such viruses are typically delivered through email. The virus hides within a file attached to an email message, and when recipients of the email open the attachment, they unknowingly unleash the virus onto their computers. News reports convey some sense of the damages caused by this one type of security violation and of the costs to businesses and other organizations associated with repairing the infected computers and restoring the lost or corrupted data. One thing these stories fail to capture, however, is how disruptive, frustrating, and costly these viruses are to the unfortunate individuals who are the victims of such attacks — individuals who rely on the Internet for their work, for the pursuit of an avocation or hobby, for recreation or entertainment, or for communication with friends and family members.

Unless you have experienced the shock and dismay of turning on an infected computer only to discover that the system no longer functions or that days or weeks of work have been lost or destroyed, it's hard to appreciate the feelings of helplessness and anger that these breaches of security and trust engender. The vast majority of Internet users are unaware of the number and variety of dangers that await them on the Internet. They log on believing that the technology that enables them to do so much — to chat with friends, play games, buy and sell stocks, and send and receive email — must also be protecting them from malicious acts, keeping their personal information safe, and ensuring their privacy. There is, however, a disturbing disparity between the perceived level of security on the Internet and the reality of that security.

The debate over how to provide some fundamental measure of security — or even what constitutes a fundamental measure of security — for individuals, organizations, and their information is ongoing, as is the debate over how and where to integrate security into the Internet's technology. Security, on the Internet and off, must provide for a wide range of functions and services in order to meet the needs of an ever growing number of Internet users and an ever expanding number of purposes for which the Internet is being used. One function of security, for example, is to control and manage access to all of our accumulating online personal information. This means providing a secure way to grant access to that information to those who should have access and to deny access to all others. Another function of security is to control and manage access to our computer. This means protecting the resources of our computer and the information stored locally on our computer, while we are connected to the Internet and even after we have logged off. Because security is (in part) responsible for defining and restricting information access, security is directly connected to our privacy on the Internet.

Our security on the Internet is also directly connected to how, when, and where we extend our trust. This means knowing that the email we just received from our sister, Catherine, is actually from Catherine, and that the address and credit card information we just submitted on a Web site to donate money to Greenpeace will actually get to that organization. Changes in the technology through the introduction of such things as improved authentication mechanisms and more extensive data protection and data encryption services will deliver greater overall security on the Internet. But the technology can only go so far. Improving security on the Internet will also demand changes with respect to how we use the Internet, our expectations and awareness of risk, and how those charged with overseeing the security and protection of our information act, are audited, and are held accountable for their lapses.

Some of the problems with security on the Internet date all the way back to its original engineering: the Internet was not designed with security in mind. Given that the creation and development of the Internet was a U.S. military project with clearly stated military objectives, including communication facilities for command and control operations that were redundant and resistant to attack, you might think security would have been uppermost in the minds of the Internet's engineers. But the computer environment back then was very different than it is today, and the early Internet comprised a very different sort of network than today's commercial and privatized Internet. Computers and the network were used for different purposes and by far fewer people from far fewer locations.

Most computers in the 1960s and 1970s were large, expensive, and locked up inside highly controlled environments. Access to computers, and to the information they stored, was strictly limited. As important, if not more so, very few people knew enough about how computers operated to pose a threat to their security. When the ARPANET started to transmit the very first packets of data across its network in 1969, there were only four computers attached to the network. This was the beginning of something big, something that would change the way we work and play, communicate, and form relationships, something that would fundamentally transform the way we live. But what the ARPANET engineers were thinking about was the present, not the future; they had more then enough problems and technical challenges to keep themselves fully occupied. Their work focused on how to keep the network and the attached computers from crashing, how to add on the next few computers, and how to convince others that they had created something useful rather than an expensive, elaborate experiment or academic toy. Security was not an integral part of this work. There was no personal information to protect. There were no intruders trying to break in (that they were aware of).

Just as the first automobile engineers and manufacturers did not consider the need for seat belts or traffic lights at intersections, the engineers of the ARPANET and the early Internet did not consider security to be something essential and necessarily integral to their designs. Furthermore, knowledge of and access to the ARPANET and early Internet was for many years confined to so few people that everyone involved more or less knew everyone else. In many respects, security cannot get much better than that. While some dreamed of a computer on everyone's desk and in every home, very few considered this likely to happen in the near future. So security was what it needed to be. It consisted of simple authentication mechanisms to distinguish individuals and to control information access. It also included logging mechanisms to record basic origination and destination information about the data transmitted across the network; this information was primarily used to augment the speed and efficiency of moving data through the network, but it was also useful for identifying the source of any one piece of data, tracing its navigation of the network, tracking down problems, and (incidentally) uncovering security threats and violations.

Then things changed dramatically and irreversibly. During the 1980s, computers became ever smaller and ever cheaper, following which they became commonplace fixtures in home and office environments. At the same time, interest in computers and knowledge of how they worked grew exponentially. During the 1990s, networking standards (e.g., TCP/IP and Ethernet) turned independent and isolated (and, relatively speaking, protected and secure) personal computers, workstations, and other types of computers into shareable, interconnected devices. Privatization and commercialization of the Internet created a master network to interconnect all of these smaller, regional networks.

The result of all of these changes is what we enjoy today: a globally distributed, networked computer environment with millions of computers in all shapes, sizes, and configurations and with untold millions of computer users connecting to the Internet from every country across the globe, each with his or her own measure of access, his or her own measure of knowledge, and his or her own measure of interest in supporting or subverting the security of the information coursing through the Internet and stored on Internet-accessible computers. Over the span of a dozen years or less, concerns over security and both perceived and real threats to security went from one extreme to the other. A fellowship of the known and generally trusted became a universe of unknown individuals with unknown intentions.

When you realize that the computer world has been transformed from one extreme to the other in such a short period of time and that pranksters, malicious individuals, and criminals exist not just in the world at large but in the world of computers and networking, you begin to comprehend the enormous importance of security on the Internet. What is more difficult to realize (and appreciate) is the difficulty of adding security into the engineering model of the Internet. The basic, working premise of the Internet is that of an open, distributed system with no central control, no single infrastructure for management, and no oversight body. This means that there's no way to mandate or overlay some technology or mechanism for establishing and enforcing security onto the Internet itself. Security solutions must necessarily begin and end on the computers that compose the Internet, which means that security must become an integral component on our computers and on those computers that offer the services provided across the Internet, such as Web servers, mail servers, information portals, online stores, chat sites, gaming sites, and online community centers.

Thinking about security represents quite a departure from contemplating other computer-related problems and solutions. Proper security measures prevent problems and attacks from occurring. Moreover, the best security mechanisms manage not to intrude into our lives; they don't require our attention and they remain out of sight. When they are working correctly, we can forget that they exist. From the standpoint of development, engineering sound security measures requires thinking about the negative side of existing computer systems, protocols, and networks. This means identifying and removing the gaps, holes, leaks, poorly written code, and even deliberately created, but hidden, back doors. It means trying to find vulnerabilities before they are exploited and providing preemptive countermeasures to prevent such exploitation. The process itself is unending, because every computer and every networking component and every service provides any number of vulnerabilities just waiting for someone to discover and exploit them.

Security on the Internet demands protecting the confidentiality, integrity, and availability of the information carried by the network and to which the Internet provides access. This means making sure that access to our information is protected, that our information remains as we left it (i.e., unchanged by others and uncorrupted), and that we can access our information whenever we choose. When you recognize how much data about you is made accessible on the Internet and how much additional data you introduce onto the Internet either through your volunteering that information or through it being collected without your knowledge or consent, you begin to appreciate how important it is to keep your information secure and private, to limit your exposure regarding the type and quantity of information that can be taken from you, and to protect your data from people and programs that may want to destroy or damage it. Security has, therefore, a large role to play on the Internet. There is no single solution because there is no one problem to resolve or one service or technology that can address all of the related concerns. Security on the Internet is necessarily many things to many people.

The following sections detail why security is needed on the Internet, how existing security measures try to address known problems and vulnerabilities, where the technology is heading, and what we might expect in the not too distant (and, hopefully, more secure) future.

Attacks

Attacks launched over the Internet occur frequently, manifest themselves in all sorts of different ways, and cost all of us a lot of money and grief. There are two basic types of Internet attacks. One type of attack targets information in transit, intercepting or otherwise interfering with our data as it makes its way across the Internet. The other type of attack targets information objects, such as the files on our computers or the information stored about us or for us in a database on a remote computer.

Ensuring the security of our information, therefore, requires protecting both the transmission of that information and the information itself. A secure Web session, for instance, (e.g., one that uses a secure implementation of HTTP, such as HTTPS) will keep our data safe as our computer communicates with the Web server by encrypting all the data transmitted during the session. The contents of the information sent and received remain unreadable by any computer other than ours and that of the Web server. Email, on the other hand, demands a different strategy. The process of transmitting the data that composes an email message is asynchronous, unlike the process of browsing the Web. There is no direct or immediate connection between our computer and that of an email's intended recipient. We must, therefore, secure the contents of the email before it begins its journey, because it may end up residing on any number of computers as it hops across the Internet towards its final destination, making the information it contains particularly vulnerable.

In general, Internet attacks can be active or passive in nature. Active attacks typically result in data loss or corruption, An example of an active attack is a virus communicated by email that makes its way onto your computer's hard drive and starts changing or deleting your files. Passive attacks are similar to eavesdropping. They involve such things as capturing your keystrokes to steal your login and password information or stealing your credit card information as it is being transmitted. Some Internet attacks ignore our information altogether. They instead target entities on the Internet, such as high-profile Web sites and government agencies. Their goal is to shut down the services offered by these organizations rather than to steal or damage the information they store.

More specific information about the most common types of Internet attacks is presented in the following sections.

The First Attacks

The first Internet attack to gain notoriety and press coverage occurred in 1986 and is described at length by Clifford Stoll in his book, "The Cuckoo's Egg." Stoll was working as a systems manager at Lawrence Berkeley National Laboratory in California when he came across some simple accounting errors in the records of several computers connected to the ARPANET. This seemingly innocuous discovery led him to uncover evidence of unauthorized access to the lab's computer systems. He started to monitor the intruders' activity in an attempt to discern what they were after and, eventually, he went in search of who they were and where they resided. His efforts led directly to the discovery of an overseas spy ring that was breaking into U.S. government computer systems in order to steal sensitive military information for the KGB. For many, including the police, the FBI, and other government agencies, this incident was a wake-up call. It told them that security on the ARPANET was lax, that information, computer systems, and the network in general were accessible to unauthorized and unknown individuals, that no one was monitoring for such intrusions, and that there were no agencies to deal with criminal behavior of this sort. Fortunately, these deficiencies began to be remedied once the full scope of this attack became clear.

Just two short years later, in 1988, Robert Morris, Jr. unleashed his famous worm on the Internet, severely disrupting network service on the Internet and crashing thousands of computers in just a few hours. This event clearly signaled the Internet's vulnerability to such simple attacks and just as clearly communicated the cost of such disruptions. As a consequence, security quickly became an even more serious concern. Even at this stage in the Internet's development — several years before the introduction of the World Wide Web — many businesses and the U.S. government were already relying on the Internet for the daily operation of their organizations. Service disruptions were not something they could tolerate; they cost money, delayed work, and needed to be prevented. One positive result of the Morris worm was the funding by DARPA of a computer emergency response team that now goes by the name of the CERT Coordination Center.

It provides a much needed means to coordinate responses to network emergencies.

Viruses, Worms, and Trojan Horses

The most obvious and common type of security threat on the Internet comes in the form of malicious programming. One simple program can quickly cause a lot of harm by damaging computer systems, networks, and the information they store and transmit. The result of such programs is lost work, data, time, and money. The openness of the Internet has greatly facilitated the propagation of malicious programs; they use the Internet as a conduit to copy and spread themselves, and we often, unwittingly, help them along.

These programs come in three distinctly different forms: viruses, worms, and trojan horses. The most common are viruses, which are self-replicating pieces of code, hidden in or attached to some harmless-looking file, and waiting for an opportunity to execute on your computer in order to damage its files, applications, or operating system. A virus can enter your computer through an infected floppy disk or CD, a file downloaded over the Internet, an email message, or through someone gaining remote access to your computer. The fastest-traveling viruses are spread through email. The virus itself is normally contained in an attachment; and when you open the attachment, the waiting, dormant virus is unleashed, either directly, through an executable program, or indirectly through an associated application, such as a Microsoft Word file that contains a virus in one of its macros. (A macro is a small piece of programming code embedded in the document.)

Unlike viruses, worms do not typically damage or delete files, nor do they hide themselves inside other programs or objects. Instead, worms are self-replicating programs that travel the network, using each computer they inhabit to copy themselves onto other computers that are accessible on the network. In the process, they consume more and more local computer resources and network bandwidth. Eventually, worms consume so many resources that the computer systems they reside on crash and the local network becomes unusable. Ironically, the very first computer worm, which was created by a Xerox engineer named

John Shoch in 1978, was designed to be a beneficial network tool. The name derives from a program called the "tapeworm" that appeared in a 1975 science fiction novel by John Brunner, entitled "The Shockwave Rider." The tapeworm is used by the book's hero to combat and destroy a malicious computer network. Shoch's creation of the first worm program was designed to automate certain repetitive functions on one of Xerox's local networks. Unfortunately, the worm developed some unanticipated and decidedly destructive behavior in the performance of its duties, which resulted in a network of crashed machines. It required many hard, frantic hours of work to eradicate the worm and then repair the network.

A Trojan horse is a malicious program disguised as something innocuous, like a screen saver or file cleanup utility. Its purpose is to collect information from your computer and send it back to the program's creator. Such programs are often used to steal usernames and passwords, and they can also be used to acquire control of your computer from a remote location.

Even though you cannot expect complete protection against these sorts of attacks, you can take steps to create a more secure computer environment for yourself. Anti-virus software is commonplace now. It's simple to install and it can even be configured to automatically check for software updates over the Internet, so that as new viruses are created your computer can remain protected with the latest countermeasures. But, ultimately, good security is also a matter of awareness. This means understanding the differences between practices that are considered safe and those that are known to be unsafe. Email attachments are a good example. Opening an email attachment from someone you don't know amounts to taking a big risk. When that attachment is in the form of an executable program (e.g., the filename ends in .exe or .bat), you are not only taking a risk, you are in effect asking for trouble. It's like inviting a complete stranger into your home and then going out for a long walk. Everything may be just as you left it when you return, or you may return to find that your possessions have been stolen and your cat has been shaved.

Phishing and Pharming

Phishing and pharming (pronounced fishing and farming) are two techniques for luring you to reveal your personal information, such as a social security number, a bank account number, or usernames and passwords for your online accounts. Phishing and pharming are a particular type of widespread and growing fraud on the Internet. They take advantage of the openness of the Internet's technology and the absence of security measures on the Internet to verify a person's or an organization's identity in order to convince you that you are supplying needed information to your bank or credit card company when actually you are handing this information over to someone else entirely.

Phishing is the older of the two fraud techniques. It takes the form of an email that seems to be from a known and reputable organization. The email may contain a notification that claims you have won something, or it may contain a warning that one of your accounts will be canceled or suspended unless you take action. You are asked to click on a link that has been included in the email; the link will allow you to login to your account and thereby accept the award or remedy the problem with your account. But the Internet site that the link takes you to is a *spoofed* version of the site you think you are visiting. It may look exactly like a site you are familiar with, but its sole purpose is to collect your personal information.

The intent of pharming, just like phishing, is to get you to visit a spoofed Internet site in order for you to reveal some amount of personal information. Pharming is a far more sophisticated and devious technique. It doesn't rely on an email to lure you into action. Instead, it relies on the *poisoning* of domain name servers, which is something entirely beyond your control and something that you would not be aware of until it is too late. Every time you enter or click on an Internet address (e.g., www.microsoft.com), that name must be converted into a corresponding Internet Protocol (IP) address (e.g., 66.14.187.92). The Domain Name System (DNS) was created to handle this conversion, and it uses specialized computers that are distributed throughout the Internet, which are called domain name servers, to perform this function. A domain name server has been poisoned when one or more of its entries have been modified. The result is that any computer consulting a poisoned domain name server for one of its modified addresses will be redirected to the IP address of a spoofed Internet site. One poisoned domain name server can affect any number of individuals, and the misdirection will remain active until the poisoning has been identified and fixed.

Crackers

Crackers are individuals who combine their knowledge of computers with a pursuit of excitement, fame, or personal enrichment to illegally gain access to corporate or government computers. Hackers are often mistaken for crackers since both groups share the same fervor for computers as well as the same mistrust of authority and big business. But hackers (generally speaking) are computer enthusiasts, not criminals. It was, apparently, the misuse of the term hacker by journalists that led the hacker community to coin the term cracker, in order to make clear the distinction between the two groups.

Crackers are the Internet's version of intruders or burglars. What they do is comparable to a criminal breaking into or circumventing a store's security in order to gain unauthorized access and steal merchandise. In their case, the merchandise is information; and if they can't locate what they are looking for — and sometimes even if they do — it's not uncommon for them to seriously damage the computers and network they have gained access to. Firewalls, sound and enforced security policies, and the constant monitoring of networked computer systems are the best, and perhaps only, defense against such intruders.

Denial of Service (DoS)

A denial of service (DoS) attack is a security problem for organizations rather than for individuals. The target of DoS attacks are the merchants and service providers of the Internet, and the goal of such attacks is to disrupt or disable an organization's ability to conduct business on the Internet. You may have encountered the result of a DoS attack when you were unable to reach a specific Web site while other sites were reachable or when you experienced a significant slowdown in network response time.

A DoS attack typically targets one or more Internet sites and uses the network against the site by flooding it with useless traffic. The net result is like continuously flushing a pipe with water so that nothing else can make its way through and nothing can come back out. DoS attacks exploit the open architecture of the Internet in general, and that of TCP/IP in particular. Information that details exactly how the Internet packages and transports data is freely available to anyone who wants it. This makes it possible — for those so inclined — to write programs that, among other things, simulate Internet traffic and direct it at one or more destinations on the Internet for the purpose of overwhelming the resources at those sites or severely limiting their ability to handle legitimate traffic and conduct business as usual. Countermeasures can be taken to limit a site's exposure to such an attack, but nothing can provide complete security and protection. New approaches are being dreamed up all the time by people of ill will, those with an ax to grind, or those who have too much time on their hands; this makes prevention all but impossible.

Internet Crime

Crime on the Internet takes many forms, and the types of attacks described above constitute the better known forms of criminal activity. Viruses, worms, and trojan horses target individuals and their use of the Internet, while crackers and DoS attacks primarily target corporate and government entities. What these different forms of criminal activity have in common is that they all cause considerable damage to computer systems, networks, and the information they carry and store, and this damage costs time and money to defend against and to repair. In effect, we all pay for this criminal activity. But the free exchange of files and information enabled by the Internet has also attracted a more traditional criminal element that consists of individuals and groups that are more interested in financial gain than in proving their abilities to defeat existing security measures or simply lashing out. This type of Internet crime typically manifests itself in some form of computer piracy or fraud; accordingly, it demands a different approach to security.

Computer piracy on the Internet is big business, in terms both of the goods being stolen and the security measures being pursued to protect against it. News reports focus on the theft of music and software over the Internet. This type of piracy, however, is not confined to individuals freely sharing material they may have purchased or otherwise acquired. It also involves businesses that have been created to sell this pirated material as if they were legitimate resellers. Both the individuals and businesses involved in this type of piracy take advantage of the file sharing facilities of the Internet as well as of the general protective sense of anonymity that pervades the space of the Internet and the Web. Meanwhile, untold numbers of businesses, employees, and artists are suffering economic losses because of this piracy. Whether or not the legal system will ever be able to catch up to the technology is impossible to say. Part of the solution, in the short term, may rest with us and with our recognizing what may be the harshest consequence of copyright infringement, namely the loss of jobs. Eventually, it may have to be the technology itself that comes to the rescue by locking products so that they can be used only by those who have purchased them.

Unfortunately, piracy over the Internet is not limited to the theft of merchandise. Intellectual property, a long-time concern of businesses and governments, has also become far more vulnerable to theft due to the Internet. Technology can provide some measure of security for this type of information through the installation of firewalls, more demanding authentication mechanisms, and various other safeguards. Limiting and controlling access, however, can only go so far. The Internet was not designed to keep information contained. So, in the end, you have to place your trust in individuals to keep the enabling technology of computers and the Internet from working against you, your interests, and the necessary security of certain information.

Fraud on the Internet, like piracy, is impossible to avoid. In many respects the Internet is an ideal breeding ground for fraud. Where else can you sell products or services without a storefront, someone to answer the phone, or even a postal address? Web pages and email are the two principal mechanisms through which fraudulent activities are conducted on the Internet. According to statistics collected by the Internet Fraud Complaint Center in the U.S., over 40% of all reported incidents of fraud relate to the online auctioning of merchandise, 20% involve either non delivery of merchandise or non payment, and over 15% stem from a Nigerian email fraud promising a share of a large sum of money in exchange for a small amount of cash up front. A wide assortment of other fraudulent activities are common on the Internet. They include credit card scams, non-existent business opportunities, advanced fee loans, and misrepresented job opportunities. No technology exists that can protect you against all the forms of fraud on the Internet or elsewhere. Your security is in your own hands; if something sounds too good to be true, follow your instincts and hit the delete button or visit another Web site.

Authentication

Most of us see security on the Internet from the perspective of authentication. Upon request, we present a username along with a password to identify who we are. After passing through this basic, but critical, security measure we gain access to specific services and information. Our identity has been authenticated; we have passed the test.

From the perspective of the Internet itself, however, authentication — and the granting or denial of access that accompanies it — looks quite different and can manifest itself in a wide variety of different forms. The smallest, most common, and perhaps most critical form of authentication occurs at the packet level. The data of the Internet is transmitted in packets; packets are the basic currency of the Internet. Therefore, it's essential to know that the data contained in each packet, as well as the information the packet includes describing where it came from, where it is going, and what it contains, has not been tampered with. The Internet relies on the proper authentication and the integrity of each and every packet it transmits. Without this baseline measure of security, the Internet would cease to function. Moreover, it is this implicit, baseline security, the same basic measure of security we implicitly rely on when we drop a letter into a mailbox, that is most responsible for transforming the Internet experiment into the ubiquitous, all-empowering engine of commerce, education, and communication that we see today.

Every packet of data transmitted across the Internet undergoes some measure of authentication. This packet-level authentication was originally engineered not to address security issues, but rather to address the more fundamental concern over network reliability. The engineering of the Internet was designed with the expectation that packets would at times be lost or damaged in transit. In other words, the network was to be considered unreliable at all times. So the Internet engineers needed to design and implement a way for computers on the network to recognize this, to authenticate packets, and to issue a request for the retransmittal of packets considered lost, altered, or damaged. Fortunately, some of the header information contained in each packet that was designed to help ensure reliable transmission of the data can do double duty and assist in validating its integrity. Recent additions to this information, which are described in more detail in the section on cryptography below, increase the authentication capabilities of packets by introducing some measure of encryption into the header information, for instance, encrypting the checksum value that stores the exact size of the packet's data. These additions serve to strengthen the security of a packet's transmission across the Internet. They do nothing, however, to reduce the vulnerability of the data itself with respect to its storage on the sending or receiving computer.

Another common, but mostly hidden type of authentication on the Internet occurs at the computer level when two computers — a client and a server — converse across the Internet. The networking protocols we use on a daily basis, such as HTTP for Web browsing, POP3 or IMAP4 for email, and FTP for file transfers, all include a handshaking process that is partly an authentication process. Our computer (typically the client) and a remote computer (typically the server) progress through a formal process of exchanging identification information and other information about their capabilities. More often than not, this process is a formality. The information is used more to establish a common ground on which the two computers can communicate and to log information about the interaction than to implement security provisions. There are, however, newer implementations of all of these protocols that are designed to implement higher, more rigorous standards for security and to provide another means of establishing more secure authentication.

Identity-Based Authentication

Usernames and passwords are the most common type of identity-based authentication. You use them in performing any number of operations on your computer that require the most basic type of security, including such things as connecting to your ISP, receiving email, logging on to a Web site, starting up an Internet chat session, and even possibly starting up your computer. Establishing a username and password can take time and it typically involves supplying some type of personal information, such as a policy or account number, a street address and phone number, or an email address. But once you have established an account, you have only to pass through a simple login form to be authenticated and regain access. Your authentication, moreover, is directly tied to an associated level and type of authorization. This means that once a system knows who you are (or thinks it knows who you are), you are then authorized to view and change some restricted amount of information (e.g., your password on the system, your email address, or your street address). You are also typically provided with some measure of privileges that enable you to use specific services on the system (e.g., email or gaming) and perform specific activities or operations (e.g., viewing an account balance, writing a check, or responding to a question or comment in a newsgroup). This is all pretty straightforward. Everything you can see and do is based on the identity presented to and authenticated by the computer system that prompts you to enter your username and password.

The problem is that this type of authentication is a weak form of security. Moreover, the closer you examine this type of security mechanism — one based on authentication by means of usernames and passwords — the more serious the problem becomes. Consider the following facts. The more accounts you create, the more usernames and passwords you are forced to record or the more you recycle the same username and password information. The greater the number of usernames and passwords, the more likely you are to write this information down onto a piece of paper and leave this sensitive information in a desk drawer, in a book, or in your wallet. The more times you recycle the same information, the more exposed you become to someone gaining access to most if not all of your accounts. Or, worse yet, you let your computer record your usernames and passwords, leaving access to your accounts open to anyone who has physical access to your computer. To make matters worse, most people choose passwords that are familiar names, and such names are easily guessed or commonly included by crackers in one of their lists of popular passwords. Good passwords should be difficult to remember. They should be long, and they should contain a mixture of letters and numbers that when put together cannot be found in any dictionary. Good passwords, therefore, can be considered yet another problem with this type of authentication, because they are more likely to be forgotten.

The most you can do with respect to maximizing your security with this type of basic identity-based authentication is to follow the advice of most security experts when it comes to creating your passwords. Create passwords that you cannot pronounce, that are at least eight characters long and contain at least two numbers, and never write them down. Unfortunately, even if you do this, there are other fundamental security problems with identity-based authentication that are entirely beyond your control and that remain largely unresolved. Many organizations, for instance, store your password in plain text on their computer systems as opposed to storing it in some encrypted form. This means that employees with access to your account information can read your password and an intruder who breaks into a computer that stores your account information can also steal your password. There is no excuse for this. It is a particularly bad business practice that puts your information at risk. Yet, it is commonly done. The reason given for storing your password in such an insecure way is that it enables an organization to email you your password should you forget it. This presents yet another problem with identity-based authentication, because plain text passwords should never be transmitted across the Internet for any reason. Doing so simply affords another easy opportunity for your password to be stolen by any number of people.

It should be apparent from the information presented above that identity-based authentication is too simplistic and problematic a mechanism to function as a secure means to verify that we are who we say we are. Too much of our personal information is already at risk. Our access to this information and our ability to manipulate it will only grow over time. We will therefore need a better, more secure system and better technology to identify ourselves electronically. We will need something more like a digital fingerprint: a means of identification that is unique to us and that is difficult or impossible to counterfeit. A complete solution will probably require integrating several different types of identification, rather than just relying on passwords. One existing solution, which is already used by many businesses, partially solves the known security problems with passwords by providing employees with a small device that they can fit onto a key chain. It displays a numeric password — linked exclusively to an employee's account — that changes every minute or so. This doesn't solve the basic identity problem, but it greatly enhances security by ensuring that you need access to this specific device in order to gain access to your account across the network. It represents a small but important step in the right direction.

Credential-Based Authentication

Certificates provide credential-based, as opposed to identity-based, authentication. They use a combination of data encryption, discussed below, and information that has been verified by a third party and then stored in a file that resides on your computer. The file functions like a digital fingerprint; it contains highly specific information about you that was designed for the express purpose of electronic identification. When you need to identify yourself, the certificate is sent as proof of your credentials.

Credential-based authentication has been around for a while, but it is still only infrequently used compared to basic password authentication. Part of the reason for its lack of widespread use rests with the encryption technology and the slow speed of its adoption and integration across the Internet. Another reason relates to privacy. Some see the use of certificates for authentication as another factor that diminishes our ability to roam the Internet anonymously. Certificates have the potential to carry more information than we may want to reveal or that we may know we are revealing, which introduces questions about how that information will be used and possibly reused. Concerns have also been raised about how to handle stolen certificates and broken encryption mechanisms. Credential-based authentication holds the promise of a more secure means to verify our identities across the Internet, but it is not yet ready for general use.

Cryptography

The future security of information on the Internet may depend on the science of cryptography and on the integration of cryptographic systems into the core technology and commonplace uses of the Internet. Cryptography is the practice of secure, and often secret, communication. It's thought that ever since writing was developed people have employed techniques and tools to conceal and protect written communication from being understood by individuals other than those for whom the information was intended. Down through the centuries, there are many examples of personal journals that were written using some form of encryption; and often the method of encryption was developed by, and known only to, the author. One well known example is the diary that was kept by Samuel Pepys in 17th century England. He encrypted particularly sensitive passages of his journal, even though he never thought that any of his thousands of diary pages would ever be seen by anyone but himself. Cryptographic systems that employ different types and levels of encryption and that typically require the use of code books or specialized encryption devices have also played an essential role in protecting the communication of messages during times of war. One of the best kept secrets of World War II was how the British managed to break the encryption produced by Germany's sophisticated Enigma device, which was responsible for changing the course of the war.

A principal part of cryptography is the cipher. A cipher is a type of key that is used to transform clear text into some encrypted, unreadable sequence of letters and numbers. In some instances, a single cipher or key can be used both to encode and decode the contents of a message. More secure systems typically employ two keys; they operate like a double lock door mechanism in which one key locks the door but a different key is needed to unlock it. Ciphers and encryption systems are normally developed by mathematicians, since they are based on complex mathematical algorithms. In the U.S., a system called the Data Encryption Standard (DES) was widely used by the U.S. government and other organizations starting in the mid 1970s. DES remained the standard encryption system in the U.S. for over 25 years. But advances in computer technology made DES vulnerable to attack. The newer computers significantly reduced the amount of time it might take to decipher a DES key. The length of DES keys, which not long ago were considered adequate protection, were now considered too short. Consequently, a new standard has been developed for use in the U.S. that relies on much longer keys. It's called AES, the Advanced Encryption Standard.

Many problems must be overcome before any type of encryption mechanism or technology will become commonplace on the Internet. First of all, encryption adds another layer onto every process that writes out or reads information. This can impact performance, especially when done incorrectly. Another problem relates to the creation and distribution of keys. Without an automated or a very simple and secure means to distribute the keys needed to decrypt the information we have protected, most people will not want to encrypt their data in the first place. Moreover, there is the considerable problem of how data can remain protected once it has been decrypted. Additional protection needs to be put in place to ensure that previously encrypted information cannot be stored or retransmitted as clear text.

Packet Encryption

When security experts discuss data encryption and the Internet they begin by focusing their attention on how information is transmitted across the Internet. They want to provide security for our information in each and every IP packet by encrypting the information contained in a packet. This is something that has been engineered but not yet widely implemented. This level of security is entirely removed from our interaction with the Internet; it takes place on our behalf, but does not necessarily require us to do anything differently than we currently do. Packet encryption happens at the network level and requires changes to the Internet Protocol itself.

Changing the Internet Protocol is a slow and difficult process. Updating the protocol specification — probably the easiest part of the process — took four years. The new version of IP, called IPv6 and known as IP Next Generation, became a draft standard in 1998. For security to be improved at the IP level it would require widespread adoption of IPv6 on old and new computers, network devices such as routers and firewalls, and other network components. But seven years later, in 2005, only a small percentage of computers and other devices on the Internet are using IPv6, and fewer still are using the new security extensions that support improved authentication, data integrity, data confidentiality, and data encryption. Any security system is only as good as its weakest link. For IP encryption to be viable, most, if not all, systems would need to incorporate its use. The benefits of enabling packet-level encryption would be manifold. But the greatest benefit would be in its ability to provide a granularity of control that could accommodate the widely divergent security needs of individuals, businesses, and government agencies.

Transport Encryption

Transport encryption secures data for transmission in the transport network layer. The transport layer, which is where TCP resides, is above the network layer, which is where IP resides, and its focus is on host-to-host communication across the Internet. Transport encryption is accomplished by breaking up a data transmission into individual, encrypted blocks of data. The details of the encryption and authentication process are handled transparently by our local computer and the remote computer we are communicating with over the Internet (e.g., a Web server). Because transport encryption is something that can be implemented by an application and does not require a user's intervention it has become a common and successful approach to ensuring the security of certain types of data transmissions across the Internet by enabling the encryption, authentication, and integrity of data streams. Transport encryption provides the necessary security for e-commerce to take place over the Internet. It enables credit card and other personal information to be transmitted safely and securely from one computer to another. The only computer that can decrypt the data that is sent through transport encryption is the computer requesting the information. So even if the data is intercepted, it cannot be read. Transport encryption was pioneered by Netscape. It was introduced in Netscape's creation of SSL (Secure Sockets Layer) and was engineered to provide a secure way to transmit sensitive information across the Web and, more specifically, to enable commerce to take place across the Web.

Public Key Encryption and Pretty Good Privacy

Public Key Encryption was developed in the late 1970s as an early solution to the problem of securing data for transmission across a network or the Internet. It employs a two key system. Both keys are created by you and are used exclusively to secure information that is sent to you. One, typically referred to as the *public key*, is used by your friends and associates to encrypt information before sending it to you across the network. The other, typically referred to as the *private key*, is used solely by you in the decryption process and is known only to you.

This combination of keys greatly increases the security of the encrypted information while simplifying the process of key distribution. The public key can be sent to anyone. It effectively locks data so that only you can unlock it. What helps make the system safe and secure, however, is that the public key does not reveal information about your private key; and once the data is encrypted, it can only be decrypted by your private key. This makes the system ideal for one-to-one personal communication, such as secure email.

A popular form of public key encryption that is employed on the Internet is called Pretty Good Privacy (PGP). It was developed by Philip Zimmerman, who released it into the public domain in 1991. The PGP software used to create public and private keys can be downloaded over the Internet from any number of sites. Its use requires a degree of manual intervention that many people are likely to find time consuming and troublesome. However, it's not hard to imagine how PGP, or comparable products, could be integrated into mail systems and other applications in a way that would make the encryption/decryption process transparent and effortless. Once that happens, many more people will routinely encrypt their personal and business-related information for safe and secure transit across a local network and the Internet.

Secure, Certified Email

Proposals for providing secure email must address two critical and independent requirements. One requirement involves encrypting the contents of a message. The incorporation of public key encryption, such as PGP, could be used to meet this requirement. The other requirement entails certifying the identity of the sender. The incorporation of digital signatures, which uniquely identity that an individual is who they represent themself to be, could be used to meet this requirement. The combination of securing information content and certifying the sender of the email would constitute a major advance beyond the existing, casual exchange of clear text email messages.

If email consisted solely of personal correspondence, there would not be such a compelling need for secure and certified email. Who questions whether the email we receive from a friend or a relative was somehow altered in transit or if the sender is being impersonated by someone else? The same question applies to the personal correspondence we send through the postal service. But email communications to and from business and government organizations make clear the need for additional security measures. The postal system created certified and return-receipt mail to satisfy these needs. Email transmitted over the Internet needs to provide the same level of security for the information it carries. Email security, however, must be embedded directly into the email itself, rather than added on to the system that carries it. This is the only way to ensure that the contents of a message are not tampered with or read by someone else, and that the identity of the sender has not been changed or impersonated. The business of providing secure and certified email on the Internet is already booming; and it's likely to grow considerably in the near future.

Trust Management

Security on the Internet, or elsewhere for that matter, must at some point interact with the definition and conveyance of trust. Trust management is a computer-based methodology for defining and negotiating issues of trust between networked services and applications. It's the security equivalent of the privacy preferences approach being developed by the W3C under the name of P3P, the Platform for Privacy Preferences Project. The idea behind trust management is to reduce the burden on us and on each application and resource we use with respect to specific, and often repeated, issues of trust. It allows us to establish standards and to configure security preferences that will manage decisions about which Internet sites, services, and applications we can trust and use securely and which ones we should avoid and deny access to. We define our security needs, and conforming applications then make the necessary security decisions on our behalf to protect our information and our computer system.

Trust management is a new type of high-level, all-encompassing approach to security. It offers a way for organizations and individuals to develop security policies, implement and exchange credentials, and build trusted relationships using a distributed and decentralized approach that mirrors the distributed and decentralized structure of the Internet. Security systems must provide the means for each of us to identify ourselves, to identify others, and to protect sensitive information so that this information is accessible only to those people who should have access to it. Security systems must also include the capacity for risk assessment. Decisions must be made based on some criteria to evaluate the credentials and information sent by an individual or organization over the Internet. Given that everything we do on the Internet — every piece of information we handle and every person we interact with — requires its own appropriate level of security and requires some corresponding risk assessment, it is not practical to make security decisions on an individual, ad-hoc basis. Creating and managing security in some systematic, configurable form seems the only realistic way to take charge of our security needs on the Internet in an all-inclusive, rather than in a piecemeal manner.

We may never need to interact directly with a trust management system. In the near future, such systems are unlikely to be purchased or used by individuals. But in a corporate or business environment, such a system could contribute significantly to lowering security risks by enforcing one or more detailed security policies throughout an organization. This could help people and applications determine who can and cannot be trusted, which actions are dangerous and which are not, and perhaps even who is entitled to perform certain actions or access certain information. Since the nature of trust is that it builds over time and develops much like a web, with one trusted relationship building on another, trust management may be the kind of system that can be integrated into the Internet over time as a basic component of its structure or a new type of service. Eventually, such a system would extend into the home environment and also offer greater wholesale security to individuals.

Protection

Since we can expect more and more of our personal information to be held in trust on remote computers, the security of our information can be measured by how well or how poorly it is protected at those remote locations. Whether we like it or not, businesses and government agencies store, manage, and share an ever-growing quantity of our personal information, including information about our finances, health, buying and entertaining preferences, and travel. It seems reasonable to expect organizations that store and handle such information to respect our privacy through measures taken to ensure the protection of this information. Just as we entrust banks to safely hold our money, and banks issue guarantees against its loss, we will need to develop the same sort of trust with the institutions that hold our personal information. They will also need to be held accountable for any loss or misuse of that information. Today, unfortunately, we have no implied or stated rights or guarantees regarding the protection of our personal information.

What may be more troubling than our lack of rights regarding our personal information is its vulnerability to theft. If you consider information theft from the perspective of a thief, you quickly realize that thieves are less inclined to rob an individual of his or her information when they could just as easily — sometimes more easily — rob an organization and walk away with the information assets of countless thousands. The news media frequently run reports on email viruses that damage computer systems and on staged attacks that temporarily shut down Internet businesses like Web portals. These malicious acts illustrate some of the vulnerabilities of the Internet and the kinds of security threats that exist. But they are child's play compared to the damage that serious, career criminal Internet thieves and terrorist organizations can and may effect.

For example, in February, 2005 criminals posing as legitimate businesses were able to steal personal information on close to 140,000 individuals from a U.S. company called ChoicePoint. ChoicePoint is a provider of identification and credential verification services that stores and resells information, such as social security numbers and credit reports, to other businesses. The billions of records that ChoicePoint stores include detailed profiles on nearly every U.S. citizen. Their security was breached by a simple circumvention of their own verification process, which resulted in their delivering personal information to the very people they were entrusted to safeguard this information against.

A different sort of security breach occurred in June, 2005 when the biggest financial services company in the U.S., Citigroup, lost computer tapes when shipping them to a credit bureau in Texas. The tapes contained personal information on nearly 4 million consumers; and since the information on the tapes was not encrypted, anyone who gained access to the tapes would be able to view that information. An incident reported by the Bank of America in February, 2005 also involved the loss of computer tapes. These tapes contained account information on 1.2 million U.S. federal employee credit cards, including some cards belonging to members of the Senate. There was no evidence in either incident that the tapes were stolen or that the personal information they contained had been used inappropriately. Nevertheless, the incidents clearly demonstrate the vulnerability of our personal information, especially when the most basic protections (e.g., data encryption) are not used.

In many ways, the solution to protecting our data is no different than that used by a bank to protect our money. The solution starts with a vault that under most conditions remains closed and locked. Access to the vault is restricted to as few people as possible; and access is monitored, logged, and audited as a further protection. Individuals are allowed into the vault through a combination of keys, one held by the organization that operates the vault and one held by the individual; access is restricted to the individual's information assets, and their behavior is audited. Multiple security devices, auditing systems, and access restrictions serve to protect our information. Most important of all, the organizations that store and handle our information assume responsibility for safeguarding these assets.

Security Policies

Information security is big business. There are organizations that train individuals and whole corporations on how to properly store, handle, and safeguard information assets. Other organizations offer products that can be used to secure data, secure Internet connections and network traffic, and install auditing and alarm systems. What any expert will tell you, however, is that the first requirement in establishing security is a clear, comprehensive, enforceable, and auditable security policy.

A security policy sets out guidelines, goals, and procedures that relate to all aspects of an organization's information. It examines the data itself, the technology used to store, maintain, and provide access to the data, how clients access their information, and how employees access that same information. It includes stated practices on such things as minimal password requirements, downloading files from the Internet, connecting to the systems at work from a home or remote computer, and the types of encryption and authentication methods to be used for employee and client accounts. It also explains what should happen in the event that security is compromised, including how to shut down systems, trace the intruder, and contact law enforcement. A comprehensive security policy not only defines security practices and procedures and specifies punishment for violations, but it also communicates the importance of protecting this information. This means that it instructs individuals who have been assigned to implement this protection about their responsibilities, expected behavior, and the importance of the data's security. This type of instruction is essential because security violations also occur on the internal side of a firewall by the very people entrusted to protect information assets. The problem of internal security violations leads us to the next security subject: auditing systems and the need for accountability.

Auditing

Auditing data access and use is one area of security for which many products already exist. Moreover, the use of auditing products, systems, and services has been common practice for many years in most business environments and elsewhere. Computers, networks, and the Internet work in a way that makes record keeping — the logging of computer operations — a simple task. Sending email, browsing the Web, chatting, and most other popular Internet activities produce log file records that capture an enormous amount of raw information. This information typically includes something to identify the individual or computer performing the operation (e.g., an IP address), the type of operation being performed, and date and time information (i.e., a timestamp). Any type of computer operation can be configured to produce records in a log file. It is, therefore, easy to monitor how an individual is using his or her computer by recording both what that person is doing on the network and what they are doing locally (e.g., which files were opened and editing, which games were played, etc.).

Auditing involves turning on and configuring record-keeping functions that track access to information, capturing data related to information access, and providing the tools to monitor and report on this captured data. A well-configured auditing environment should be able to set off alarms when atypical or questionable behavior occurs and provide the means to track and identify security violations. It should also include the ability to reconstruct events from the captured data so that it can produce a report listing all the operations performed by an individual during a specific time frame. Even the best auditing systems, however, cannot provide absolute protection against the theft of data or a break-in by an intruder. But only by dedicating time and resources to auditing computer systems and monitoring network activity can a security violation be found and hopefully stopped in a timely manner. Trust is a wonderful thing, but you'll want your information, like your money, stored in a secure location that has safeguards in place to protect your data and that regularly audits its systems to make sure those protections are working.

A Secure Internet World

Security experts will tell you that in an ideal, secure Internet world every individual and every host computer would have some sort of certificate (like a digital fingerprint) that would uniquely and securely identify them. Packets traveling the Internet would all be encrypted, thereby eliminating the worry about that data being intercepted and read. Applications would automatically handle the technical details about security, freeing us from the tedium of encrypting data, deciding who to trust, and negotiating security policies and from the worry of changed, misrepresented, or stolen information. Organizations would have advanced auditing systems to watch over our personal information and protect it against any mishandling, unauthorized access, or outright theft.

Achieving good security is a difficult balancing act. You have to weigh information access against the protection of information. You have to measure the open, empowering nature of the Internet against its equally open, global nature and its exposure of your personal information. You have to grant your trust while knowing that criminals exist who want nothing better than to abuse that trust. You have to acknowledge that information warfare exists, at the corporate and government levels, and whether or not your information is secure may be determined by who has the better offense or who has the better defense, who is your friend and who is your enemy. You might even catch yourself wondering: are the computer geeks on my side better than the computer geeks on their side?

Java: Connecting All the Dots

3

Java in Brief

Much like the creation of the Internet and the World Wide Web, the creation of Java, and the inspiration behind it, was both utterly new and filled with far-reaching consequences. The short, but event-filled history of Java is directly tied to, and in many respects parallels, that of the Internet and the World Wide Web. But perhaps the most remarkable characteristic that these three highly inventive, popular, and extremely influential creations share is that they all evolved into something quite different from what their creators had intended or even imagined.

So, what is Java? In its simplest terms, Java is a programming language. It was developed by Sun Microsystems, a computer hardware company that helped create the market for computer workstations. Sun's workstations were developed for use in academic and scientific computing environments. They were (and are) used in work related to networking, the Internet, and the Web. But, just as the Internet and the Web eventually migrated into the commercial sector and became an integral part of the business computing environment, so did Sun, its workstations, and Java. Like other computer programming languages, Java enables programmers to bring their ideas to life by writing instructions that control how a computer interacts with a user's actions, how it retrieves, stores, interprets, and manipulates information, and how it manages resources (e.g., computer memory, file systems, a connection to a network). These instructions take the form of Java program code.

Java program code must conform to the particular constructs and specifications of the Java language. The Java language consists of a complex body of rules as well as a rich vocabulary of keywords and predefined objects. These objects constitute the basic building blocks of the language. Some objects are highly specific in how they are defined and in what they were designed to do; they require only the most minor additions or customization (if any) in order to perform some common and basic task (e.g., printing text on a screen for the user to see or forming a query statement that can be processed by a database). Other objects are purposefully general in their definition and design; they assist the programmer in building virtually anything, from a small one-of-a-kind program (e.g., a filter to automatically delete unsolicited emails) to a large complex application (e.g., a Web browser or Web server).

Think of the Java language and its objects in the context of a hardware store. If your project is relatively small and simple, you may find precisely what you need already packaged for you in one box; all you will require are a few basic tools and some time to assemble the parts. If instead your project is large and complex, you may need to find a unique assortment of pipes, fittings, screws, nails, wood, stone, and adhesive; you will also need to engineer how to assemble all the parts so that they work together safely, consistently, and as expected. The popularity that Java has achieved is in large part due to its ability to accommodate both circumstances. It facilitates the creation of small and simple utilities, tools, and programs by supplying a large library of predefined objects that can be used as-is or altered and extended quickly and easily to satisfy highly specific requirements; and it enables the creation of any size application by providing the tools and building blocks to construct virtually anything.

In some respects, Java is not all that different from a human language with its particular alphabet (symbols or characters), grammar, vocabulary, and library of published material. Programs written in Java are composed of layer upon layer of abstractions, which is also true of how we use language to convey meaning through the abstractions of words and sentences. Programs consist of simple statements that build upon themselves (like sentences in a paragraph) and incorporate other statements (like the inclusion of a quotation), and collections of statements (like the reference to an article or a book), to create ever larger and more complex objects and functions. Where Java differs from the languages we use in order to communicate is in the precision of its definition and application. There are, for instance, no regional dialects; nor can you bend or break the rules and expect your program to run.

Computers, and the environment in which they function, are unforgiving of mistakes and omissions. Carrying out their operations, whether for the purpose of processing information, transmitting data, or anything else, demands a strict adherence to any and all rules and requirements. Simply put, the purpose of the Java language is to enable programmers to control the functions of a computer and, therefore, the language precisely defines what a programmer can and cannot do. Programming languages are utter artifice: man made, abstract creations designed to collect, store, and manipulate data and that aspire towards the same precision as the language of mathematics. Accordingly, Java's evolution, definition, and standardization as a language is both highly controlled and precisely documented.

Java has been used to build everything from simple, dancing cartoons and interactive games to mini-applications like streaming information tickers and stock portfolio managers, to independent applications like word processors, Web browsers, and Web servers, to all-encompassing e-business solutions, to the chip-based controls in *smart* appliances. Part of Java's power and popularity derives from its inherent versatility. But its greatest appeal and its greatest value derives from it being designed with networking, the Internet, and the Web in mind.

More than likely you have come into contact with Java (possibly without even knowing it) in one of its earliest and most common forms: a Java applet contained on a Web page. Applets are relatively small, self-contained programs written in Java that are responsible for many of the animations and much of the interactive page content (e.g., games and collaboration/communication tools like chat) and streaming content (e.g., information tickers and real-time stock trading tools) that transformed the Web into a dynamic, powerful, and entertaining environment. Java applets are commonly used to turn simple, static Web locations into engaging and interactive destinations that retain our interest and keep us returning to these locations again and again.

One key feature that made these small, Java programs different and new relates to how and where the applets were designed to run. Java applets are transferred over the network (a local intranet or the Internet) to your computer and run locally, using the memory and other resources that are on your computer. This approach contrasts sharply with other Web-based programming models, in which programs run on a remote Web server and simply exchange data between the Web site and your computer. Java applets use the network as both a delivery mechanism for the program and a communication medium that sends and receives data related to the running of the program. This means that you and your computer interact directly with the applet, which also means that the applet can access and take advantage of features on your computer that server-based programs can at best approximate from their remote locations. This approach considerably broadened the scope of what your computer, the Web, a network, and the Internet could do.

First through applets, and later through more broad-based programming that ran independent of a Web browser, Java brought executable content onto Web pages in a safe, simple, and architecturally neutral manner. Executable content meant liberation from the tight confines of HTML, overcoming the necessary, but unfortunate limitations of its markup. Java programs were limited only by the restrictions of the Java language, not by those of the far more restrictive browser environment. Moreover, Java managed to provide its benefits in a way that did not compromise the security of your computer. This capability was critical, because Java programs were copied onto your computer and ran in its environment. Finally, Java did not make demands on the type of computer or operating system you were using. Java programs were designed to be free of the dependencies common with other programming languages; they would run on virtually any computer architecture, regardless of the computer's manufacturer, the specifics of its hardware, or its operating system.

Much of the beauty and power of Java is its architecture-neutral engineering, as is explained in the following section. At the core of the Java programming model is that a program should be written once and run anywhere. This freed programmers from worrying about the differences between, for example, a Macintosh PC, a Windows PC, and a Unix workstation. Those differences, many of which are considerable, would be handled by Java outside of and separate from the code that a programmer would write. With Java, programmers could for the first time create a single program that would execute and function the same way across different architectures, whereas before they were forced to write for a specific architecture, or to painstakingly write individual programs for each architecture they wished to support. As a result, Java simultaneously reduced the effort required to write a program and increased its potential for use and widespread distribution.

Java evolved from an architecture-independent programming language into a large and sophisticated development platform consisting of the programming language, many different libraries and toolkits, and various Application Programming Interfaces (APIs) — highly detailed, open standards allowing for different implementations of commonly requested features and components. As such, Java serves to encompass and interconnect all types of information and data operations common to conducting business today and has, in the process, helped to fuel the growth of e-business and, in particular, of e-commerce. Java functions to unify the data of e-business with the existing and emerging computer and networking technologies, establishing what is commonly referred to as a distributed enterprise computer environment. This environment mimics the efficiencies, economies, and general strengths that have played a key role in the successful global operation of the Internet on the smaller scale operation of a business. Java's presence and functionality are distributed, like those of the Internet. Java's goal is interoperability, as applied to hardware, software, and information, like that of the Internet. Java's credo, as expressed by its promise of "write code once, run it anywhere," is architecture independence, like that of the Internet. But Java goes one step further than the Internet; it aspires towards architecture irrelevance.

Java accomplished all this by evolving from its original client-side model, with applets and large-scale applications that ran on our computers, to reach out and encompass the server side, where it is now often employed to manage the content of Web servers and much of the surrounding information infrastructure of databases, messaging systems, and productivity tools. This evolution enabled Java to become singularly capable of understanding all the information wants and needs of any business model and providing for them in just about any networked computing environment. The Internet provided a common and efficient communication infrastructure for interconnecting computers on a network and handling the transmission of information across the network. The Web provided a common and simplified information management system for accessing and publishing information. Java provided a common and powerful language for accessing, controlling, and interacting with all the components of the Internet, the Web, the computers that constitute the Internet and that power the Web, and all the applications, peripheral devices, and information that can be found on the Internet.

In summary, Java has developed from adjunct programming for a Web page into a unified standard for creating distributed applications that is capable of understanding and directly employing most elements of the Internet and the Web, while mimicking the distributed nature of the Internet. For many, this means that Java is not just cool; it is a force to be reckoned with.

The History of Java

Java's beginnings were small and humble in comparison to what it has become. Its history loosely dates back to 1990 and the formation of a group of engineers at Sun that would come to be known as the Green Team. Many of these gifted engineers had been involved in the creation of a product called NeWS, a graphical windowing system for the Unix operating system. When Sun failed to take the necessary business steps to promote the product, and a rival, less sophisticated windowing system called X instead became adopted as the standard, one engineer, James Gosling, communicated his disappointment with Sun management directly to Sun's CEO, Scott McNealy. In response to Gosling's complaint and to other factors, Sun funded the Green Team and gave its members an open mandate to pursue their interests heedless of any business concerns and without immediate oversight by the company.

In 1991, members of the Green Team directed their attention to household appliances and the growing use of microprocessors in everything from toasters and blenders to VCRs, telephones, and televisions. They noticed that while these devices were growing more sophisticated, with an ever increasing number of controls and features, they were not becoming any easier to operate. There was no intelligence at work to assist consumers in using these more advanced, feature-rich devices; consequently, many of the new capabilities they offered — and that were largely responsible for a device being purchased — remained unused. The never-programmed VCR clock, with its frozen, flashing time of 12:00, offers the most common example of this basic failure. Worse yet, no thought had been given to a common interface or language that would allow these devices to interact with each other, share information, or operate in unison. But it was not difficult to envision how and why such an interconnection could prove valuable and become a potentially successful selling point of such devices. Consider your television, VCR, and cable box, each with its own remote control, and each control with its own unique keypad and functions. They represent a lot of duplicated cost as well as duplicated functions; yet all three devices interconnect and work together at many levels. But the only intelligence available to help them interconnect and interoperate is yours.

Members of the Green Team envisioned devices that were part of their own network, interconnected through a common language and a common set of instructions and definitions that enabled each device to recognize and understand the features and properties of the other devices on the network. On such a network, when you inserted a tape into the VCR, it turned on the television, adjusted the volume, dimmed the lights, and started playing the movie. The action of inserting the tape implied the other actions (i.e., pressing the power button on the television's remote and pressing the play button for the VCR). When the telephone rang, it would signal the VCR to pause the tape. When the microwave finished popping a bag of popcorn, it would cause the tape to pause and display a message on the television stating that the popcorn was done. These same capabilities, in which knowledge and devices are interconnected at various levels, are included as part of the planning for a future World Wide Web that is referred to by some as the Semantic Web. But the Green Team was thinking about these capabilities before the Web was born.

They determined that to create this network they would require a programming language capable of enabling different devices from different manufacturers to talk to one another. They began by examining the existing programming languages to see which, if any, they might be able to adapt to suit their needs. They first considered the C++ language — a popular, object-oriented programming language that had evolved from an earlier language called C — as a starting point. But C++ is a compiled language, which means that the language instructions that make up the programming statements must be processed for a particular architecture before they can be interpreted by a device. Program compilation diminishes a program's portability, because each device (or architecture) requires its own unique set of compiled instructions. Instead, they wanted one set of instructions for all televisions or all microwaves. They also wanted a language that would support incremental updates in order to simplify the process of updating instructions, adding features, fixing problems, and so on. A compiled language could not meet these requirements, and the other languages they examined were also compiled. Accordingly, they set out to create a new language. Years later, that language would be named Java.

By incorporating many of the best features from several languages, including C++, LISP, and Smalltalk, they managed to create a robust language that Gosling named Oak, because an oak tree was the first thing he saw outside his window when a name had to be chosen. To deal with the issue of portability, they built a virtual machine (VM) to act as intermediary between the Oak language programs and the surrounding environment of the computer or microprocessor. The VM functioned as an abstraction of a particular device (e.g., a personal computer or the thermostat of a heating system) and its features. The VM isolated the Oak program from the operating environment of the device, allowing the program to treat general conditions, like raising or lowering a volume control, while the VM translated the general instructions into the highly specific instructions implemented differently by each manufacturer. Since only the VM would interact with the program, one program could run on any number of like devices. A separate VM would have to be created for each distinctly different device, but this was a reasonable tradeoff against needing to create a separate program for each device. Moreover, creating a VM for larger, multifunctional devices, like computers, made the tradeoff seem that much more favorable since such devices could be expected to run any number of different Oak programs.

They created a prototype to show Sun management what the company had been spending its money on. What they built was something like the Swiss Army Knife of remote control devices, something that could control the interconnected devices in a smart home. They named it *7, after the code sequence used on their telephone system that allowed any telephone to answer any other telephone that was part of the system. Its first physical form was described as follows:

> *7 was digital particleboard, assembled from an almost shocking array of bits and parts. It was a teensy Sharp television, a set of Nintendo Game Boy speakers, some Sony Walkman connectors, a Sun workstation's innards, a couple of *batteries from hell*, and a military spectrum radio, all held together by solder and prayers, and emceed by a perky cartoon fella named Duke, who leaped about its screen pointing things out *7 had no keyboard. Users navigated and managed it by poking and twiddling their fingers across its face.[1]

McNealy and others viewed the prototype in September, 1992. They were quick to recognize the immense value of the work that the prototype represented, and this led to a series of changes. The Green Team was dissolved and in its place a business unit called First Person was formed. It was time for more formal arrangements with more specific and more practical plans. This meant scrapping the idea of a network of smart home devices. It was considered too expensive a proposition and not something appliance manufacturers were even remotely ready for. However, interactive television (ITV) was considered by many the next big thing in the early 1990s, and Oak seemed tailor-made for it.

ITV is often referred to as "the Web that never happened." Commercialization of the Internet was just starting. Cable television was already entrenched and its popularity was rising quickly. Internet access was slowly but surely gaining popularity. Everyone had a television, but far fewer people also owned a personal computer. Consequently, it seemed that the most expedient way to bring new multimedia services into the home environment was through cable television. The objective was to offer a television-based service that was interactive and that included the communication and information access services of the Internet. ITV would, for example, combine new entertainment services, like video on demand (i.e., being able to select and pay for movies through the television's remote), with the capability of shopping for such things as clothes, furniture, and electronics.

Unlike other typical household appliances, which cost less than one hundred dollars, ITV boxes, which cost several hundred dollars, could easily absorb the extra twenty-something dollars that an embedded Oak microprocessor chip would cost. Best of all, from Sun's perspective, the success of ITV would lead to large expenditures for computer servers to house and supply all the resources that ITV would provide. Such servers constituted the principal revenue stream for Sun's computer hardware business. But, in the end, consumer interest did not match that of the media giants and the cable and telecommunication industry experts. Oak continued to languish in relative obscurity, an exciting new language waiting for the right application and the right moment.

What Sun and the creators of Oak were waiting for, without yet knowing it, was the advent of the World Wide Web. Commercial and consumer focus in the early 1990s centered on the personal computer; and the growing popularity of the personal computer led to an increasing interest in multimedia applications. Combining text and graphics with audio and video components, animations, and special effects was quickly becoming as popular in the business environment as in the home. With the arrival of the Web and the first browsers, interest in multimedia rose to new levels. Oak seemed well suited to the multimedia capabilities of the personal computer. But to many of the engineers at First Person, who were always thinking ahead, exploring how to apply the capabilities of Oak on desktop computers was a step backward. Nevertheless, Patrick Naughton, one of the lead engineers, used

Oak to write a very basic, but functional, Web browser in July, 1994. He took Oak in the direction of the Internet by means of the Web, and there was no turning back after that.

Oak, everyone quickly acknowledged, was a natural fit for the Internet; it was almost as though it had been designed with the Internet in mind. After all, what these engineers had been thinking about from the start was a generalized model of networked communication between any number and type of discrete objects. Wasn't this also the basic model of the Internet? Instead of toasters and televisions and microwaves, their new network model would contain computers and other connected devices, across the ever-growing Internet or within a company's or home's internal network, or intranet. Oak was conceptualized as being embedded in the network. It was conceived as something that was fundamental to a network and that tied everything together (that connected up the dots, and more) through the intelligence represented in its programming model.

Starting in September, 1994, the Oak team, now functioning under the name Liveoak, turned Naughton's prototype into a fully functional browser in a few weeks. The browser was named WebRunner in tribute to one of the group's favorite movies, "Blade Runner." Meanwhile, the first applet was created by Jonathan Payne. Its function — a box was programmed to turn itself red — could not have been simpler. But it made a loud and lasting statement regarding the potential of what they had created. Others joined in, and soon they had their old, animated friend from *7, Duke, waving his hand in a browser window. This was followed by bouncing and spinning coke cans and then the bouncing head of Jonathan Payne. At the time they were doing this, in 1994, a Web page that mixed text and graphics was considered state-of-the-art. The engineers of Oak were looking at the future of the Web, and in some respects that of the Internet, too, and they knew it.

Then the first source of conflict emerged. The team felt that Oak, the language, the browser, everything, should be openly available and free for the taking. Netscape was giving its browser away; it was freely available for anyone to download. They figured that success would be measured, for Netscape's Navigator browser as well as for Oak, by the speed with which the product gained acceptance and its ability to acquire early dominance of the market. Netscape, however, was not giving its source code away. You could download the browser and use it as much or as little as you liked. But you couldn't change it, adapt it, or see how it was constructed. Moreover, Netscape had its own plans for bringing in revenue, plans that were helped by giving away its browser and using it to brand the company name in the marketplace. The situation with Oak was very different.

Compared to the resources that Netscape allocated to the development of its browser, the resources that Sun allocated to Oak were very small. But the goal for Oak to operate on many different architectures, especially the various and very popular Windows and Macintosh architectures, was just as lofty and perhaps even more difficult to attain. The engineers of Oak realized they would need help — a grassroots kind of help, a quintessentially Internet kind of help — to get VMs built for each of the different computer architectures that were popular at the time. Security was also a factor for Oak. Applets run on an individual's computer, and because they are executed locally, it was essential that guarantees about an applet's inability to harm a person's computer hardware, operating system, or files be understood, accepted, and believed. The only way to convince people of this was to let them see for themselves what was in the code. Enabling other people to help build VMs and convincing people that Oak's security measures were sound required giving people free access to the source code. Moreover, the team also wanted to make sure that Oak did not become another casualty of uninformed, short-sighted corporate business practices, something that many of them feared because of their earlier experience developing NeWS. They figured that once Oak was out there — on the Internet and in the hands of others — it would live on despite what Sun management (or others) wanted.

The team members were nervous, and rightfully so. They had already been burned once. Moreover, there was the painfully obvious business question that even they could not avoid or overlook: how do you make a business out of giving something away? Worse yet, they weren't talking about giving away an application. They were talking about giving away a whole technology. Their general philosophy and their concerns were much the same as those expressed by the early Internet engineers and the creator of the Web. But the management at Sun had the foresight and wisdom to provide the free reign that the team requested. No doubt Sun co-founders Bill Joy and Scott McNealy shared some of that Internet-inspired vision and spirit of public domain technology that benefited everyone that was so ingrained in the team. Consequently, an alpha version of Oak was released by Sun in December, 1994. The language and the browser were placed on a server available for download outside of Sun's firewall. Shortly afterwards, realizing that Oak and WebRunner were already trademarked, the group brainstormed to find new names. The name they finally agreed on to replace Oak was Java and the name to replace WebRunner was HotJava.

The crucial turning point for Java came during the spring of 1995. First was the well-planned press leak, orchestrated by the project's long-time marketing person, Kim Polese. It was March 23rd and on the front page of "The San Jose Mercury News" was the story line, "Why Sun thinks HotJava will give you a lift," accompanied by a glowing endorsement from Netscape's Marc Andreessen. This was followed in May — at the annual SunWorld conference — by the announcement of a deal between Netscape and Sun to incorporate Java into Netscape's Navigator browser. The combination of the media attention, the partnership with Netscape, and the demonstrations at the conference showing animations of Duke, interactive crossword puzzles, stock portfolio tickers, and many more such exciting, inventive creations, made it clear to most people that Java was now the next big thing.

The Java Language and Environment

If you tried to do much with Java in 1995 you quickly understood both its promise and its problems; it offered an empowering new approach to programming, but it was not quite ready for mainstream use. Apart from the problems caused by the simple facts that it was new, that it had bugs, that it made demands on your computer in terms of memory and processing power that most computers could not yet tolerate, the additional fact that Java was network-based meant that it also made demands on your network connection. With a local area network and a high-speed Internet connection, which, if you were fortunate, you might have at work, it functioned well enough. But with a home connection to the Internet via an ISP and a modem, a Java applet more often tried your patience than it amused or entertained you. Faster computers with more memory and faster connections to the Internet resolved most of these problems. What's amazing, however, is how many people recognized back in 1995 the transforming effects that Java was going to produce. Some people even envisioned that Java would help eliminate the stranglehold on the development of new software applications produced by the Microsoft Windows and Intel CPU association often referred to as Wintel.

A Java application, which was written once but could run anywhere, threatened to upset one of the main constructs behind choosing which type of computer or computer architecture to purchase. This applied to home computer purchases and to computer purchases made by businesses. Microsoft's operating systems, for instance, are considered by many to be inferior to those of its competitors, such as the operating systems produced by Apple and Sun. Yet computers running Microsoft's operating systems and its applications dominate the market. One reason for this is that Microsoft-based systems run the greatest number of applications, and they often come packaged with most of the software that people routinely use.

With the coming of Java, the operating system in general, and Microsoft's operating systems in particular, suddenly became far less significant factors in deciding which computer to buy. Consequently, Microsoft's stranglehold (whether real or perceived), especially with respect to the desktop computer market, was threatened by Java's architecture-neutral approach to application development and deployment. Moreover, Java introduced the notion of network-based applications that you paid for only when you wanted to use them, thereby eliminating the need to purchase software outright. Many people had been eagerly waiting for something like this, which had the potential to upset the existing balance of power, return control to the individual, and restore competition to the marketplace.

When you examine the Java language, three prominent features are apparent. These features, which led many to believe that another technology-based revolution was about to take place, happen to be the same three features that contributed to the enormous popularity and amazing growth of the Internet. First, the Java language is an open standard, no different in effect than the open standards that define the Internet, like TCP/IP. By making Java an open standard, Sun created a level playing field. Sun was also drawing a sharp contrast between itself and Microsoft by emphasizing its commitment to the grassroots, open source development environment of the Internet. Microsoft's technology, which consisted of the code for its operating systems (e.g., Windows 2000 and Windows XP) and applications (e.g., Word and Excel), was proprietary and controlled exclusively by Microsoft. With Java, no one had the upper hand; not even Sun. The infrastructure was there for everyone to see and for everyone to use in constructing whatever they envisioned.

Second, Java is inherently extensible. The object-oriented composition of the language, combined with a feature called inheritance, enables you to build new objects quickly, simply, and safely. Inheritance functions much as you might expect; its purpose is to pass on qualities, features, and instructions as defined in some body of code (e.g., a file or a collection of files) for its use in a program. It enables you to take an existing object that defines some data, behavior, or condition, inherit all of its properties, and then easily amend or expand those properties in a way suited to your specific purpose. Like Java, the Internet's composition is inherently extensible. The Web — a service on the Internet — is an excellent example of this. The definition of URLs for the Web (a URL specifies the location of an object on the Web, such as an HTML page) builds on the Domain Name System (DNS) of the Internet, which names and locates Internet objects such as our computers. URLs inherit all the features and functionality of DNS and extend them to identify Web objects housed on the Internet. The facility of inheritance in Java allows you to easily build on the work of others, thereby reducing the time it takes to build new products, while increasing their quality and reliability.

Third, Java keeps its complexity hidden from us. Its design allows its technology to remain transparent. This dates back to *7 and the Green Team's requirement that objects on the network should be able to talk amongst themselves and figure things out without our intervention. You put a tape into the VCR and it does everything else for you, without any additional instructions or assistance. The same is true of a Web page that contains, for example, a Java applet that streams an information ticker across your screen with the latest news headlines or football scores. With respect to the Java applet, you do nothing; everything is done for you. The applet transfers automatically from the Web server to your computer. It executes (i.e., starts running) automatically, without requiring you to press a button or type in a name. It then displays its scrolling ticker window through your browser. As time passes, it automatically sends data back to the Web server in the form of a short message asking for updated information, which then gets transferred to your computer and displayed in the ticker. There is no need for you to know that Java is there, doing all this in the background. Its operation is deliberately seamless and hidden.

The Internet functions in much the same seamless, transparent way. This is one reason why so many people have a difficult time understanding what the Internet is and how it works and distinguishing the Internet from its services like email and the Web. The Internet was engineered so that its complexity was layered, with most of its layers hidden from view and outside the scope of our direct interaction. You click on a button to send an email message. You don't need to see, know about, or understand the communication that occurs between your computer and the mail server at your ISP, or the further communication between your ISP and the destination for your email. What do you care that the "I love you" expressed in a message to your significant other gets packaged up as zeros and ones, is stuffed into IP packets with header information about the message source, its destination, and the other packets that compose your message, and is then whisked away via TCP across any number of network nodes on the Internet. We would all go back to pens and paper and the mail system of the postal service if we had to know about and think about all these things. No, all you have to do is click that button; all those other events happen on your behalf, silently, effortlessly, invisibly.

Java does not just share certain properties and design considerations with the Internet. Its greatest significance is its distinction as a programming language *for* the Internet. It promises to deliver a future in which the network is the computer and the applications we use and the data we store are housed on the network and are available when needed from any number of networked devices. The Internet allowed us all to become connected across its endless, distributed, adaptable network. The Web established an information space, providing a simple means for us to find, collect, and publish information. Java provides the Internet a programmable intelligence that is as architecturally neutral as the Internet itself, enabling applications and data to be fully portable rather than locked into one architecture or one computer.

Java and E-Business

Java evolved over the latter half of the 1990s from a limited, but promising language for creating small, client-side mini-applications called applets, designed to run within the confines of a browser window, into a rich, robust language and programming environment for creating independent, large-scale applications. The core language was substantially improved by Sun during this period. Moreover, a wide range of toolkits, libraries, and APIs were produced by Sun and many others; these extended the reach of the language and facilitated the process of building Java applications. In a word, Java matured.

During this same period, as the Web grew exponentially and the terms dot com, e-commerce, and e-business entered our common vocabulary, Java became the platform of choice for companies seeking to bridge the gaps between the Internet, the Web, and their business operations. IBM was one of many companies to embrace Java and, in doing so, under the leadership of its CEO, Lou Gerstner, it changed the way it conducted business while it changed the business it was in and how it generated revenue.

Before Gerstner's arrival at IBM in 1993, IBM was the industry giant of mainframe computer technology and proprietary operating systems. IBM was in many ways as antithetical to the revolution taking place on the Internet — and the one poised to take place on the Web — as Microsoft, if not more so. Coincidentally (or not), IBM was in dire straits; it was heading towards oblivion, as the computing world in which it did business had been transformed — in no small part because of the Internet — and IBM had failed to change along with it.

Under Gerstner's leadership, IBM reinvented itself. As IBM changed over the remainder of the 1990s, it discovered that its future was directly tied to that of the Internet; and it adjusted its focus accordingly. In the process, IBM embraced Java and placed it at the center of its e-business solution with a product called Websphere. This meant that one of the largest computer hardware, software, and services organizations in the world recognized that Java was critical to the goal of dominating the e-business market; it adopted Java for its own use and for resale to others. Consider the following statement Gerstner made in the spring of 2000 at IBM's annual meeting of stockholders.

> Let's start with software. If the Net has made one thing explicit, it's that integration is the name of the game. Companies are going to build competitive advantage by driving a level of integration never seen before and never possible before -- integration of business processes and integration of the computer applications that support them -- everything the business does from the point of customer contact all the way to manufacturing, service, support and on out to their supply chain partners. Everything connects.

> So more and more customers are realizing that e-business isn't about spinning off some part of the company and calling it a 'dot-com.' It's not about creating one dot. It's about connecting all the dots within the enterprise. This demand for increasing levels of integration is in turn driving demand for software to provide that integration -- particularly in the layer called middleware, which accounts for 75 percent of everything customers spend on software.[2]

Gerstner's comments, made seven years after he took control of the company, reveal his understanding that the Internet, e-business, and the integration of information were central to the interests of IBM customers and the business community at large. For IBM, Java took on a significant role in connecting all the dots, within the company and for its customers. IBM was neither the first nor was it alone in recognizing the potential of Java and adopting its technology. But its action rang out loud and clear.

What was it about Java that helped bring about the creation of e-business and that integrated the information and operation of a business with computers and the Internet? The answer, like so many others related to the Internet and the Web, centers on the elimination of barriers. The Internet eliminated geographic and technological barriers between computers. The Web eliminated geographic and technological barriers between information. Java took this concept one step further and eliminated the barriers between the resources that composed the Internet, the information that composed the Web, and pretty much everything in between.

Think about it this way. The Internet was built, grew, and continues to evolve because it was purposefully designed to be unaware of and unconcerned with the data that it carries, the computers that are attached to it, and the people using it. It provides and defines the infrastructure, but it is detached from the infrastructure's specific, daily use. For example, the Internet doesn't know and doesn't need to know anything about the Web to allow the Web's technology to make use of it. Similarly, the Web knows about the Internet; the definitions for HTTP and the URL depend on that understanding. But the Web is purposefully disconnected from the information it carries. Whether a Web page contains the Gettysburg address, a photo of Madonna, the Beatle's song "Let It Be," a crossword puzzle applet, or all of the above, is irrelevant to the Web, its purpose, and its functionality.

Java, on the other hand, knows about and can interconnect everything. It knows all about networking in general and the Internet in particular. It knows all about the Web, including URLs, HTTP, and HTML. It knows about XML and databases, fonts and colors, audio and video properties, and more. Java understands and interconnects data, devices, and applications on one system, across a network of systems, or across the Internet. Meanwhile, it doesn't care if your computer equipment is from IBM, Dell, or Sun, if your database software comes from Oracle or Sybase, or if your data center is in Wichita, while your offices are located in San Francisco and Poughkeepsie.

Java can run the Web server that takes your book order. It can communicate with your credit card company to validate your card number, expiration date, and billing address. It can connect to the warehouse database to check that the book is in stock and then issue a transaction that processes your order, allocates one of the books to you, and so on. In doing so, Java effectively unifies the merchant's data across all organizations and all points of access in the business. The warehouse manager, using her computer and specialized interface to check on book stocks, will see precisely the same information as the telephone operator taking an order over the telephone, or you checking on a book's availability through the Web site.

This sort of integration was possible before Java, but it depended on a complete uniformity of equipment or the expensive tailoring of components, that is, a turnkey system designed exclusively for the needs of a particular business. Such systems typically required highly specific types of hardware and software, along with specialized programming to interconnect all the components. It is precisely such costs and such restrictions that Java promises to eliminate, thereby allowing you to buy and incorporate into your system a wide variety of computers, databases, and network components. Java runs anywhere and connects all the dots, and it manages to do this seamlessly, hiding the complexity.

Such integration means more than cutting costs and giving a business more choices in terms of the equipment it chooses to buy. It also provides the means to isolate data from the business rules surrounding its use and to reduce the ways we duplicate information and the ways we interact with it. One way Java achieves this is by helping to separate business logic from issues related to information storage, access, and display. This encapsulation and separation of information is the key to building, managing, and profiting from a fully integrated e-business, whether or not it is commerce-based.

For example, Java can help you isolate specific product information, such as a book's title, author, publisher, and ISBN (unique identification), from the business logic that contains calculations for determining the book's shipping costs or margin of profit. It can also isolate this data from issues related to who can access such information or how the data gets displayed to different employees in the company or to different customers on the Web site. Java can do all this without making specific demands on the type of Web server you are using, or the particular database providing persistent storage of the data, or the types of computers used by your employees. One day you might use HTML to display the information on your Web site, the next day you might use Java Server Pages (JSP) or perhaps XML. Such changes can be made and consolidated through Java, leaving the underlying data and its associated business logic unchanged, and also leaving unchanged how your customers or employees view and interact with the data.

Java is capable of weaving all these separate components together behind the scenes according to the business logic programmed to the specific needs of the business. Such a system can be as simple or as complex as you need it to be. It can grow as your business grows and can easily adapt as new technology gets introduced. Java facilitates all this by being architecturally neutral, object-oriented and component-based, distributed and portable, robust and secure. The technology of Java is far from intuitive or even easy to explain. But what it lacks in these areas it more than makes up for in terms of what it can do in the right hands.

Java Everything

Java wants to be everywhere. Eventually, it may come full circle and take up residence on microprocessor chips in our microwaves, televisions, and telephones. Chips are substantially cheaper and far more common today than they were when the Green Team was created; and now networks are everywhere, at work, in our homes, carried in our backpacks and handbags, and even clipped onto our belts. Why not Java, too?

Sun provides Java in three separate platforms, in order to accommodate the three different networked computing environments that currently exist. The first platform is called the Standard Edition, also known as J2SE. This platform is designed for those building and deploying client-side Java applications. These applications are the independent programs we can download and run on our computers, such as Java word processors and painting applications, notepads and recipe managers. Such programs promise one day to replace the shrink-wrapped software that we buy in stores or that is packaged with the computers we buy. They can be pulled off the network when we want to install them and updated across the network when new features are introduced or patches are needed to fix existing problems. In a business environment, they offer still greater advantages. A single technical support person can install these programs in one place on the network. Employees can then pull programs down to their computers as needed, or a Java program can push the programs down to the client computers across the network at night or over the weekend. Java provides the necessary tools; the network becomes the delivery mechanism.

The second platform, and by far the largest and most sophisticated, is called the Enterprise Edition, also known as J2EE. J2EE is where Java and the power and efficiencies of e-business meet. J2EE focuses on server-side information management. It enables an organization to identify and distribute all its business information into separate, modular, re-usable components for the purposes of storage, sharing, transfer, display, updating, and security. J2EE also provides a wide range of networked services that function to interconnect these distributed components as needed. These services are used, for example, to extract information from a database (e.g., retrieve account information, like a mailing address, when a customer clicks on a Web form to pay for a purchase) and then place that information into something called a JavaBean component (a type of basic, reusable data container), which is then read by the Web server to display the data. The bottom line is that J2EE handles the infrastructure of information management — the basic framework and organization of information — allowing you to focus your attention on improving the business logic, the component that controls the use and value of that information.

The third platform is called the Micro Edition, also known as J2ME. This is the realm of Java appliances, devices that range from smart cards that pop in and out of computers, toys, and a wide assortment of electronic devices, to telephones and pagers, to set-top television boxes that manage cable or satellite services, to car navigation systems. J2ME is a Java optimized for the features and properties of small, dedicated electronic devices. Introducing Java into the operations of these devices will, at the very least, integrate these devices into an encompassing network, enabling them to share information and be controlled remotely. But it will also make such devices more adaptable, enabling them to be repaired or enhanced as needed. For example, a Java-powered car navigation system on a wireless communication network could easily keep you informed of road conditions as you drive along from location to location, or automatically update its maps for a city you are about to enter. The possibilities are endless.

If Java is going to be everywhere, in applets and in full-blown applications, in servers running Web sites and clusters of networked computers handling the information needs of e-business, in appliances in our homes and offices, what about a simple Java computer terminal to replace the personal computers that many people find troublesome, clumsy, costly, and difficult to use? Sun and IBM tried to introduce such machines, powered by a Java operating system, into the business environment in 1998. They promoted the machines as a way to lower a business's costs for purchasing computers and greatly reducing, even eliminating, maintenance costs. Their Java machines did not require client data backups, software or operating system updates, or even software installations, because all the applications and data were stored remotely, on larger, centrally located and centrally maintained computers, unlike most personal computers that stored data principally, if not exclusively, on a local hard drive. Consequently, the total cost of ownership for such machines was substantially lower than it was for comparably powered personal computers. The timing, however, was not right for such a leap forward, particularly given the continued dominance of Microsoft desktop applications; the project was canceled the following year.

It is only a matter of time before Java terminals, or comparable devices, find a place in both business environments and the home. Such devices are capable of mimicking the look and feel of today's personal computers, but they will be easier to maintain and update and less costly to purchase. More importantly, they can be produced as a basic network appliance that connects us to the Internet and that frees us from concerns about losing or corrupting data on a local disk drive, becoming infected with a virus, or being frustrated by misconfigured applications. Finally, such devices effectively extend the Internet in a fully integrated and vendor-neutral manner right onto our desk, into our kitchens, and anywhere else we may want to access information or communicate.

In a way, Java is leading computing in general — and networked computing in particular — both backward in time and forward. Java provides the means to turn the Internet, business intranets, and even home computer networks, into the type of client-server model that flourished when large, expensive mainframes ruled the computing world. Back then, you might have anything from a dumb terminal (i.e., a monitor with a keyboard), to a PC, to a workstation on your desk; and everyone used the resources of one or more centrally located, mainframe computers. These mainframes ran applications and provided computing services with greater power, speed, and efficiency than anything that could be put onto a desktop. But this client-server model lost out to the seemingly less expensive and more distributed model of personal computers.

Today's typical computing environment, in which resources are duplicated on everyone's computer, gross inequities and incompatibilities are common from computer to computer, installation, configuration, and maintenance costs are high, and use of the network itself is extremely limited, cries out for change. Java can bring the lost, client-server model efficiencies back into business computing and, for the first time, into home computing. It can reduce application costs, and allow applications to be shared and accessed across the network. Through J2EE, Java provides a powerful server environment that makes it easier for businesses to maximize use both of their data and of their networked environment, while removing common incompatibility issues and hiding the complexity of the technology. Best of all, Java provides a common, robust language through which devices large and small, from any manufacturer and running any operating system, can communicate, share information, and function together across any network. This makes Java the language of the Internet.

Internet Access: The Digital Divide and Beyond

The Digital Divide

The digital divide is a new name for an age-old issue: the gap between the *haves* and the *have nots*. The technology of the information age has added a new dimension to this separation. Access to and knowledge of computers and the Internet — or the lack of such access and knowledge — has become another means to categorize, differentiate, and divide both individuals and groups, as this chapter explains.

The importance of this divide depends on your perspective and on your understanding of the technology. If all you see in this new technology is another way to shop, correspond, chat, play games, or listen to music — activities that undoubtedly constitute a large percentage of computer and Internet use — then the digital divide may not seem all that significant. If, on the other hand, you view computers and the Internet as enablers and equalizers; if you recognize the importance of the technology as a new and powerful tool for communicating and socializing, a rich and vast resource for accessing information and entertainment, and a revolutionary advance in performing business transactions; if you believe that the Internet and its array of services have the potential to help break down the barriers between nations, peoples, races, age groups, economic classes, and the sexes; if you acknowledge the unlimited capacity of this technology to offer new and exciting educational and employment opportunities; then the digital divide is an important issue that you may want to better understand and, ultimately, see eliminated.

The U.S. Department of Commerce has been actively measuring the use of computers and the Internet, as well as the disparities in their use, since the mid-1990s. Other organizations, like the Center for Democracy and Technology and Eurostat, have been examining the digital divide by documenting its changing composition and exploring its ramifications in Europe, Asia, and elsewhere throughout the world. Overlooking, for the moment, any differences of opinion related to the reasons behind the digital divide, all of these organizations agree on one key point: there exists a fundamental incongruity between the egalitarian, democratizing potential of the Internet and the very large number of individuals, and specific groups of individuals, who either cannot afford access to the Internet or who cannot locate some type of free access (e.g., through a local library or community center). Governments, commercial and non-profit organizations, and others are working in just about every region of the world to redress this problem by making available some type of affordable or community-based, free access to the Internet. But it's clear that, even with such efforts, the digital divide is not going to disappear for some time to come.

A large number and wide range of factors are responsible for creating the divide. One principal factor is the affordability and accessibility of telephone service. The telecommunications infrastructure varies considerably from country to country. In wealthy, highly industrialized countries, such as the U.S., Canada, Japan, and France, telephone service is inexpensive and reliable, it's available everywhere, and it's generally regarded as a necessity. In poorer, less industrialized countries, such as Afghanistan, Bangladesh, and Sri Lanka, telephone service is expensive, the quality of service is lower (which has a greater impact on data communications than on voice communications), it's not available to a large percentage of households, and it's generally regarded as a luxury. Easy and inexpensive access to reliable telephone service is responsible for bringing Internet access into the homes (and businesses) of millions of people across the globe. Of equal importance is that a lack of such access is keeping many millions of others on the other side of the digital divide.

Inexpensive, reliable, and ubiquitous telephone service, and the local availability of free Internet access, are responsible for lessening the overall digital divide. But by themselves they are not able to eliminate the divide; nor are they able to address many of the less apparent but more entrenched causes of the divide. Even in wealthy countries, such as the U.S.; where nearly all homes have telephone service, there are striking divisions in the population with respect to who uses (and who does not use) the Internet and from what type of location access is obtained (e.g., home, work, or some public facility like a library). Moreover, there are striking disparities with respect to the types of activities for which the Internet is used, how much is understood about the technology, and how much attention is paid to concerns over growing use of the Internet with respect to the privacy and security of one's information and other online dangers. These differences constitute a more subtle aspect to the digital divide.

Studies of the digital divide reveal that geography, income, and race all play a role in determining which side of the divide one may be on. Age, gender, education, and employment are also contributing factors. Another factor is the newness of the technology. Different segments of the population adopt (and adapt to) technological innovations at different speeds. For instance, studies reveal that the older we are, the more likely we are to resist radical changes in our daily routines, work habits, and lifestyle. And few innovations (technological or otherwise) have resulted in as many radical changes as those stemming from the introduction of personal computers and the Internet. Disabilities are another factor affecting the composition of the digital divide. Computers, the Internet, and associated technologies contain the potential to improve the quality of life of individuals with disabilities by offering them new employment, educational, and social opportunities and thereby lessening the impact of their disability. For now, however, most people with disabilities remain on the far side of the digital divide, waiting on the technology to address their needs.

The following sections explore some of the different demographic groups that are represented in the divide. Each group has its own unique set of factors contributing to which side of the divide members find themselves, and the acceptance or rejection of the technology by members of each group also has its own unique set of ramifications. For instance, children born into the digital information age embrace the technology without question, while adults often find the new technology intimidating, inaccessible, or simply uninviting and uninteresting.

This chapter also explores what it means for so many individuals to have access to the public, free, and uncensored information space that is such a large and integral part of the Internet. Controversies are growing surrounding open access to the Internet, especially through community-based terminals like those installed in public libraries, as is the debate over restricting or filtering the information available through public Internet terminals and the impact of such censorship with respect to the First Amendment of the U.S. Constitution. The chapter ends with tables of U.S. census data that contain a breakdown of Internet use by gender, age, education, race, and other factors, over a period of several years. First, though, a quick overview is presented of some of the statistics related to the composition of the digital divide and the ways in which the Internet is being used.

The Numbers

Regardless of predictions, the Internet is charting its own course. That course belies the existence of any map. The Internet's dynamic and unpredictable development is one of its most distinctive and significant characteristics, and it is one that has far-reaching consequences for the composition of the digital divide. In the course of a few years, for instance, between the late 1990s and 2002, both the number of individuals who owned a computer and the number of individuals who used the Internet increased far beyond anyone's expectations. One result of this change was that certain measurable aspects of the divide in the U.S. and elsewhere, such as differences in use between urban and rural locations and between some racial groups, were reduced to the point that they were no longer considered significant.

Numbers tell a story all their own. Data compiled in the U.S. and abroad about computer and Internet use provide the necessary foundation of information from which to explore the digital divide. This data contains records about who is accessing the Internet, where this access is taking place (e.g., a home, a place of business, a library), and what activities are being pursued.

It is important to recognize, however, that these numbers are constantly changing. At best, they present a snapshot in time. Moreover, both the technology and makeup of the Internet are highly dynamic. They are also closely interconnected; that is, changes in one (e.g., advances in wireless network technology) can rapidly and radically affect the other (who is using the Internet and how it is being used).

The following information summarizes the most significant figures relating to the use of computers and the Internet in the U.S. This information was derived from U.S. statistics compiled in late 2001 and again in late 2003 by the U.S. Census Bureau.[1] The numbers from 2001 indicate:

- Use of the Internet is increasing at a rate of two million new users each month.

- More than half the country's population is online, while two-thirds uses computers.

- Teenagers and pre-teens show the highest saturation of computer and Internet use, with 90% using computers and 70% using the Internet.

- Sizable increases in annual growth rates among lower-income households, minorities, and rural populations over the course of a year or two have lessened the divide with higher-income households, whites, and urban areas, respectively. The highest changed growth rate was seen in households of single mothers with children.

- Higher-speed, broadband Internet connections are slowly growing in popularity for home Internet access, but 80% of all home connections are still through dial-up services.

- Nearly half the U.S. population uses email.

- Roughly one-third of Internet users search for product or service information, seek out health information, and make purchases online.

- Individuals with computer and Internet access at work are roughly twice as likely to have a computer and Internet access at home as those who don't use them at work.

In 2001, the amazing rate at which individuals were joining the Internet was having the greatest impact on the composition of the Internet. Two years later that rate had slowed considerably, and it was the rising use of broadband Internet connections that was having the greatest impact on the composition and use of the Internet. The numbers from 2003 indicate:

- Households with Internet connections rose by 12.6% during the two years between the surveys (between September 2001 and October 2003).

- Households with broadband Internet connections more than doubled during that same period (rising from 9.1% to 19.9%), while households with dial-up connection declined by over 6%.

- Nearly one-third of the U.S. population (31.9%) accesses the Internet every day, and 90% of these individuals access the Internet from their home.

- Email remains the most popular service of the Internet; nearly all Internet users send and receive email.

- The gender gap in overall Internet use has been eliminated, although older age groupings still show more male than female users. (It's interesting to note that the gender gap still exists among Europeans, with a measurable difference of 6-7% more male than female users. This difference, however, drops to 2% in the 16-24 age grouping.)

- Some gaps remain pronounced, as evidenced by continued differences in use measured by age groupings, race, education level, finances, and location.

- Individuals with disabilities remain predominantly on the far side of the divide.

- Broadband Internet users are more likely to access the Internet on a daily basis and they are more likely to engage in a wider variety of activities on the Internet.

- Reasons given by individuals for not having Internet access at home are: not needed/not interested (41.6%), too expensive (22.9%), no computer or inadequate computer (22.5%).

The 2001 and 2003 statistics reveal that demand for computer and Internet use is amazingly high and continues to grow at a considerable, but slowing pace across all segments of the U.S population. These same statistics also reveal that, while a significant percentage of the U.S. population may be online, there is another large segment of the population (over 40% in 2003) that remains offline, either through choice or through circumstance.

The following chart reinforces this picture of growth and of the basic divide. It also indicates a strong and ever-increasing correlation between home computer ownership and Internet access, with nearly every home computer now connecting to the Internet. The advent of personal computers in the 1980s changed the landscape of computers, their use, and their significance. Less than twenty years later, it is networking — and the Internet in particular — that is responsible for changing that landscape all over again.

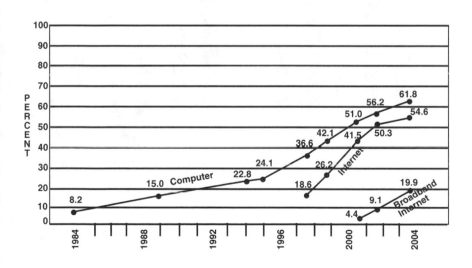

Figure 1. Computer and Internet Access in U.S. Homes

Some basic Internet usage numbers collected from European countries both in and outside the European Union (EU) in 2004 speak to a different element of the digital divide, one related to geography. These statistics, as shown in the following chart, measure general Internet access from any location, rather than from just work or the home. They reveal a considerable and surprising disparity. Even among these industrialized countries, where one might expect to find only modest differences with respect to the adoption of new technologies, there is nearly a 70 point difference in use separating countries with the greatest and the least Internet usage.[2]

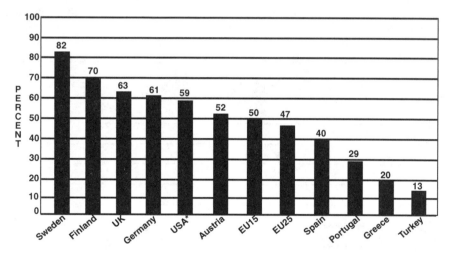

*Note: USA numbers are from October, 2003. All other numbers are from January, 2004.

Figure 2.   General Internet Use in Europe

Perhaps more important than the differences between these countries is the clear indication of how many people overall remain beyond the Internet's reach, or for whatever reason choose not to go online. These numbers include an EU25 average (average use across the expanded, 25-member EU) of over 50% and 80% and higher in Greece and Turkey. Upon examining less industrialized nations across Africa and Asia, it becomes even more apparent that the global Internet and the World Wide Web are in actuality far less global than their names and their promises suggest. Geography and fundamental economics are more responsible for keeping people on the far side of the digital divide than any other factors. Unfortunately, politics also plays a role. These factors will take the greatest time and the effort to address.

There are some two billion people on the planet who do not have any access to reliable electricity. To many, providing these people with Internet access makes as much sense as giving them a refrigerator or a microwave oven. Technology advocates argue, however, that the issue here is more subtle. It should not be a question of one or the other. They envision the Internet as another means to combat poverty, through making such fundamental deficiencies and needs known to the community at large, effectively using the infrastructure of the Internet to better network our societies and cultures, and to provide opportunities, for instance, for education and employment, where before they were few or none. The world seems a smaller place now that information courses around the globe as fast as the speed of light. But this effect is largely an illusion, precisely because so many parts of the world remain on the far side of this technological divide. Who knows what changes may come when the Internet becomes truly global and the Web lives up to its name.

A more manageable and localized geographical factor with respect to Internet use involves where people access the Internet. You might think that community-based Internet access, such as that provided by libraries or civic organizations, plays a considerable role in extending access to a greater portion of the population. But if you look at the breakdown of Internet access locations in the U.S., as shown in the following chart, the statistics strongly support the understanding that home access has been, and may continue to be, far more responsible for the Internet's growth than access from public terminals.

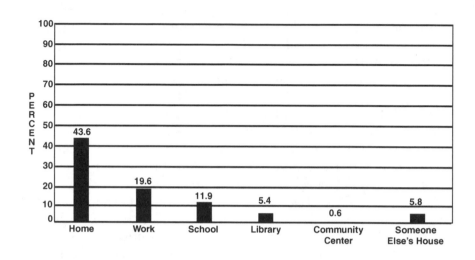

Figure 3. Breakdown of Internet Location Access in the U.S.

The numbers showing the distribution of access tell one story. That story is largely one of privilege, in which individuals and employers purchase access to the Internet because they can afford to and because it provides some personal or professional economic gain or it satisfies some other need. But many people view Internet access as more than just another commodity to buy and sell, because they see far more to the Internet than a privatized, commercialized network of services, information, and products. They look to the numbers to reveal where and how much progress is being made on providing public Internet access. They regard these numbers as a more compelling story about usage of the Internet and about the digital divide.

Public Internet access, which is provided in schools, libraries, and community centers, speaks more to the fundamentally egalitarian nature of the Internet and its relevance outside of work and the home. Many regional governments have made it their priority to bring Internet access into every local school and library. Local and national organizations, as well as international organizations like the United Nations, are pursuing a similar path to bring public Internet access to as many people as possible.

These efforts communicate a clear understanding of the importance of equal and free access to the Internet and its resources, for purposes of education and exploration, training and the hope for better employment, communication with friends and family, and any number of other activities.

Finally, a look at how people are using the Internet tells yet another part of the story.

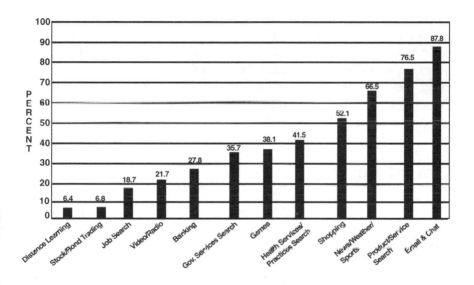

Figure 4. Breakdown of Internet Activities in the U.S.

It's no surprise that email still constitutes the most common use of the Internet; it's unlikely this will change any time soon. Much of the remaining activities consist of browsing the Web in search of information or in search of something to buy. When broadband access becomes far more commonplace than it is today this breakdown will probably change in favor of more media-rich services, like streaming audio and video, and more dynamic, interactive environments through which people will meet, exchange ideas, and interact, either for entertainment or for work (think of the Multi-User Dimensions, or MUDs, discussed in *The Internet Revolution*).

It's impossible to determine which story being told by all these collected statistics is most compelling. Is it the phenomenal, widespread growth of computers and the Internet? After all, personal computers have only been available since the 1980s, while the commercial Internet and the Web have only been available since the mid 1990s. Or is it the lessening, but still prominent disparity with respect to who has access to the Internet and what this means potentially in terms of education, employment, and other areas, like access to information about events as those events are happening? It's hard to deny that the Internet offers something for everyone. But it still has many obstacles to overcome before it can include everyone, before it becomes as approachable and as easy to operate as a telephone or television, and before it contains the necessary controls to protect young eyes from inappropriate, and perhaps damaging, information and interactions. Some of these issues are explored below.

Born into an Internet World

Teenagers and pre-teens make up one extreme of the digital divide, where the gap is narrowest and an understanding of the consequences of using the technology is far less than it should be. Teenagers and pre-teens grew up with computers and accept them without question or hesitation. Many enjoy access to the Internet from their home; and, in the U.S. and elsewhere, most children can access the Internet from their school. For them, the Internet is more like a natural extension of the telephone. The Internet is a destination where they meet friends, interact together through gaming environments, locate information related to school work or other activities, and explore the world. They have no frame of reference that allows them to understand the substantial and widespread changes that computers and the Internet have effected over the last decade or two. They have no fear of the technology and, at best, only the smallest appreciation for the types of danger and the inappropriate information that awaits them on the Internet. Nevertheless, school-age children, more than any other group, have the highest percentage of Internet use. They typically access the Internet on a daily basis; and their use is soaring. Look at the following numbers.

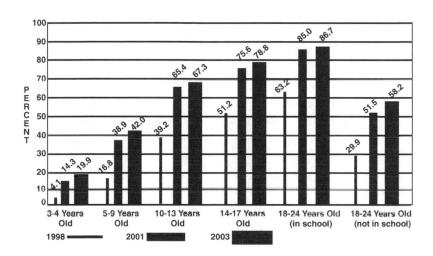

Figure 5.   U.S. Children/Young Adult Internet Usage

Parents have always had to contend with controlling their children's exposure to unsuitable images, language, and information. Television was the first technology that made this task more difficult. The creation and greater distribution of music that contained explicit and sometimes racist or misogynist lyrics increased the difficulty of this task still more, as did the release (and growing popularity) of computer games with excessive violence and sexual content. But monitoring and controlling a child's access to certain types of movies, or to news reports of the latest disaster or terrorist attack, or to inappropriate music and games, while hardly simple or foolproof, pales in comparison to monitoring and controlling a child's use of the Internet. Moreover, the exposure produced by movies and other forms of entertainment is an anonymous, passive, one-way experience. But use of the Internet is neither anonymous nor passive. Nor are the dangers of cyberspace limited to images, language, and information that is unsuitable for children; cyberspace also contains people. To complicate matters, the Internet also has the capability of extracting as much information from its users as it delivers to them.

Parents must contend with the following dangers in attempting to safeguard their children's use of the Internet. First, content on the Internet is unfiltered and offensive material is common. This material can take the form of pornography and other sexually explicit images and information. It can also confront Internet users (children and adults alike) in the form of Web sites that advocate hate, promote violence, and present overtly racist views. Even with content filters installed, it's not currently possible to avoid some kind of exposure to such explicit and offensive material. Content filters can, at best, only limit exposure to this material. More importantly, the Internet lacks any kind of rating system that might be used to identify and categorize Internet site content in a universal and uniform manner. It would be impossible to enforce such a system, even if it were to be established, given the distributed and global nature of the Internet.

Second, individuals on the Internet are often not who they represent themselves to be. Everyone has some sort of alias. It's a necessary part of the technology. For most of us, our alias is some sort of transparent representation of our identity, such as a favorite nickname, our initials, or some variation on our first and/or last names. For others, an alias is a simple and effective way to conceal one's true identity. Moreover, individuals who prey on innocent children commonly represent themselves as children as they strike up a relationship within a chat room or through email.

Third, a child's use of the computer and his or her Internet access are rarely monitored. Many adults relinquish their control directly to their children either because they are on the far side of the divide, they are uniformed about or intimidated by the technology, or for any number of other reasons. But even when a parent exerts some control, he or she cannot be there every minute. Children typically access the Internet on a daily basis, and not just from home, but from school, and perhaps from the library or a friend's house. Rules at school and at home that restrict when and how a child can access and browse the Internet are becoming more common, and they can help. But the Internet is still very much an unregulated and unfiltered environment, filled with people and information that most adults would prefer to avoid. Children who follow all the rules and who have the best intentions can still come across objectionable Web sites by accident and they can easily be deceived into thinking they are chatting with a friend when that person is actually a complete stranger. These incidents happen to adults, and there is no reason to think children are immune. But children are far more impressionable and far more at risk.

Fourth, how many children understand that they should not reveal any personal information, such as their full name, address, or phone number, when they are asked to do so? Nearly every Web site solicits this information routinely and repeatedly. Most adults don't bother reading a Web site's privacy policy page. Does anyone expect that children will read and follow this information or that they will refrain from filling out a Web site's form that promises they could win some prize because they are under a specified age? Most children are naturally trusting; and the friendly environment of a computer and the protection they typically feel when they use it at home or in some other secure environment serve to reinforce that trust.

Laws like the Children's Online Privacy Protection Act (COPPA) have been established to protect children on the Internet. They have, among other things, made it illegal for companies to collect personal information from minors, thereby broadening the burden of responsibility for protecting children on the Internet to include the Internet site owners. Recent lawsuits of several high-profile companies that were illegally collecting personal information from minors are helping to spread awareness about the commonness and consequences of these dangers to children. They also demonstrate that some protections are finally taking shape on the Internet. These protections, however, are few and far between. Children can unwittingly find trouble on the Internet with amazing ease, and the global reach of the Internet makes enacting and enforcing laws a means of partial protection at best.

Fifth, children are more and more the primary targets of online advertisers. Marketers are well aware of both the vast numbers of school-age children on the Internet every day and the money they command. Moreover, children are fully at ease with the technology. Unlike many adults, they have no qualms about purchasing items online or concerns over privacy issues related to typing in credit card and other personal information. But how much targeted marketing is too much? Sneaker companies and soda producers want nothing better than to establish a relationship with a consumer at an early, impressionable age and secure what they hope will be a consumer for life. The stakes are high. Advertising campaigns on the Internet may resemble more familiar forms of advertising delivered through television, radio, magazines, and newspapers. But any similarities are purely superficial. Advertising on the Internet is surprisingly intrusive. It tracks information about our movements on the Internet and our interests and preferences without our knowledge or consent. And it doesn't differentiate between children and adults. It's personal and potentially very dangerous.

Finally, a child's use of the Internet can quickly and easily start to replace other, very important activities, including reading, sports, and socializing with friends. The Internet offers its own unique form of social environment. This is especially true for children who are more inclined to spend many long hours in chat rooms or playing online, interactive games. But socializing on the Internet can become a substitute for socializing at home and elsewhere, leading to increased isolation. Adults are also susceptible to this behavioral effect of the Internet. Phone calls, social gatherings, and business meetings may get replaced by email, Internet chatting, and online meetings. There is something very safe, comforting, and easy about interacting with others over the Internet. But the ramifications of these behavioral changes are more profound when it comes to children. The Internet cannot replace a touch football game, a visit to a theme park, playing video games in person with friends, or the simple, intimate experience of sitting in a comfortable chair with a good book.

Born into a World of Typewriters and Card Catalogs

On the other extreme of the digital divide (when examining use of the Internet according to age groupings) are the generations of individuals who never used computers at work and to whom navigating information resources meant pulling out and thumbing through the seemingly endless rows of wooden drawers that housed the card catalog at the public library. While more and more seniors (people aged 60 or more) are discovering and learning to appreciate the value of Internet access, far more seniors remain offline (on the far side of the divide) than are going online. Additionally, seniors constitute a demographic grouping whose needs and interests are often overlooked or misunderstood on the Internet. The following chart illustrates the basic disparity in Internet use broken down by age.

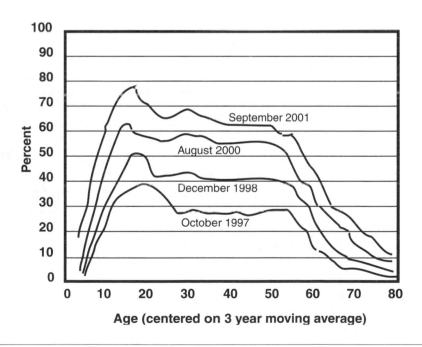

Figure 6. U.S. Internet Usage by Age Group

The reason for the low, but growing numbers of seniors on the Internet is due to a combination of factors. Unlike other demographic groupings of the digital divide, in which geography and finances play a pivotal role in making a decision about Internet access, for many seniors it's the technology itself that stands in the way. The same technology that offers the promise of a richer, better-connected, more engaging lifestyle is a hurdle all its own that needs to be faced and overcome.

Different age groups of the population welcome and adapt to large-scale changes at dramatically different rates. Technological innovations, as epitomized by the personal computer, the Internet, and the Web, often manifest even more extreme differences. Seniors were the last group to discover the technology of the Internet and to start utilizing and adapting the technology to suit their interests and needs. But like other groups that lagged behind the younger, more affluent part of the population that took to the Internet early on and in large numbers, seniors are now starting to become a specific demographic grouping to be targeted.

If you didn't grow up with computers and you never used one at work, there's no denying that you must confront the burden (or rise to the challenge) of learning about the technology of computers when you decide to purchase one and bring it into your home. If you decide to use your new computer to go online, as nearly everyone does, you must additionally learn how to navigate the Internet and the Web, each of which provides its own, unique challenges. Unfortunately, there is little about the operation of a computer that is intuitive. On the contrary, all aspects of interacting with a computer, and by extension interacting with the Internet, are contrived. On the positive side, computers excel at providing self-paced tutorials. They can teach you everything you need to know, as quickly or as slowly as you want to learn it. Surveys have shown that the vast majority of seniors now on the Internet identify themselves as self-taught, or as having taken a class in order to get started. On the negative side, even the best computers can be temperamental, respond badly to unexpected or hostile behavior (as many people can personally attest), and they have been known to test the patience of saints and sinners alike. Knowing all this, what argument do you use, with yourself, your parent, or your grandparent, to take the plunge and bring one of these unfamiliar and expensive devices home? A computer is not going to replace a worn-out television or radio, or bring something into their life that they felt was lacking. It's something entirely new, different, foreign, and unfriendly.

Ironically, the best answer to this question may be the Internet itself, effectively compounding the need to learn about computers with the need to learn about the Internet. But how do you argue that everyone should have access to a computer and the Internet, when not many years ago we all managed to live our lives comfortably without both? The most compelling argument will require a demonstration. You might begin by demonstrating the simplicity and speed of communicating through email. You might then demonstrate the fun and immediacy of interacting with others in a private or public chat room. This should make the revolutionary communication features of the Internet abundantly clear. You might provide a tour of the Internet's many information services. You could demonstrate the speed and versatility of search engines, the information integration and customization of Web portals, the helpfulness of newsgroups, and the breadth of information provided by online libraries. This should produce a convincing argument for how the Internet is responsible for inciting an information revolution. You might also introduce the purchasing possibilities of e-commerce by visiting a selection of virtual storefronts and browsing the merchandise auctioned and sold by individuals.

No matter how you go about demonstrating the Internet, the result is the same: the Internet sells itself because it has something for everyone. Often the difference between a senior (or anyone) expressing no interest in the Internet or dismissing it outright and someone who has crossed the divide and taken himself or herself online has to do with whether or not that person has discovered on the Internet some of those activities that interest them off the Internet (e.g., collecting stamps, playing cards, listening to music, monitoring the weather). The services and benefits of the Internet are hardly limited to the young.

The helping hand — and the strong opinions — of an enthusiastic child or grandchild or some other younger, experienced Internet user is frequently responsible for getting a senior onto the Internet. But once on the Internet, seniors are finding their own uses for the Internet, many of which are different than those of younger users. Seniors are less likely to frequent chat rooms, download music, or play games on the Internet. Instead, their focus is on accessing information related to the news and weather, travel, hobbies, health, and medical information, getting maps and directions, and interacting with financial services for account transactions and stock quotes. Not surprisingly, however, even among seniors, email is the most widely used service of the Internet.

What many Internet businesses and organizations have yet to discover is that not only are seniors coming online in ever larger numbers, but that, as individuals, they are spending as many or more hours online as younger users. They are also spending more money on the Internet; seniors account for a considerable (and growing) percentage of Internet transactions. Despite the facts that a sizable number of seniors are online, that their interests and activities are far more varied than is commonly realized, and that they are spending more time and more money online, marketers, information purveyors, and others in the business of catering services to and selling merchandise to Internet users have been slow to acknowledge their presence. Consequently, the special interests and needs of seniors have been largely ignored.

It's not difficult to design Web sites that will appeal to a large, diverse audience. But the vast majority of sites are overly complicated in design and use busy page layouts, dark colors, and small typefaces that seniors (and others) may find unattractive or, more importantly, hard to read and navigate. It's also not difficult to present a site in a selection of different styles; each style might include a format and features (e.g., a larger typeface and larger images) that was geared towards a specific audience. Individuals could then choose the style that best suited their needs or interests. But only a small percentage of sites offer such a feature, and only some of these sites have taken the time to test out their styles with seniors. It would seem that largely twenty-something Web designers and their managers have a great deal to learn about seniors, their interests, the money and power they command, and their needs.

Compared to other groups, seniors are likely to be less patient when an Internet site is slow and less forgiving when they encounter technical problems. Familiarity with the technology — something far more common with younger Internet users — doesn't just breed contempt; it also, unfortunately, breeds a certain degree of acceptance with respect to the technology's infrequent, but difficult to avoid glitches, interruptions, and deficiencies. Seniors have higher expectations and a lower tolerance for problems. If they can't easily find what they need, they move on quickly to another site and a potential sale is lost. If they have one bad experience at a site, they tend not to return. They are also more protective of their privacy and more resistant to parting with personal information. Seniors constitute a growing, demanding, and largely overlooked segment of Internet users. They are waiting on the purveyors of the technology, the service providers, and the e-commerce sites of the Internet to take notice of and recognize their place on the Internet.

Disabilities and the Internet's Challenge

People with mental or physical disabilities remain another largely overlooked group of existing and potential Internet users. The reason for this may be due to stereotyping or, as with seniors, it may stem from a general lack of understanding regarding their wants and needs. People with disabilities often face an additional obstacle to crossing the divide that most people would never consider an obstacle: the technology itself may be more a hindrance than a help, depending on the nature of their disability. Computer and Internet access for many individuals with disabilities is not simply an issue of availability, it is also an issue of accessibility. It is a question of whether or not the hardware and software supports their limited abilities to operate the computer and to interact on the Internet.

Computers and computer software, like other commodities, are purposefully designed to be usable by some generic, majority demographic. In other words, design decisions are made so that most individuals will experience little or no difficulty in operating these products. Keyboards, mice, and display screens function reasonably well for individuals with good manual dexterity and good eyesight. The same can be said of most computer operating systems, application interfaces, and Web sites. But what about individuals with diminished, failing, or lost eyesight? And what about individuals who don't possess the fine dexterity required to use most keyboards and mice? And what about individuals with limited language skills who may not be able to grasp the basic but necessary concepts that the designers of Web browsers, email applications, and other tools build into their products and that they require us to learn?

These individuals should not be ignored by the technology. They should, instead, be embraced by it; they should be welcomed onto the Internet and added to its diversity. The means to make this happen is (ironically) the technology itself. One of the most powerful aspects of the technology of computers, computer networking, and the Internet is its adaptability. There are no limitations on the types of devices or programs that can be built. Voice recognition software, for example, can take the place of a keyboard and mouse by allowing individuals to make selections and to enter information by speaking commands into a microphone. But, to date, little progress has been made with respect to recognizing and addressing the needs of individuals with disabilities and to helping others whose capabilities are not suited to using the standardized computer technology commonly available today.

The private sector, along with public organizations and some government agencies, is working to build specialized hardware and software components to assist those with disabilities with using computers and the Internet. One such effort is being promoted by the Web Accessibility Office of Industry Canada. Its goal is to address the needs of Canadians with disabilities and those with literacy deficiencies through its initiative called Web-4-All. Web-4-All is a package of assistive and adaptive technology that makes Web content available through sight, sound, and touch. The package allows users to customize a computer interface to compensate for one or more specific disabilities or limitations, such as impaired vision or restricted movement. After the interface has been customized, a user can save these settings using smart-card technology so that these same preferences can be used again at the same location or at another location using the same adaptive technology. (Smart cards are credit-card-size memory sticks that can store various sorts of personal information and that can be easily carried from location to location and from device to device.) The smart card technology then configures an associated suite of assistive software and hardware components.

Smart-card technology is ideally suited to the public access Internet terminals commonly found in libraries and community centers. Both this technology of storing personal information and preferences so that it can be carried and used on various computers and the technology that allows for the customization of computer interfaces can be used to accommodate a wide variety of special needs. Web-4-All is already in use in communities across Canada. It is also being used as part of a similar program in Australia, enabling participating public libraries to offer Internet access to vision-impaired individuals as well as to those with cognitive disabilities or other types of physical disabilities. The Australian program incorporates 21-inch screens, wheelchair-accessible desks, and a screen-magnifying program, as well as virtual keyboards and text decoders.

Web-4-All is a perfect example of inclusive technology. Inclusive technology is driven by an engineering process that addresses the specific needs of specific types or groups of individuals. Consider the design of a mouse in this regard. The purpose of a mouse is simply to locate and select objects on a screen. There is no requirement that dictates its physical shape or characteristics. For many years, however, only one generic mouse design was produced by all the manufacturers that sold computer systems and by those manufacturers that sold peripheral devices, such as keyboards and mice. No effort was made to produce variations on the design that might be better adapted to one individual as opposed to another, such as a mouse that was optimized for left-handed individuals. Eventually, the need for different mouse designs and for other devices that could perform the same functions as a mouse became known as more and more people encountered difficulties in using the original mouse design.

It's common now to find dozens of styles of pointing/selection devices, each with its own particular features and functionality, each meeting the particular needs of a specific type or group of individuals. Some people still prefer the original mouse design that fits under your hand and is moved on your desk. Others prefer the eraser-head type found in the middle of a keyboard, the trackball type located at the base of a keyboard, or one of the many ergonomically-designed mice that promise to reduce fatigue. This type of design customization, or inclusive technology, is the same type of effort behind Web-4-All and other like-minded projects focused on the disabled.

Slowly, the same sort of product diversity that developed in mice is starting to appear in other types of computer components. And some of these components are being designed for individuals with specific disabilities or impairments, such as a device that allows someone to type by turning their head to direct a light beam onto individual keyboard letters. More software products, too, are showing signs of developing inclusive technology that can be customized for individuals with special needs. Speech recognition software, for instance, has improved considerably over the past few years and many products now include the ability to learn as the program is being used as a means to accommodate the unique speech characteristics of the user. Such software addresses the needs of someone who may not be able to use a keyboard, but it also addresses the needs of any individual who may feel more comfortable or more productive in interacting with his or her computer in this manner. The widespread application of this same sort of multi-audience, adaptive approach to software engineering and design has yet to occur. One main reason for the slow progress is cost; this type of product takes more time and effort to develop. Another reason may stem from a lack of understanding of what is needed and of how many people are waiting for this enabling and more adaptive technology.

But with increased participation by the business community, and more community- and government-sponsored programs, computers and the Internet can have a transforming effect on the lives of millions of disabled individuals. The technology has the potential to greatly improve their ability to work, communicate, socialize, and contribute to their community. It offers them the means to pursue further education that otherwise might not have been available. It can, in many cases, help them build richer lives that are more closely interconnected with family, friends, co-workers, and others. These benefits of the technology are available to everyone, but to those who may — for whatever reason — have impaired mobility or sight, have limited dexterity, or have any number of other conditions that may limit their opportunities for education, employment, recreation, or socializing, these benefits can dramatically affect their quality of life.

Libraries, Internet Content, and the First Amendment

No better place exists to help narrow, and even eliminate, the digital divide than the public libraries found in most communities (even if the numbers don't yet confirm this). In many respects, the free, open access to the Internet provided by public libraries most closely embodies the egalitarian spirit of the Internet. Public libraries and the Internet were built by our tax dollars and provide equal, unregulated access to a wide variety of information resources. Both serve the public good. Both welcome individuals to browse the information they house, to search for information on a particular subject, or to locate a specific resource. Both also serve as community centers, with the library functioning as a physical location where individuals can gather in person and with the Internet functioning as a virtual location where individuals can exchange messages, meet in a chat room, play games, or interact in any number of cyberspace environments.

The Internet access provided by public libraries, however, is not without its share of controversy. Much of that controversy (in the U.S.) surrounds the uncensored content of the Internet, the protection of freedom of speech stipulated in the First Amendment of the Bill of Rights to the United States Constitution, and the restrictions a public library can or must impose — if any — on the types of services and information that a library patron may be subject to when accessing the Internet from one of its public terminals. The First Amendment states:

> Congress shall make no law respecting an establishment of religion, or prohibiting the free exercise thereof; or abridging the freedom of speech, or of the press; or the right of the people peaceably to assemble, and to petition the government for a redress of grievances.

At the heart of the controversy is protecting minors from exposure to indecent or patently offensive material on the Internet while upholding the freedom of speech guaranteed by the First Amendment. The Internet terminals at public libraries, which are equally accessible to minors and adults, brought the matter to the attention of the Supreme Court of the United States in 1997 in an appeal's case between then Attorney General, Janet Reno, and the American Civil Liberties Union (ACLU). The ACLU challenged the provisions of censorship expressed in the government's Communication Decency Act, which would have enforced information access restrictions at the Internet terminals provided at public libraries. Many considered this the first test case of how the principle of free speech would be applied to the new communication and information delivery medium of the Internet. The Supreme Court's finding was in favor of the ACLU, the First Amendment, and the protected right of freedom of speech. Subsequent cases, however, such as the U.S. versus the Library Association in 2003, have produced opinions of an opposite nature, such as one observing that the government's demand for content-filtering software at public libraries does not violate the First Amendment. As a consequence of this ruling, the government can withhold funding from libraries that fail to install content-filtering software.

Such findings are supposed to clarify the law, which they may well be doing. What they are not doing is resolving or even addressing the fundamental issues. Far more important (to most of us) than any existing, debated, or proposed legislation is getting answers to many commonly asked questions about access to the Internet through publicly-funded Internet terminals. Do or should the same Constitutional protections that apply to the books lining the shelves of public libraries now also apply to information accessed over a library's Internet terminals? Can or should the government prohibit public libraries from using software that blocks or filters information content, even though such software is most typically used to prevent access to sexually explicit material? Can or should it mandate the installation of such filters? No matter how you pursue answers to these questions, the argument always returns to the issue of freedom of speech. Public libraries are meant to be places of inclusion. They are access points to any and all information, not to some percentage of that information; and it matters less how much or little information content gets excluded than that some quantity of information — from a specific author or source or belonging to a specific category or genre — is deliberately being made unavailable to the general public.

The questions surrounding the issue of information access through a library's Internet terminals and the protection of freedom of speech are complicated by the fact that children — not just adults — use these terminals. Can freedom of speech be protected while also protecting a child's (and parent's) right to avoid offensive or inappropriate content? Can content filters solve this problem? Content filters operate through various mechanisms to achieve their goal of restricting access to certain types of material. Databases are used to track sites considered unsuitable for minors. Rating systems established by third-party organizations (e.g., commercial, educational, and non-profit groups that independently analyze and categorize sites according to their content) are used to identify a site's appropriateness along the lines of movie and computer game ratings. Keyword or other content scanning techniques are used to identify sites that might contain unsuitable material. A content filter could be designed specifically for use in public libraries. It could be installed with some sort of switch that turns the filter on or off based on the age of the user or some other basic criteria. But no filtering software is going to satisfy everyone's wants or needs. Moreover, the First Amendment expresses a fundamental right. Once that right is abridged, it is forever diminished.

The closer you examine the controversy surrounding the freedom of speech and the use of content filters, the more complex it becomes. Since the Internet does not — and cannot — impose any rules or provide any guidelines to categorize the content made accessible across its network, it is virtually impossible to engineer software to automatically and without fail distinguish, for instance, pornography from art or historical images or medical material. Worse yet, once content filtering software has been installed on a computer, it is impossible for the user of the terminal or the librarian to know exactly what material is being filtered out, who has made the decisions about the types of content being excluded, or how such decisions were made. So not only is the engineering of content filtering software necessarily flawed, but there is always going to be some element of subjectivity in any filtering process. Another part of the controversy concerns the librarian. The librarian cannot be expected to take on the role of the parent while a child is using the library's equipment. Only parents have the right and responsibility to control their child's access to information.

It may not be possible to find a solution that will satisfy everyone's needs. Many steps have been taken to help the situation, but it's clear that still more are needed. The First Amendment protects freedom of speech and our right to access any material we seek. One approach that fully preserves that protection favors the enforcement of new child-protection laws relating to pornography and obscenity that force purveyors of such material to establish their own safeguards and barriers to prevent children from accessing their sites. Most of these barriers are based on a proof-of-age concept, such as requiring individuals to provide credit-card information before being allowed access to the site. The basic idea is sound. It shifts the burden of responsibility and the legal accountability of protecting minors from offensive and inappropriate material to the information providers, freeing libraries and other organizations from the need to restrict access or filter content. But far more work still needs to be done with respect to both the methodology and implementation of these barriers, and many questions still exist regarding who, how, and where one draws the line separating acceptable from unacceptable material.

Another approach to protecting children from objectionable material on the Internet amounts to another — albeit very different — shift in the burden of responsibility. Rather than leaving children, or adults for that matter, alone and unguided on the Internet, many librarians are applying their considerable knowledge, skills, and experience with locating and providing information to locating and accessing information resources on the Internet. By customizing browsers on their library's computers and by creating one or more Web sites or portals for their library, librarians are combining their knowledge of the Internet's resources with their knowledge of the particular needs and interests of their library's patrons.

The goal of such efforts is to help guide the users of a library's public Internet terminals through the Internet's resources and to help them more easily locate the information they seek. Who better to navigate the vast information resources of the Internet than a librarian? By creating collections of reviewed Internet sites and by establishing well-managed and well-maintained home pages and Web sites for their library's patrons, librarians are effectively extending their services from the library book shelves onto the Internet. Librarians can create sites for children and sites for adults, and they can create local-interest sites that meet the specific information needs of the local community and that promote the interests or services of the local community, such as a town's fishing or lumber businesses or its natural resources. In the process, the First Amendment remains untouched and the two information environments — one digital and the other paper — become integrated and complementary.

This still leaves open the question of how to make it possible for parents to monitor and control their children's access to the Internet, wherever it occurs. One solution may take the form of a smart card of some sort. Imagine an information card (as opposed to a credit card) that carries on it basic identity information as well as enforceable preferences related to the types of information or activities that can be accessed on the Internet. A parent would program the preferences of the card and the child would need to swipe the card to access any type of public Internet terminal, such as a terminal at the local public library or school. The preferences on the card would need to communicate with Internet access software, which would in turn rely on some sort of categorization of Internet sites, their available information, and their services. To get around the unregulated and distributed nature of the Internet, the approach might be one of inclusion rather than exclusion or filtering. For instance, sites might be rated by parental organizations and approved for certain age groups; and these sites would then be enabled on the identity card, while other sites would be automatically excluded. The strength of such an approach is simple: parents alone remain responsible for restricting, or not restricting, information access for their children, not librarians, school teachers, or others. It will, however, take time to develop and implement standards that libraries, schools, community centers, and other organizations will be able to adopt and install on their computers for this approach to work.

U.S. Census Data on Internet Use

The following tables present a breakdown of several years of census data collected in the U.S. on Internet use. The data speaks for itself with respect to the remarkable increase in use across all segments of the population and the effect of increased use on the composition of the digital divide.[3]

Table 1: 1997-2001 U.S. Usage Statistics

	1997-2001 U.S Internet Usage Statistics										
	Oct. 1997 (thousands)		Dec. 1998 (thousands)		Aug. 2000 (thousands)		Sept. 2001 (thousands)		Internet Use (percent)		
Category	Internet Users	Total	Internet Users	Total	Internet Users	Total	Internet Users	Total	Oct. 1997	Dec. 1998	Aug. 2000
Total Population	56,774	255,689	84,587	258,453	116,480	262,620	142,823	265,180	22.2	32.7	44.4
Gender											
Male	30,311	124,590	43,033	125,932	56,962	127,844	69,580	129,152	24.3	34.2	44.6
Female	26,464	131,099	41,555	132,521	59,518	134,776	73,243	136,028	20.2	31.4	44.2
Race/Origin											
White	46,678	184,295	69,470	184,980	93,714	186,439	111,942	186,793	25.3	37.6	50.3
Black	4,197	31,786	6,111	32,123	9,624	32,850	13,237	33,305	13.2	19.0	29.3
Asian Amer. & Pac. Isl.	2,432	9,225	3,467	9,688	5,095	10,324	6,452	10,674	26.4	35.8	49.4
Hispanic	3,101	28,233	4,897	29,452	7,325	30,918	10,141	32,146	11.0	16.6	23.7
Employment Status											
Employed [b]	37,254	130,857	56,539	133,119	76,971	136,044	88,396	135,089	28.5	42.5	56.6
Not Employed [b,c]	9,012	72,911	14,261	73,891	21,321	73,891	28,531	77,268	12.4	19.5	28.9
Family Income											
Less than $15,000	4,069	44,284	5,170	37,864	6,057	32,096	7,848	31,354	9.2	13.7	18.9
$15,000-$24,999	3,760	32,423	5,623	30,581	7,063	27,727	8,893	26,650	11.6	18.4	25.5
$25,000-$34,999	5,666	33,178	8,050	31,836	11,054	31,001	12,591	28,571	17.1	25.3	35.7
$35,000-$49,999	8,824	38,776	13,528	39,026	16,690	35,867	20,587	36,044	22.8	34.7	46.5
$50,000-$74,999	13,552	41,910	19,902	43,776	25,059	43,451	30,071	44,692	32.3	45.5	57.7
$75,000+	16,276	36,572	24,861	42,221	36,564	52,189	44,547	56,446	44.5	58.9	70.1
Educational Attainment											
Less Than High School [d]	516	29,114	1,228	29,039	2,482	28,254	3,506	27,484	1.8	4.2	8.8
High School Diploma/GED [a]	5,589	57,487	10,961	57,103	17,425	56,889	22,847	57,386	9.7	19.2	30.6
Some College [a]	10,548	42,544	16,603	43,038	24,201	44,628	28,321	45,420	24.8	38.6	54.2
Bachelors Degree [a]	11,503	27,795	16,937	28,990	21,978	30,329	24,726	30,588	41.4	58.4	72.5
Beyond Bachelors Degree [a]	7,195	13,863	9,635	14,518	12,104	15,426	13,633	16,283	51.9	66.4	78.5

1997-2001 U.S Internet Usage Statistics (continued)											
	Oct. 1997 (thousands)		Dec. 1998 (thousands)		Aug. 2000 (thousands)		Sept. 2001 (thousands)		Internet Use (percent)		
Category	Internet Users	Total	Internet Users	Total	Internet Users	Total	Internet Users	Total	Oct. 1997	Dec. 1998	Aug. 2000	Sept. 2001
Age Group											
Age 3-8	1,748	24,445	2,680	24,282	3,671	23,962	6,637	23,763	7.2	11.0	15.3	27.9
Age 9-17	11,791	35,469	15,396	35,821	19,579	36,673	25,480	37,118	33.2	43.0	53.4	68.6
Age 18-24	7,884	24,973	11,356	25,662	15,039	26,458	17,673	27,137	31.6	44.3	56.8	65.0
Age 25-49	27,639	101,853	41,694	101,836	56,433	101,946	65,138	101,890	27.1	40.9	55.4	63.9
Male	14,679	50,177	20,889	50,054	27,078	50,034	30,891	50,020	29.3	41.7	54.1	61.8
Female	12,960	51,676	20,806	51,781	29,356	51,913	34,247	51,871	25.1	40.2	56.5	66.0
Age 50+	7,712	68,949	13,669	70,852	21,758	73,580	27,895	75,272	11.2	19.3	29.6	37.1
Male	4,560	31,252	7,356	32,248	10,989	33,561	13,757	34,438	14.6	22.8	32.7	39.9
Female	3,152	37,697	6,313	38,604	10,769	40,019	14,138	40,834	8.4	16.4	26.9	34.6
Geographic Location of Household In Which the Individual Lives											
Rural	n/a	n/a	19,274	65,828	28,889	67,980	35,751	67,642	n/a	29.3	42.5	52.9
Urban	n/a	n/a	65,313	192,625	87,591	194,640	107,072	197,537	n/a	33.9	45.0	54.2
Not Central City	n/a	n/a	41,881	116,091	56,773	118,641	69,342	120,724	n/a	36.1	47.9	57.4
Central City	n/a	n/a	23,432	76,534	30,818	75,999	37,730	76,813	n/a	30.6	40.6	49.1
Household Type In Which the Individual Lives											
Married Couple w/Children < 18	27,664	103,791	41,462	110,295	57,122	112,920	64,714	104,337	26.7	37.6	50.6	62.0
Male Householder w/Children < 18	1,143	6,284	1,995	7,868	2,825	8,186	3,389	7,400	18.2	25.4	34.5	45.8
Female Householder w/Children < 18	4,041	27,327	6,219	27,877	9,866	30,034	13,140	29,032	14.8	22.3	32.9	45.3
Family Household w/o Children	15,240	77,612	21,660	72,155	29,199	70,521	41,397	81,996	19.6	30.0	41.4	50.5
Non-Family	8,293	39,381	13,220	40,199	17,442	40,884	20,136	42,333	21.1	32.9	42.7	47.6

Source: U.S. Bureau of the Census, Current Population Survey supplements, October 1997, December 1998, August 2000, September 2001. Notes: [a] Age 25 and older. [b] Age 16 and Older. [c] Both people who are unemployed and people not in the labor force.

Table 2: 2001-2003 U.S. Usage Statistics

The following table contains statistics about Internet use from any location by individuals age 3 and older. It also contains statistics about broadband Internet use from home in 2003.

Internet Access: The Digital Divide and Beyond

2001-2003 U.S. Usage Statistics			
Description	Internet Users(%)		Broadband Household(%)
	Sept. 2001	Oct. 2003	Oct. 2003
Total Population	55.1	58.7	22.8
Gender			
Male	55.2	58.2	23.9
Female	55.0	59.2	21.8
Race/Ethnicity [a]			
White [b]	61.3	65.1	25.7
White Alone	n/a	65.1	25.7
Black [c]	41.1	45.6	14.2
Black Alone	n/a	45.2	13.9
Asian Amer. & Pac. Isl. [d]	62.5	63.1	34.2
Asian Amer. & Pac. Isl. Alone	n/a	63.0	34.7
Hispanic (of any race)	33.4	37.2	12.6
Employment Status			
Employed [e]	66.6	70.7	26.0
Not Employed (unemployed or NLF) [e]	38.0	42.8	16.1
Family Income			
Less than $15,000	25.9	31.2	7.5
$15,000-$24,999	34.4	38.0	9.3
$25,000-$34,999	45.3	48.9	13.4
$35,000-$49,999	58.3	62.1	19.0
$50,000-$74,999	68.9	71.8	27.9
$75,000+	80.4	82.9	45.4
$75,000-$99,999 [f]	n/a	79.8	36.8
$100,000-$149,999 [f]	n/a	85.1	49.3
$150,000+ [f]	n/a	86.1	57.7
Educational Attainment [g]			
Less Than High School	13.7	15.5	5.9
High School Diploma / GED	41.1	44.5	14.5
Some College	63.5	68.6	23.7
Bachelor's Degree	82.2	84.9;34.9	
Beyond Bachelor's Degree	85.0	88.0	38.0
Age Group			
Age 3-4	17.6	19.9	22.0
Age 5-9	41.0	42.0	24.1
Age 10-13	66.7	67.3	25.8
Age 14-17	76.4	78.8	28.3
Age 18-24	66.6	70.6	25.5
In School	85.4	86.7	33.8
Not In School	54.0	58.2	19.0
Age 25-49	65.0	68.0	25.9
In Labor Force	68.4	71.7	26.8
Not in Labor Force	47.1	49.7	21.1
Age 50+	38.3	44.8	15.9
In Labor Force	58.0	64.4	22.6
Not in Labor Force	22.2	27.6	10.1

2001-2003 U.S. Usage Statistics (continued)			
Description	Internet Users(%)		Broadband Household(%)
	Sept. 2001	Oct. 2003	Oct. 2003
Location of the Person's Household			
Rural	54.1	57.2	
Urban	55.5	59.2	
Urban Not Central City	58.8	62.5	
Urban Central City	50.3	54.0	
Household Type In Which the Individual Lives [h]			
Married Couple w/Children < 18 Years Old	63.5	65.3	29.3
Male Householder w/Children < 18 Years Old	46.8	50.3	19.4
Female Householder w/Children < 18 Years Old	46.6	51.4	14.8
Households without Children	51.8	56.7	20.7
Non-Family Household	48.3	53.1	17.3
Location of Internet Use			
Only At Home	19.0	19.0	
Only Outside the Home	11.8	11.6	
Disability Status			
Between 25 and 60 and In the Labor Force			
Multiple Disabilities	54.8	58.9	14.2
Blind or Severe Vision Impairment	56.2	63.7	21.6
Deaf or Severe Hearing Impairment	59.6	72.1	25.8
Difficulty Walking	60.5	64.2	22.4
Difficulty Typing	62.8	64.4	26.0
Difficulty Leaving Home	73.2	67.8	20.8
None of these Disabilities	67.0	71.0	27.4
Between 25 and 60 and Not In the Labor Force			
Multiple Disabilities	25.5	27.9	10.9
Blind or Severe Vision Impairment	40.3	40.0	14.4
Deaf or Severe Hearing Impairment	30.9	47.9	25.6
Difficulty Walking	26.3	33.1	11.9
Difficulty Typing	28.8	34.3	8.9
Difficulty Leaving Home	24.0	26.1	12.0
None of these Disabilities	47.0	52.5	23.4
Over Age 60			
Multiple Disabilities	6.7	8.3	5.9
Blind or Severe Vision Impairment	9.6	23.0	11.0
Deaf or Severe Hearing Impairment	18.7	23.6	6.2
Difficulty Walking	17.3	20.7	6.6
Difficulty Typing	13.5	26.1	9.6
Difficulty Leaving Home	7.5	10.5	6.3
None of these Disabilities	26.4	34.2	10.9

Source: U.S. Bureau of the Census, Current Population Survey supplements, September 2001, and October 2003. Notes: n/a = Not Available. [a] In 2003 respondents were able to choose multiple racial categories. Thus, 2003 race data are not strictly comparable with data from previous surveys. [b] For 2003, "White" should be read as "White alone or in combination with other racial categories, non-Hispanic." [c] For 2003, "Black" should be read as "Black alone or in combination with other racial categories, non-Hispanic." [d] For 2003, "Asian Amer. & Pac. Isl." should be read as "Asian American and Pacific Islanders alone or in combination with other racial categories, non-Hispanic." [e] Age 16 and Older. NLF=Not in the labor force. [f] The October 2003 Current Population Survey had income categories above $75,000 that were not previously available. [g] Age 25 and older. [h] The male and female categories refer to family households where a spouse is not present.

Table 3: 2001-2003 Non-Internet Usage Statistics

2001-2003 Non-Internet Usage Statistics		
Description	Non-Internet Users (%)	
	Sept. 2001	Oct. 2003
Total Popluation	44.9	41.3
Gender		
Male	44.8	41.8
Female	45.0	40.8
Race/Ethnicity [a]		
White [b]	38.7	34.9
White Alone	n/a	34.9
Black [c]	58.9	54.4
Black Alone	n/a	54.8
Asian Amer. & Pac. Isl. [d]	37.5	36.9
Asian Amer. & Pac. Isl. Alone	n/a	37.0
Hispanic (of any race)	66.6	62.8
Employment Status		
Employed [e]	33.4	29.3
Not Employed (unemployed or NLF) [e]	62.0	57.2
Family Income		
Less than $15,000	74.1	68.8
$15,000-$24,999	65.6	62.0
$25,000-$34,999	54.7	51.1
$35,000-$49,999	41.7	37.9
$50,000-$74,999	31.1	28.2
$75,000+	19.6	17.1
$75,000-$99,999 [f]	n/a	20.2
$100,000-$149,999 [f]	n/a	14.9
$150,000+ [f]	n/a	13.9
Educational Attainment [g]		
Less Than High School	86.3	84.5
High School Diploma / GED	58.9	55.5
Some College	36.5	31.4
Bachelor's Degree	17.8	15.1
Beyond Bachelor's Degree	15.0	12.0
Age Group		
Age 3-4	82.4	80.1
Age 5-9	59.0	58.0
Age 10-13	33.3	32.7
Age 14-17	23.6	21.2
Age 18-24	33.4	29.4
In School	14.6	13.3
Not In School	46.0	41.8
Age 25-49	35.0	32.0
In Labor Force	31.6	28.3
Not in Labor Force	52.9	50.3
Age 50+	61.7	55.2
In Labor Force	42.0	35.6
Not in Labor Force	77.8	72.4

2001-2003 Non-Internet Usage Statistics (continued)		
Description	Non-Internet Users (%)	
	Sept. 2001	Oct. 2003
Location of the Person's Household		
Rural	45.9	42.8
Urban	44.5	40.8
Urban Not Central City	41.2	37.5
Urban Central City	49.7	46.0
Household Type In Which the Individual Lives [h]		
Married Couple w/Children < 18 Years Old	36.5	34.7
Male Householder w/Children < 18 Years Old	53.2	49.7
Female Householder w/Children < 18 Years Old	53.4	48.6
Households without Children	48.2	43.3
Non-Family Household	51.7	46.9
Disability Status		
Between 25 and 60 and In the Labor force		
Multiple Disabilities	45.2	41.1
Blind or Severe Vision Impairment	43.8	36.3
Deaf or Severe Hearing Impairment	40.4	27.9
Difficulty Walking	39.5	35.8
Difficulty Typing	37.2	35.6
Difficulty Leaving Home	26.8	32.2
None of these Disabilities	33.0	29.0
Disability Status		
Between 25 and 60 and In the Labor force		
Multiple Disabilities	45.2	41.1
Blind or Severe Vision Impairment	43.8	36.3
Deaf or Severe Hearing Impairment	40.4	27.9
Difficulty Walking	39.5	35.8
Difficulty Typing	37.2	35.6
Difficulty Leaving Home	26.8	32.2
None of these Disabilities	33.0	29.0
Between 25 and 60 and Not In the Labor Force		
Multiple Disabilities	74.5	72.1
Blind or Severe Vision Impairment	59.7	60.0
Deaf or Severe Hearing Impairment	69.1	52.1
Difficulty Walking	73.8	66.9
Difficulty Typing	71.2	65.7
Difficulty Leaving Home	76.0	73.9
None of these Disabilities	53.0	47.5
Over Age 60		
Multiple Disabilities	93.3	91.7
Blind or Severe Vision Impairment	90.4	77.0
Deaf or Severe Hearing Impairment	81.3	76.4
Difficulty Walking	82.8	79.3
Difficulty Typing	86.5	73.9
Difficulty Leaving Home	92.5	89.6
None of these Disabilities	73.6	65.8

Source: U.S. Bureau of the Census, Current Population Survey supplements, September 2001, and October 2003. Notes: n/a = Not Available. [a] In 2003 respondents were able to choose multiple racial categories. Thus, 2003 race data are not strictly comparable with data from previous surveys. [b] For 2003, "White" should be read as "White alone or in combination with other racial categories, non-Hispanic." [c] For 2003, "Black" should be read as "Black alone or in combination with other racial categories, non-Hispanic." [d] For 2003, "Asian Amer. & Pac. Isl." should be read as "Asian American and Pacific Islanders alone or in combination with other racial categories, non-Hispanic." [e] Age 16 and Older. NLF=Not in the labor force. [f] The October 2003 Current Population Survey had income categories above $75,000 that were not previously available. [g] Age 25 and older. [h] The male and female categories refer to family households where a spouse is not present.

Table 4: 2003 Internet Use by Percent of U.S. State Population

2003 Internet Use by Percent of U.S. State Population			
State	Total Population	Lower Bound	Upper Bound
Alabama	4,435,532	50.5	55.8
Alaska	634,207	69.3	73.8
Arizona	5,382,335	61.0	66.2
Arkansas	2,670,197	47.1	52.7
California	35,490,299	55.6	57.9
Colorado	4,489,372	63.0	67.2
Connecticut	3,441,856	64.7	69.0
Delaware	576,188	56.7	61.4
Florida	16,352,570	56.2	59.2
Georgia	8,435,441	53.7	58.8
Hawaii	1,215,507	53.4	58.7
Idaho	1,327,338	59.5	64.9
Illinois	12,697,160	56.7	60.0
Indiana	6,135,518	56.6	61.0
Iowa	2,923,456	61.2	65.8
Kansas	2,696,591	61.4	66.1
Kentucky	4,027,467	54.0	59.2
Louisiana	4,424,416	47.1	52.8
Maine	1,270,136	62.2	66.7
Maryland	5,408,755	62.8	67.3
Massachusetts	6,454,814	60.3	64.6
Michigan	10,047,160	57.1	60.7
Minnesota	5,017,883	66.8	71.1
Mississippi	2,825,852	39.7	45.5
Missouri	5,592,374	58.1	62.8
Montana	896,273	57.1	62.8
Nebraska	1,725,102	62.3	67.2
Nevada	2,126,219	53.2	57.9
NewHampshire	1,261,524	68.2	72.6
NewJersey	8,646,566	60.8	64.4
NewMexico	1,848,212	48.9	54.7
NewYork	19,379,829	55.5	58.0
NorthCarolina	8,163,417	53.0	57.2
NorthDakota	628,358	62.0	67.0
Ohio	11,372,776	56.8	60.4
Oklahoma	3,427,054	52.7	57.9
Oregon	3,491,795	59.7	64.6
Pennsylvania	12,175,267	58.0	61.3
RhodeIsland	1,055,249	55.6	60.0
SouthCarolina	4,022,423	49.8	55.0
SouthDakota	752,836	61.8	66.4
Tennessee	5,715,727	53.0	58.6
Texas	21,697,942	53.2	56.0
Utah	2,360,737	67.2	71.9
Vermont	611,658	63.6	68.2
Virginia	7,111,123	61.2	66.0
Washington,DC	793,708	57.6	63.9
Washington	6,030,976	65.7	70.3
WestVirginia	1,769,062	49.0	54.0
Wisconsin	5,401,673	61.9	66.2
Wyoming	490,644	66.0	70.8

Source: U.S. Bureau of the Census, Current Population Survey supplements, September 2001, and October 2003.

Table 5: 2003 Household Internet Connection Types

Description	Total Internet Households (thousands)	Dial-Up Telephone		Cable Modem		Digital Subscriber Line (DSL)		Mobile, Phone, PDA, Pager		Satellite		Fixed. Wireless (MMDS)		Other	
		No.	%	No.	%	No.	%	No.	%	No.	%	No.	%	No.	%
Total Pop.	61,481	38,593	62.8%	12,638	20.6%	9,335	15.2%	138	0.2%	195	0.3%	252	0.4%	329	0.5%
Family Income															
< 15,000	3,681	2,555	69.4%	584	15.9%	477	13.0%	9	0.2%	10	0.3%	12	0.3%	32	0.9%
15,000-24,999	3,839	2,786	72.6%	600	15.6%	418	10.9%	1	0.0%	10	0.3%	9	0.2%	15	0.4%
25,000-34,999	5,855	4,137	70.7%	921	15.7%	694	11.9%	21	0.4%	11	0.2%	27	0.5%	43	0.7%
35,000-49,999	8,867	6,213	70.1%	1,391	15.7%	1,138	12.8%	25	0.3%	25	0.3%	38	0.4%	37	0.4%
50,000-74,999	12,429	7,918	63.7%	2,531	20.4%	1,814	14.6%	24	0.2%	33	0.3%	43	0.3%	65	0.5%
75,000-99,999	7,774	4,440	57.1%	1,919	24.7%	1,321	17.0%	7	0.1%	26	0.3%	28	0.4%	33	0.4%
100,000-149,999	5,811	2,726	46.9%	1,771	30.5%	1,207	20.8%	16	0.3%	43	0.7%	28	0.5%	21	0.4%
150,000+	3,753	1,482	39.5%	1,242	33.1%	961	25.6%	14	0.4%	22	0.6%	18	0.5%	15	0.4%
Not reported	9,472	6,335	66.9%	1,680	17.7%	1,305	13.8%	21	0.2%	14	0.1%	47	0.5%	70	0.7%
Household Type															
Mar Couple w/ Child < 18	19,934	11,914	59.8%	4,574	22.9%	3,205	16.1%	25	0.1%	67	0.3%	82	0.4%	67	0.3%
Male Hhldr w/ Child<18	1,229	751	61.1%	258	21.0%	204	16.6%	1	0.1%	5	0.4%	3	0.3%	7	0.6%
Female Hhldr w/ Child<18	4,181	2,833	67.8%	702	16.8%	606	14.5%	12	0.3%	9	0.2%	7	0.2%	12	0.3%
Family Hhldr w/ Child<18	21,852	14,323	65.5%	4,152	19.0%	3,023	13.8%	57	0.3%	83	0.4%	97	0.4%	119	0.5%
Non-Family	14,284	8,772	61.4%	2,952	20.7%	2,297	16.1%	43	0.3%	32	0.2%	63	0.4%	125	0.9%
Region															
Northeast	12,113	7,066	58.3%	3,339	27.6%	1,565	12.9%	27	0.2%	25	0.2%	24	0.2%	68	0.6%
Midwest	13,953	9,168	65.7%	2,752	19.7%	1,790	12.8%	31	0.2%	27	0.2%	70	0.5%	116	0.8%
South	20,927	13,782	65.9%	3,820	18.3%	3,013	14.4%	33	0.2%	74	0.4%	99	0.5%	106	0.5%
West	14,487	8,578	59.2%	2,727	18.8%	2,966	20.5%	48	0.3%	70	0.5%	59	0.4%	40	0.3%

Source: U.S. Bureau of the Census, Current Population Survey supplements, September 2001, and October 2003.

The Dot Com Bubble, and Life (So to Speak) at a Dot Com

5

The Dot Com Boom

The latter half of the 1990s brought the dot com boom, a short, intense period of commercial investment in Internet companies and their technology. It's difficult to determine exactly when it started. Many of the ideas that inspired the creation of these sometimes innovative, always highly speculative Internet-centric companies date to 1994-5, a time when exuberance over the World Wide Web was still young but spreading quickly. This relatively quiet, early period was immediately followed by several frenetic years of Internet gold fever, fueled largely by inventive, but underdeveloped and overly optimistic business plans. From 1996 through 2000, the dot com ideas, their mostly young, inexperienced, entrepreneurial creators, and their associated business plans intersected with a wealthy and eager venture capital community. In the process, the dot com companies acquired many millions of dollars of funding through unbridled and highly uninformed speculation and investment. The dot com boom was born. The term dot com, incidentally, derives from the .com Internet domain names purchased by these companies for their presence on the Internet. The .com suffix is used by commercial Internet entities, while other suffixes (e.g., .edu for educational entities and .gov for government entities) are used for other types of organizations.

During the boom, dot com startups (i.e., business ventures in their earliest stage of development) were formed at a furious rate. Each went out in search of financing and used the investment capital it secured to build and then grow the business. Many focused their sights on going public through an initial public offering (IPO), trying to recreate for themselves the meteoric rise in company value made famous by Netscape, Amazon.com, and the IPOs of many other Internet-based companies. But the boom was quickly followed by the dot com bust, felt by many in 2000 and continuing on well into 2001 and beyond. Eventually, this period of dramatic speculation and growth followed by an equally dramatic failure rate came to be referred to by the media as the Internet, or dot com, bubble.

Frantic, speculative bubbles like this one are nothing new. They date back to the 5th century and the collapse of the Roman Empire, and possibly earlier. For instance, the Great South Sea bubble of the early 18th century consisted of financial projects that promised investors unimaginable profits through securing trading monopolies in the South Seas. These baseless investments were further incited by the highly popular travel logs of sea captains and picturesque maps of lands in the newly discovered world. But the only action this bubble ever evidenced was in the trading of its stock, in which many lost their fortunes, including Sir Isaac Newton who lost some 20,000 pounds. Newton was quoted as saying in regard to his loss: "I can measure the motions of bodies, but cannot measure human folly." The greatest speculative bubble in U.S. history was the mania for buying stock in the 1920s, which led to the market collapse of 1929 and to the Great Depression that followed. Boom periods spurred on by new technology, like the dot com boom, include those of the railroads in the 1840s, radio in the 1920s, transistor electronics in the 1950s, and biotechnology and home computers in the 1980s.

Leading up to and stoking the dot com boom in the first half of the 1990s were the following:

- The commercialization of the Internet.

- The invention and exponential growth of the World Wide Web, along with the immense popularity of Web browser technology.

- The emergence of local, affordable Internet service providers (ISPs), followed quickly by the addition of Internet access through existing online services (i.e., proprietary computer networks that predated the commercialization of the Internet) like America Online, Compuserve, and Prodigy.

■ The widening and deepening role of computers in our personal and professional lives.

The dot com boom and subsequent bust resulted from a growing interest in and attention to the Internet, its technologies, and its transforming effect on our access to and communication of information. The wildly escalating use of the Internet by individuals, businesses, government agencies, and other organizations prompted many entrepreneurial individuals to take notice of the Internet and its potential. The Internet promised to change many of the fundamental assumptions of business; and those who understood this new, high-tech world, could predict (they thought) where it was heading, and could figure out how to exploit it expected to become exceedingly rich.

For many, it all started with a simple idea, like an online grocery store with home delivery, a virtual mall of high fashion clothing, or a one-hour delivery service for books, video rentals, and other products purchased online. Each of these ideas used the Internet as the business's engine of commerce: its means to connect with consumers and provide products or services without the imposed time and geographic constraints of brick and mortar establishments. Meanwhile, the Web provided a simple, customizable, and highly effective browser-based interface to the Internet that nearly anyone could quickly understand and use. Moreover, the Web offered an inexpensive and easy-to-learn technology with which to present a business's goods and services over the Internet.

The dot com ventures created online product catalogs, storefronts, tellers, and phone operators, and they empowered the customer to interact with the various operations of the business on the customer's terms rather than on those of the business. The Internet and the Web appeared to make old ideas new, like providing a better way to buy books and music, and any number of other products, through a virtual storefront. They also appeared to make new ideas feasible, like making money through online rebate and coupon programs, or using the Internet to connect individuals directly with their local government bureaucracy to pay parking tickets or file a building permit.

With the stage set, the race was on to be first and then to be biggest. Those who were first had the chance to garner both media attention and a large, fresh, eager customer base. The general idea was to get noticed and to build a following of loyal customers as quickly as possible. The immediate goal was not to make money. Profitability was projected as something that would naturally and eventually come at a later date. The business needed to brand its company name with consumers, develop its product or service, build its customer base, and be willing to lose a lot of money in the process. The ultimate goal was considered market share: first creating or building the market, and then dominating it. In the virtual realm of the Internet, there was not a lot of room for competition. The business had to reach and hold the number one or number two position in any particular market to be considered successful.

Consider the story of Theglobe.com, a Web portal that began as an idea for an online community in 1994 in the dorm room of two Cornell University students, Todd Krizelman and Stephan Paternot. Its IPO on November 13, 1998, made history on Wall Street as the value of the company rose over 600 percent in the first day of trading, taking the stock price from $9 to a high during the day of $97. Two short years later, Krizelman and Paternot, the inexperienced co-CEOs who had become minor celebrities as well as paper multi-millionaires, stepped down from their positions of leadership to hand control over to seasoned executives as the company tried to save something of itself. Meanwhile, the stock had fallen to 53 cents.

During its short but frenzied history, Theglobe.com never showed any profit. If anything, the meteoric rise in its valuation as expressed by its stock price utterly destroyed any presumed correlation between share price and corporate profitability or corporate assets. The numbers simply didn't add up. The company burned through millions of dollars of capital as it created and grew its Web portal business, all of which was based on the inflated promise of future profitability and the expectation of a huge, loyal base of customers. Through intense and unrealistic market speculation, it acquired overnight a market capitalization of nearly a billion dollars. In early 2000, Theglobe.com was considered one of the 100 most visited sites on the Web (i.e., it was extremely successful at inciting interest and getting people to load one or more of its pages). But income predictions never materialized and by year's end the company reportedly lost over $100 million against less then $30 million in revenues. When the new Internet economy never materialized and sober financial practices returned, Theglobe.com collapsed under the weight of its own debt, a failure that was helped along by poor management and unrealistic predictions.

The general story of Theglobe.com illustrates more the rule than the exception, as hundreds of other dot com startups followed a similarly pronounced trajectory. The majority of companies that constituted the dot com boom were built on ideas that sounded good in presentations and looked good on paper. But when subjected to extended scrutiny and to the harsh realities of a competitive and unpredictable marketplace, these companies failed to perform. Even the small number of startups that were founded on relatively conservative and practical ideas could not withstand the coupling of unsound business practices and unrealistic expectations.

The Dot Com Bubble Bursts

As exaggerated investor expectations came face to face with the marketplace realities of the Internet, over 800 Internet companies declared bankruptcy or ended their Internet activities between January, 2000 and July, 2002. The number of failures started to increase rapidly in the first quarter of 2001; and the failure rate peaked in the middle of 2001. It all started in the business-to-consumer (B2C) sector as the stock market started to plummet, cash got scarcer, and investors started to reign themselves in. The B2C failures quickly bled over to the business-to-business (B2B) sector as these software and services organizations also began to lose revenues at an accelerated pace.

The majority of failed dot com businesses were content providers or e-commerce sites, such as news and entertainment providers, e-merchandisers, and B2B marketplaces. The following are some general observations regarding why these failures occurred:

- **Everything takes time.**
  Investors grossly underestimated how long it would take dot com innovations to be adopted. This wrong assumption in turn greatly accelerated the rate and amount of capital invested, which led to "the inevitable bubble and bust."

- **New products/services don't simply replace the old ones.**
  History shows that people don't quickly change their buying habits. Innovations don't overtake a market and eliminate existing popular products and services; at best, they find their own place and slowly build market share.

- **Getting there first meant, for some, getting there too early.**
  Many new product and service offerings believed all the hype for broadband Internet access while ignoring the realities of how few people actually had such access. Good offerings or not, these products were expensive and the potential market was small.

- **Copying business models doesn't ensure success.**
  Many startups envisioned the Internet as little more than a superhighway to consumers. But they failed to grasp anything more about the technology or to understand the realities of how people actually used the Internet. Taking an existing business and throwing it onto the Internet did not necessarily mean you would increase sales at minimal additional cost. The same was true of taking existing content for a magazine or other media and recreating it on the Internet. Many such attempts failed to exploit the powerful *pulling* force of Internet users who wanted and expected to search and explore, to find and refine information tailored to themselves. Taking a catalog of clothing and copying it to the Internet, for instance, ignored what the technology could do and what the online consumer wanted.

- **Giving things away costs money.**
  For a while, bringing people to your web site was job number one. Many businesses offered some sort of free goods, rebates, or coupons to entice people to visit, and especially revisit, their site. The more *hits* they received, the more advertising revenue they generated. Others made their

money through relationship management, which involved joining merchandisers with web site owners to help generate more traffic for web site purchases. And others profiled their *visitors* and resold this information. The premise was based on low operating costs, very low margins, and an ever increasing base of Internet sites and merchants. So, as the bust began, these companies that depended on each other to generate revenues fell fastest of all.

- **Knowing your audience doesn't equate to profitability.**
Some startups regarded the Internet's ability to collect information about its users as a means to cater to the needs of specific rather than generalized audiences. The technology of the Web facilitates something called *narrowcast* marketing which, as contrasted to the broadcast marketing of television advertising, uses demographic information collected on you to target products and services specifically to you. But catering to more specific audiences demanded offering a far larger selection of products from which to choose; and, in the end, high startup and infrastructure costs combined with low margins to spell disaster for many of these companies, including Webvan, an online grocer, and ValueAmerica, an online retailer.

- **Bigger is not necessarily better.**
The old rules for investing large amounts of money to build a business often did more harm than good when applied to an Internet startup. Overfunding led to attempting a too rapid expansion of business, which in turn led to the need for more money and a larger infrastructure, and so on. Costs grew while very few saw any profit; and the greater the debt, the shorter the trip to bankruptcy.

- **Business interdependencies require time, money, and more time.**
Buyers and sellers on the Internet somehow needed to grow simultaneously, to build each other up. eBay couldn't exist without a large user base of both buyers and sellers; but it took eBay a lot of time and money and good management to reach critical mass and become successful. Most attempts,

such as B2B marketplaces and B2C reward programs, fell far short of making the equation pay.

- **Forecasting the Internet's future is more than the sum of its technology.**
  The Internet is writing its own history. Its history to date provides clear evidence that its path, and the expectations and predictions about it, have diverged widely and often. Email was a by-product of the creation of the ARPANET — not something that was planned; from its inception, email has been responsible for more Internet traffic, and for bringing more people onto the Internet, than anything else. The Web was created to facilitate the sharing and publication of research; it is largely responsible for the creation of e-commerce. The Internet is a highly dynamic environment and too many *good ideas* in dot com business plans did not take into account the shifting tides of the Internet, its technologies, and the people who travel it.[1]

Ultimately, the reasons for failure were as diverse as the businesses and the people who ran them. Nothing about the Internet or the Web was capable of rewriting basic business precepts. The dot com bubble stands as a testament to that fact.

Life at a Dot Com, Sort Of

My own experience at a dot com began in October, 1999, when I accepted the position of Director of Software Engineering and Development at a small Internet startup called Linkshare. Located in New York City, Linkshare is an affiliate management organization. It was established in 1996 by twenty-something, sibling New York lawyers, Heidi and Stephen Messer. This was the height of the dot com boom. Startup dot coms were issuing IPOs every week; and the frenzy was such that most company valuations were doubling, tripling, quadrupling, or more, pretty much overnight. Linkshare was hiring experienced individuals to facilitate its second growth phase, and to help prepare for its own, highly anticipated and much vaunted IPO.

Company Background

At the time I joined Linkshare the company was still relatively small, with a total head count of under fifty people, most of whom were located at the New York City office. The company was already well established in its niche of affiliate management and had no more than a half dozen serious competitors, the best known of which were probably BeFree and DoubleClick. Like many other dot coms of the time, Linkshare had reached the point where they needed experienced professionals in order to transform their startup into a more traditionally managed business. This was especially true with respect to its technology and its operational infrastructure. These areas had suffered considerably during the first couple of years of operation, as much from the frantic pace of conducting business over the Internet as from the inexperience of novice programmers and novice managers. Aside from financial issues surrounding basic money management and the business's revenue stream, the areas of technology and operational infrastructure were most critical to the ultimate success or failure of any dot com.

Prior to my joining Linkshare, I had worked for fifteen years in the computer industry, primarily with large, established corporations like AT&T Bell Laboratories and Lucent Technologies. Over the years I performed a wide variety of jobs, including system and usability testing, application design and development, project management and systems engineering. A common thread connecting most of these jobs was the element of networking. This work came to include the networking technology of the Internet and, later on, the information management technology of the World Wide Web. One of my specialties was finding ways to improve the coordination of work, the sharing of equipment and information, and the communication capabilities within one or more organizations in one of these large corporations. Each organization comprised several groups, and groups were often spread out across several floors in a single building and sometimes they were separated by many miles across several building locations. Networking was key to the success of this work.

Networking computers represented the starting point. Next came networking the applications and resources commonly employed in the work performed by each group and each organization. Ultimately, this translated to networking people and all the information at the heart of their business activities. It didn't matter if a group was producing documentation or building circuit boards, there was always a way to introduce or expand on networking in their environment in order to improve on the way work was being done, how information was being shared, and how people communicated. Accordingly, I was always looking out for what was coming next, like the latest wave of networking products, a new type of email collaboration tool, or the World Wide Web. I would try to determine how best to incorporate these emerging technologies into the existing networking and computer environment to facilitate the work at hand. Taking the job at Linkshare was quite a departure from this type of eclectic, forward-looking work.

Along with other similarly structured dot com companies in the business of affiliate management, Linkshare aggressively courted merchants. A merchant was a purveyor of products or services, such as a clothing and sporting goods retailer like L. L. Bean, a telecommunication company like AT&T, a computer manufacturer like IBM, and so on. Merchants wanted to reach out through the Internet (e.g., through Web site advertising) to promote their company and its products and to direct individuals back to their Web site. Linkshare's objective was to get these companies to sign on exclusively with them in much the same way that advertising agencies execute exclusive agreements with their clients. Through Linkshare and its network of affiliates, these merchants could then promote their products and services more effectively and in a more managed and trackable way. They chose their affiliates from Linkshare's existing network, and they entered into a contract with each affiliate, specifying precisely how the affiliate would be compensated for directing consumers to the merchant's own Web site. To a lesser extent, Linkshare also courted the affiliates, the Web site owners, to join their affiliate network for free. More affiliates meant a larger network, which in turn helped to attract more merchants, and ultimately led to more transactions on the Linkshare network.

Over the course of a few years, Linkshare's network of merchants and affiliates had grown quickly, much as the Internet and the Web had grown over the same late 1990s period. By the time I arrived, the company had some 200 merchants on board, and tens of thousands of affiliates. With their network established, Linkshare's business model effectively centered on tracking all activity on their network, providing performance information to the merchants and affiliates, arranging for payments, and assisting affiliates with setting up the links (primarily banner advertisements with hidden tracking codes) on their Web sites. Not unlike the telephone companies, Linkshare primarily made their money from transactions on their merchant-affiliate network; and the more transactions, the greater the revenue. While this was clearly a great asset during the dot com boom, when the bubble burst it naturally blew a large hole through Linkshare's business model, just as it did through those of other dot coms that relied directly on the interdependency of Web-only or Web-centric businesses. Like a deck of cards, one dot com failure affected others. Affiliate management organizations like Linkshare, with their narrow business niche and their basic *share the wealth* approach, were particularly vulnerable to such large fluctuations.

When I joined Linkshare, the company consisted of some forty or more people, almost all of whom were under thirty. For most of these individuals, this was their first job. Fortunately for me, the company was in the process of moving from an exceedingly cramped location on Madison Avenue to what at the time seemed a spacious new location that consisted of an entire floor in a building close to Union Square. This area of New York City had recently taken on the name of Silicon Alley in acknowledgment of all the new technology-based dot com companies that had taken up residence there. The old location contained two to three times the number of people that the office space was designed to handle, and to pass through the front door typically required one of the account executives to move her chair out of the way. Nevertheless, everyone there seemed energized and excited about their work and the company's future, including the CEO's overweight dog, a pug named Brutus, who was constantly in search of food. This excitement, combined with the understanding that they were moving, prompted me to take a chance and enter the fray.

The Technology

My focus at Linkshare was the technology. As I quickly came to appreciate, Linkshare's technology was relatively small in scale and surprisingly simple in terms of its specific functions and overall operation. The technology and the modest computing environment in which it operated stood in sharp contrast to the large-scale leading (often called bleeding) edge technology and the complex, high-tech computing center environments I was used to working with. The challenges in working with and adapting Linkshare's technology, however, proved anything but simple or small.

First, and the only part of the technology unique to their particular business, were Linkshare's programs and methodology for tracking impressions and click-throughs. An impression is produced when an advertising banner is shown to you. A click-through, a far more significant event in terms of making money from affiliate management, occurs when you click on a banner to visit the merchant's site. Both of these events need to be recorded somehow, capturing the event along with related information about you, the merchant's program, the affiliate, etc., to some sort of log file for later compilation, reporting, and analysis. Program code contained in Web site banner advertisements can include hyperlinks to programs located on a third party's Web site in order to collect and track information in the process of showing the banner or as part of your clicking on the banner. This was Linkshare's basic approach.

Incidentally, Linkshare received a United States patent for describing and defining their general methodology for performing these tracking functions. Linkshare's patent, like many others granted to dot com startups, is less invention or new technology than it is a formal depiction of how existing, mostly standard Web technology can be applied to satisfy a new business function or condition. These types of patent grants have evoked a great deal of discussion about the need for changing how patents are awarded, given the new types of technology that have emerged, either on the Internet or because of its existence, and the generally shallow understanding of this technology in the legal community.

The simple programs that performed these functions were responsible for collecting most of the raw data central to Linkshare's business. This data contained the core transaction information that fed the rest of the business functions. These programs, therefore, enabled Linkshare to determine how much compensation each merchant needed to pay each of their affiliates in a network that contained many thousands of such relationships. They also helped the merchants to determine the effectiveness of their programs and enabled the affiliates to understand which merchants and programs were providing the best revenues for their efforts. Accordingly, these programs needed to process their information quickly, write out the data without any significant failure rate, and be available and working 100% of the time, or as close to that as possible. This may seem like a lot to demand of a program. But this kind of programming was commonplace on the Internet and off. Its functionality was little different than that included with standard Web server software to handle the server's need to record its transactions in log files.

The remainder of the technology at Linkshare was largely the same as it was at other Web-centric dot coms. One Web interface was designed to serve the needs of their merchants. Through it, the merchants could create advertising programs, approve affiliates, produce charts and reports based on the collected data, and so on. Another Web interface was designed to serve the needs of their affiliates. Through it, the affiliates could apply to merchant programs, acquire the link code and banners for each program they participated in, produce charts and reports based on the affiliate side of the collected data, and so on. These interfaces employed the same basic Web constructs used by any number of Web sites. They were simple and unsophisticated, written in basic HTML, and used a popular, interpreted programming language called PHP to generate the dynamic content specific to each affiliate and merchant, such as showing their business's name on each Web page. The content itself was housed in several large relational databases that constituted the final core element in Linkshare's technology; and PHP provided the mechanism through which to connect the user's actions on the Web interface, for instance a merchant's request to see a report on affiliate payments, with the information collected in the database on all transactions related to that affiliate.

While there are many good, bad, and indifferent ways to implement this general technology scenario, these core elements are commonplace in most Web businesses and dot coms. The business needs a Web interface through which to interact with its clients or consumers. It needs forms on that interface through which to collect information. It needs a database, or some corresponding data storage and retrieval application, in order to provide persistent storage of data about and for its clients or consumers. It also needs some type of embedded language or specialized program to function as an on-demand interpreter, retrieving and storing data in response to the actions being executed on the Web site (e.g., someone adding an item to a shopping cart or filling out a form to open an account). More than anything else, the technology of the Web itself comprised the foundation that built Linkshare, just as it was our growing use of the Web, and the growth of e-commerce in particular, that kept Linkshare afloat.

Step One: Discovering Where Things Stood

When I arrived at Linkshare in the fall of 1999, I inherited a small team of some half-dozen friendly and hard working programmers. Over the course of a few short, hectic years, they had managed to build a functional system that took care of the business at hand. The merchants and affiliates had their respective Web interfaces, while behind the scenes an assortment of programs did the grunt work of tracking the impressions and click-throughs, consolidating data in a database, running reports on demand, and so on. In many ways it seemed an impressive feat. I was used to working from detailed project plans, feature specifications, and a collection of other process, engineering, and development documents. The programmers who created the assorted programs and interfaces at Linkshare had no such help. But a working system is one thing. A system that has been planned out and engineered, coordinated, developed according to strict guidelines, documented, debugged, and meticulously tested is something else altogether.

My job was to take a system that had developed organically and haphazardly, and that included no documentation (not even commented code), and create from it a stable platform on which to further develop the technology of the company. This was, at least, the first mandate I gave myself. When I looked at the big picture before me, however, and tried to identify a starting point for the work, I quickly became lost and confused. I knew there was a collection of programs, databases, and computers tirelessly working on Linkshare's behalf to collect input, handle many thousands of transactions, and display information, but it was going to be a job in and of itself just to identify, categorize, and collect all the parts. When I looked more closely and started to review specific programs and code samples, I discovered something more. It was apparent that there had been little or no communication among the members of the small team of programmers that had written the code, despite the fact that the work was done by only five or six people all sitting together in a room no larger than a small bedroom. To make matters worse, the code was written with little to no regard for modularity or reuse. This was in many respects the problem with the largest and longest lasting impact.

Imagine that you want to write a simple program to turn a light switch on and off. If you understood the value of code modularity and reuse, you would regard the light switch in terms of its most general characteristics. You would, for instance, write a generic function to read the condition of the switch and tell you if it was in the off or on position, and another function to flip the switch to the opposite position when the position it was in was not the position the user had selected. Such a simple and generic program could then be applied to any light switch. Moreover, it might easily be used for other similar applications, like opening or closing a garage door or turning a heating system on or off.

The program code at Linkshare had understandably been written in haste and without any kind of coordinated effort or planning. Each and every operation had its own individual program; any common ground between operations — and there were many places where it existed — failed to take advantage of using a single function (i.e., one common block of code) to accomplish the common task. Some programs were identical in all but name and location. This suggested, at first glance anyway, that they were performing the same operation for different purposes or in different capacities. More often than not, however, this was not the case, as was quickly discovered when work commenced to enhance, consolidate, and document the code and parts of the system started to break. In other cases, two or three or four programs showed themselves, upon close examination, to be only slightly different from one another. But no apparent need or reason was expressed in the code or by the programmers for such minor differences. More disturbing still, some programs were apparently written to perform exactly the same function, yet their code was remarkably different.

After several weeks of studying the Linkshare program code, I was unsure of how and where to begin. It soon became clear to me, however, that the greatest obstacle was not going to be the apparent problems and limitations of the existing system, but the attitude and expectations of Linkshare's enthusiastic, but inexperienced young executives. They had no concept of the state of their technology compared to that of other companies. But I couldn't fault them for that. They had no frame of reference, no means to determine if what they had developed was good or bad, sound or unsound, modular and easily enhanced or linear and dangerous to tamper with. None had any substantial experience working in the computer industry, nor did they have any business experience with the Internet or the Web apart from what they had gained by creating Linkshare. This was not uncommon at a dot com startup. But it wasn't a good situation either.

The executives of Linkshare wanted to pursue a fast and competitive course of action to expand the company's position in the market; and they were full of ideas about new features and better service for their clients that they wanted to implement as soon as possible. This was a perfectly reasonable and valid perspective, and it had succeeded in making them a force to be reckoned with in the highly competitive area of affiliate management. The dot com revolution was nothing if not exceedingly fast paced. If you wanted to win, you had to be first; and you had to keep growing as fast as you could. But where they saw a robust, fully functional system I saw a system ready to collapse; and it had taken me the better part of two months, consisting largely of long hours of investigative work, just to reach this conclusion. This wide difference in our perspectives was, in a word, a problem. This particular chasm never completely closed during the time I was there.

I had inherited the following conditions. There were programs that sometimes worked, but at other times they failed utterly, and for no apparent reason. Each of the programmers lived in his or her own world, writing code without any regard for what the others were doing. This meant that each was reinventing the wheel, or copying large sections of existing code and calling it their own. Worse yet, it meant that changes made on the system by one programmer could easily and adversely affect other existing programs, which happened often and without anyone taking responsibility. But the single greatest problem was that the system as a whole was effectively one large black box containing an unknown number of smaller black boxes.

It was, for instance, one thing for me to interview candidates for jobs and explain what the company did and how the system generally worked. It was another thing altogether to take new hires and sit them in front of terminals, give them jobs to do, and then walk away. There was no road map to describe the system components and how they worked together. There was no central storage of the code that comprised the system, or any comments in the code to help someone understand what a particular program did or how it worked. There was no history of how the programs were developed or what changes were implemented as bugs were fixed or new features were added. There was no assigned or understood ownership of individual programs or components, something that would instill a sense of accountability, assist with resolving technical problems faster and more effectively, and enable technical information to be documented and shared.

These were the problems I had to address, while at the same time I had the CEO and others happily and feverishly describing to me the wonderful new features they wanted me to build. I clearly recall during my first few weeks at Linkshare staring out the train windows during my commute into and out of New York City and trying to reconcile this disparity. I realized that the solution was going to be, at least in the beginning, some middle ground. Rather than confronting the issue head on (that would come later, in no uncertain terms), I set out to give them something of what they were after, while working simultaneously to put some controls and processes in place to carry the work, and the technology, forward.

Step Two: Planning and Getting Started

In the late 1980s and into the early 1990s I was fortunate enough to work for AT&T Bell Laboratories in Summit, New Jersey. The organization I belonged to built the Unix System V operating system, one of the leading-edge operating systems of the time. It ran everything from large mainframes to desktop workstations and contributed significantly to the operation and growth of the Internet and later the Web. We were roughly 500 people, divided into a dozen or so departments, and housed in a single, three-story building; and together we planned, engineered, prototyped, built, documented, tested, debugged, packaged, and supported this very large and complex product. What enabled all these people to work together so effectively towards one goal were process, coordination, communication, and teamwork. It was the knowledge and understanding I gained there that I attempted to apply to the situation I faced at Linkshare, albeit on a far more modest scale.

I began by creating some basic infrastructure. First on my list was addressing the problem of not knowing the names, locations, and relationships of all the files and programs that composed the system. Part of my solution to this problem was to introduce a source code control system. With this application, we were able to house all the code in one place, establishing a central repository for all the program files, and organize the files into different components or modules. Equally important, the system would also function to track changes to the code as programs were modified and developed. Installing and configuring the system, however, proved easier than convincing the staff of programmers to use it. This process took time, some figurative hand slapping, and repeated pleas that they recognize the importance of using such a system to improve the quality of the software we were developing and to establish some measure of accountability. The system also made it possible (and easy) to back out newly introduced changes that resulted in unexpected behavior (i.e., bugs) by reverting to a previous version of the code. I figured that if we could get all the program code into this system we could understand for the first time what we had to work with. Also, we might be better able to estimate precisely what we needed to do in order to stabilize the basic technology that ran the company.

Next on my list was very basic documentation. Even well-written programs must be read carefully, typically line by line, to understand and follow what they do, how they function, and what purpose they serve. Poorly written programs require time-consuming study and tedious note-taking if they are to be understood. There is no good excuse for not including some basic comments in any program, no matter how short or simple, even if those comments include only the name of the original author, the program's purpose, a listing of key features, the types of information the program accepts or needs, and what, if anything, the program outputs or modifies. Such basic program commenting, as most programmers quickly learn, helps the program author as much as anyone else. This new demand also did not go over well; it was some time before it was fully implemented and, finally, appreciated. It was, however, a bare minimum effort that, in my long-term view, would directly impact the time, effort, and cost of maintaining and developing the fundamental technology of the company and, therefore, also impact the company's ability to compete.

At this stage, still managing to sidestep most of the demands for new and exciting features from the CEO and the marketing side of the business, I pushed forward with one more necessary piece of the basic infrastructure. This piece had to do specifically with how the company handled the reporting and repair of program bugs and with how it was failing to identify and resolve larger, more serious recurring failures in the system. I was concerned about the impact of these technical problems on the existing client base as well as their effect on the broader issue of software engineering, development, and maintenance within the company. No program, no matter how well written or tested, is entirely free of bugs. If nothing else, there will always be a case that no one anticipated when a user or a computer performs some action that causes the executing program to do something unexpected and perhaps harmful. Linkshare code had more than its fair share of bugs. But given the development environment — or lack thereof — and the relative inexperience of the staff, this was to be expected and was certainly the norm among dot coms.

But having bugs is one thing. Hearing your clients report them and repeatedly complain about them is another thing entirely. What Linkshare needed was a company-wide means to collect information about such problems and then track their progress and resolution. This called for the creation of a process that both the technical and non-technical members of the company could use to report problems. Everyone needed to be on the same page with respect to this issue so that we could present a unified front to the clients and work together as a company to quickly and efficiently resolve the problems. This process, in turn, required an associated application to embody and enforce it. The application would be used by everyone in the company from the CEO on down. Through it, problems would be reported, tracked, and resolved. Meanwhile, the application would build a problem/resolution database from the collected information that could be used to improve the overall system.

I introduced a modification request (MR) system into the Linkshare environment to track information about reported problems with the system and create the process to make sure problems were resolved quickly, efficiently, and according to their severity. I had had experience engineering and integrating MR systems into similar environments. Such systems function to track problem reports from their inception (e.g., a phone call or email to an account executive from an unhappy merchant or affiliate) through their various stages of assignment, analysis, and review, all the way to their final approval and closing. MR systems are critical to the success of any organization that has a product or service with a sizable, and hopefully growing, user population.

MR systems directly link a problem to a client, to one or more specific programmers assigned to investigate the problem, and to specific blocks of program code that are modified to resolve the problem. They also collect descriptive information that provides a history of both the problem and the resolution. Duplicate problems are quickly recognized and grouped together. Reports can be generated to show which components or features of the product may be weaker than others. Management can better understand how time and money is being spent on support of the product, which might lead them to recognize the importance of devoting resources to functional and usability testing of the product. In a word, MR systems are indispensable in any software development environment.

We configured the MR system at Linkshare to include different types and levels of access. Who you were in the company and what job you performed determined whether or not you could assign MRs, for instance, or review aggregate reports, or close MRs. But everyone could enter a new problem into the system and stay informed about its basic progress. A typical MR was entered into the system by an account executive using information supplied by one of his or her assigned clients. The MR system included a Web interface, which meant that account executives (and others) could use a browser to access the system's Web forms to enter the MR information and to watch the MR progress through its various stages. A development manager would review the new MR and then determine whether to accept or reject the issue and who to assign it to (if accepted), based on the type of problem or how other MRs had been assigned. That same manager would also review the resolution information entered by the assigned programmer before closing or re-assigning the MR. Meanwhile, the account executive knew which programmer to speak with if he or she had a question or wanted to know the current status of the work. The account executive was also better informed when he or she needed to communicate with the client about the the problem and its resolution. On a larger scale, the MR system enabled account managers (and others) to run a wide variety of reports, such as one showing all problems reported by a specific merchant or affiliate or one showing all problems of a particular type, like a login failure. This feature made it easier to determine which issues were general in nature, and which specific to their accounts or to particular parts of the system.

The MR system at Linkshare proved crucial to keeping the Web interfaces and supporting programming operational, while satisfying customer complaints. It also helped foster a greater understanding of technology issues across the entire company, and a wider awareness of both the strengths and weaknesses of that technology. Best of all, the system was the first and only means to connect up everyone in the company and drive them collectively towards the same goal: building a better product for improved client satisfaction and establishing a far more stable platform upon which to add all those new and exciting features that everyone wanted.

All things considered, the system exceeded my expectations. It made me realize how important it was to involve everyone in the company in a common forum focused on improving and advancing the company's product and image. Some of the simplest and best ideas for such improvements, incidentally, came from people outside of the product development or technology areas, for example, from the account executives and the customer support staff. After all, they were working directly with the clients and with the product; and they often knew best where the product was succeeding, and where it was failing. More subtly but equally important, the MR system also narrowed the chasm between my perspective on the state of the company's technology and that of the company's founders and other executives. They could now see for themselves the nature and the number of the problems being encountered by the clients, as well as better understand the efforts being extended to correct those problems. I no longer had to open my mouth; the data spoke for me.

Step Three: Introducing Process and Engineering

With a reasonable infrastructure in place, and with a process — embodied by the MR system — through which system changes, even minor enhancements, could be approved, managed, and documented, the stage was set for new development. But here, too, I insisted on and pushed through substantial changes in the way such efforts took place. Prior to my arrival, and for a few months afterwards, new product features were described, discussed, and developed entirely in email exchanges. Often, as the programmers attempted to determine if and how a particular feature could be built, and frequently while they were in the process of writing the code, the basic definition of the feature would change. Or, just as often, the person requesting the new feature would suddenly want something else altogether. To complicate matters, a person who did not understand the technology (which included all of the product development and marketing staff at the company) could not begin to fathom the impact of such changes on the development effort and schedule.

Trying to conduct product development in this way (which was hardly unique to Linkshare) presents too many problems to list. But one of the biggest problems, and the one that had to be addressed first, was that the person or group requesting a new feature had no understanding of how easy or difficult it was going to be to engineer, develop, and integrate the feature. To fix this, and other closely associated issues, product development would need to formally document what they wanted, explain who was going to use it and what benefits were expected, and organize these requests in some order of priority with respect to the other ongoing technical projects. To achieve this end, I introduced the product management group to a features specification template commonly used in the computer industry. Through it, I explained, they could define their requests. It didn't matter if the request was two pages or twenty, provided they included the requisite information.

Once a features specification had been completed, it was reviewed by the development group to determine how much effort would be required to implement the new feature and to see what, if any, technology issues were involved. A meeting was then held with members from both groups to discuss the specification; and this exchange of information typically led to very positive and critical changes, as concept and technology came head to head. The specification was refined accordingly; and eventually it was finalized and frozen. The new feature was now properly documented and understood, and the effort needed to implement it had also been assessed and acknowledged. When members of product management later told me that writing the specifications helped them to refine and clarify the features they wanted to add to the system and that reviewing the specifications helped them to better understand the technology, I knew I had managed to effect some positive change.

When it came time for the programmers to produce their own, corollary specification, a requirements document detailing how they were going to write the code to implement the new feature, understanding and appreciation were far less forthcoming. Most programmers are not terribly fond of producing any documentation. They would much rather be writing code than sentences and paragraphs. But eventually I managed to instill some acceptance and appreciation of the need to create a requirements document. A few programmers even managed to grasp the importance of producing such documentation. Writing a requirements document forces a programmer to conceptualize all the individual objects of code before sitting down to write the code itself, prototype the new feature, and debug its operation. It's like writing an outline before one begins to compose an essay. Even the simplest requirements document can contribute significantly to the overall quality of any software. It seems like more work, but if done correctly it should reduce development time and, more importantly, help to produce a far better product.

Step Four: Building the Future

During the time I was instituting these changes at Linkshare, I was also interviewing and hiring programmers as fast as I possibly could. I quickly learned that general aptitude, good communication skills, a strong desire to learn new things, and overall intelligence were far more significant factors in determining whether or not a new programmer would succeed at Linkshare than highly specific skills with a particular programming language or Internet protocol. I managed to put together a cosmopolitan team of men and women, some young, some not so young, with individuals who hailed from Russia, Germany, Japan, China, India, and the U.S. My happiest memories from Linkshare relate to watching this talented, diverse group of people become a team, freely helping each other to understand and resolve complex technical issues. What was best about the company was evidenced by their commitment to quality and the generally happy demeanor they displayed even when things became stressful, as they often did.

Technically speaking, the most challenging project during my tenure at Linkshare involved a joint venture with Mitsui and Company, Ltd. of Japan, one of the largest multinational corporations in the world. Linkshare and Mitsui had struck a deal that called for recreating the Linkshare product for use in Japan. This meant, among other things, building Web interfaces, creating new databases, and adapting all of the ancillary programs and technology to work with and display the Japanese language in addition to English, and the yen in addition to the dollar. But that was just the beginning. Aside from the myriad technical issues, it also meant localizing the whole product for a Japanese audience. What one culture views as acceptable and understandable, another may find offensive, ambiguous, or even incomprehensible. Even the use of color is viewed differently by different cultures. Consider the icon used on many Web sites in the U.S. to represent a post box for email. Many people in the United Kingdom are more likely to interpret this icon as a bread box. That's just the tip of the iceberg.

When I started to think about the scope of this endeavor, all sorts of basic, technical questions presented themselves. For instance, all the text that appeared on the Linkshare Web site, or that was stored in the database, or that was used for reports, and so on, was distributed or, more exactly, sprinkled throughout hundreds of HTML files, program code fragments, database tables, and elsewhere. Before we could get the text translated, which itself was not an easy or straightforward task, first we had to get it all located, extracted, and stored in one, central place. We also had to create a whole new methodology to tag, store, and later retrieve this information when needed. We also needed a means to know when someone wanted to see Japanese, as opposed to English, text. Hardest of all, Japanese is what's called a double-byte language; and it has three separate alphabets, broken into two groups. These features, simply put, make it about as different from English as you can get. Such differences impacted how we would need to store and display text; and it increased the demands on the systems we used for our Web servers and databases.

While the language issue was one large and difficult factor in adapting the system for use in Japan, localization proved just as difficult. Every country represents phone numbers differently. The U.S. has social security numbers; other countries employ different systems to uniquely identify their citizens. Postal codes in the U.S. have five digits, with an optional four digit extension; every other country has its own unique way to represent geographic zones for their postal systems. These differences, and dozens more just like them, affect the Web interface, the database, programs that collect and verify and exchange data, and so on.

Managing to complete this project was a difficult and stressful challenge for my team. In the end, both the U.S. and the Japanese products benefited greatly from the effort. It forced far greater modularization of the technology; and since it entailed such close scrutiny of both the code and the representation of the product to the clients, many long-standing problems were finally found and fixed in the process. Think about this issue the next time you visit a Web site. The Internet and the Web are global resources that function well to dissolve many of the barriers between peoples and nations. But we do not all speak, or for that matter read, English; and to many the symbol for a question mark or the icon for a post box represents something else altogether.

Step Five: Moving On

I suspect that the various conflicts I experienced at Linkshare were not uncommon at other dot coms, at both successful ventures and failures. In the end, such conflicts typically culminate in discussions about the right way, the wrong way, my way, and the highway. That best describes the termination of my employment at Linkshare, as the dot com bubble burst, business started to sour, and heads along with expenses started to roll (i.e., less revenue equaled less employees, which equaled layoffs). Most of the experienced managers brought in to Linkshare over the previous two years left in the course of a few months. It's hard to find that balance between the drive for more and better features and the need for quality, stability, and reliability. While it is always good practice to aspire to reach this balance, it is far more typical that one side gets sacrificed in the pursuit of the other.

Overall, my dot com experience was as exhilarating as it was exhausting. Working twelve to fourteen hour days, six to seven days a week, for nearly two years ends up taking its toll. It is something of an understatement for me to say that it felt good waking up one morning and realizing that my life at Linkshare was now part of my past. I think back, however, to some of those early Monday morning company meetings held by the CEO. We all crammed into a conference room as he described the state of the business and endeavored to infect us with his enthusiasm about the bright, rich future ahead. He said books would be written about the dot com pioneers, and Linkshare and everyone in that room would be a part of those books. It's possible that my little story is not exactly what he was anticipating. But, for what it's worth, it is my story.

The Internet as Community

6

The Internet as Community

If the Internet were just another way to locate and purchase merchandise like the latest catnip-soaked toy for your favorite Siamese cat, who would bother with it? What if the Internet were just another, albeit faster, way to send mail or an alternative to the telephone that also allowed you to chat with friends, family, business associates, and others? What if the Internet were just a huge information network, an online version of your local library that came directly into your home or business, or simply another source of entertainment, bringing you still more broadcast channels of radio, television, and movies? How many people would take on the additional and considerable expense of buying a computer and paying for monthly online access just to visit an Internet filled with merchandise and fact sheets, greeting cards and magazines, music and videos? And how many people would spend hours and hours of their time online every week surfing this shopping-information-entertainment network?

What brings millions of us to the Internet is that the Internet is full of people. What keeps us there, what makes the Internet appealing and even compelling — whether or not we have acknowledged it — is that interactions with other people on the Internet are integral to our use of the Internet. Simply put, we extend our presence through the Internet's distributed network and myriad services, and the Internet provides a space where we can meet and connect with other people, where we can share our ideas, insights, and dreams, where we can learn from others, and where we can become part of something larger than ourselves. It's a place to form and develop relationships — with individuals, with groups of individuals, and with organizations — that fuel our interests and that help us share and promote our goals and aspirations.

Because the Internet is full of people and because we use its services to communicate, share information, and form and develop relationships, the Internet's space — cyberspace — is rich with communities. All sorts of community structures thrive on the Internet. They have been an important and popular part of the Internet since its earliest days. As we shall see, these Internet communities are something utterly new in both concept and form. Their impact, which is likely to be far-reaching, can be felt today, but it cannot yet be measured or understood. Moreover, these Internet communities are something that has changed, and continues to change, the way we interact as individuals. They enable us to combine our voice with the voices of others in order to grow, be heard, become empowered, and effect change.

The Internet itself is often described as a community. When we join the Internet (i.e., when we connect to the Internet and go online) we become part of that community, not simply as a member or constituent, but as a unique, active, contributing participant and, if we choose, as a vocal, influential, and even controlling, participant. Just as our individual computers effectively constitute the Internet, forming and reforming its vast network as we come and go, so it is with us as individuals in constituting the Internet's community as we post emails, exchange thoughts and feelings in chat rooms, play games with remote friends or strangers, browse the Web, take part in newsgroups, subscribe to services, publish our journals, sell our creations, and so on. We, personally and uniquely, go online.

On the Internet, we interact in our private associations of friends, family, business associates, and acquaintances. We join organizations that match our interests. We become members of like-minded groups of people. We use the Internet's services — email, chat, bulletin boards, Multi-User Dimensions (MUDs, or cyberspace gaming and socializing environments), the Web, and other services — to share information, exchange ideas, and interact with other members of these groups and with the group as a whole in order to promote a common cause, provide comfort and support, or for any number of other reasons. In doing so, we form, and enter into, a variety of online communities that themselves make up the larger Internet community. We are, in the process, changing our definition of community through our use of the Internet; that is part of the Internet's power, part of the revolution it brings. Because of the Internet, the communities we belong to are no longer tied to where we live, nor are the groups we interact in dependent on in-person, face-to-face meetings.

For someone who is limited in who they can interact with or in how they can interact with others because of the remoteness of their location or perhaps a physical disability, the virtual communities made possible by chat, newsgroups, MUDs, group blogs, Web sites, and other Internet services offer riches and rewards that most of us cannot truly appreciate. But even for the rest of us, the Internet's virtual communities are empowering. That's because, if nothing else, they speak to the value and uniqueness of the individual: they validate that we all have something to contribute and a voice that should be heard and a vote that should be counted. The Internet makes this validation possible because its technology enables us to do so much more than we could do before its creation and because its egalitarian composition gives each of us equal standing. All the factors that keep us apart, that pigeonhole and stereotype us, that drown out our voice or don't allow us through a door in the physical world, or IRL (in real life), either don't come into play or are greatly diminished in their effect in our interactions on the Internet. In the Internet's realm, in its community, we are all equal, and we all enjoy equal opportunities for pursuing knowledge, joining a struggle, voicing our dissent, or even claiming that our recipe for clam chowder or lobster gumbo is the very best.

Individuals are not alone in establishing or participating in community structures on the Internet. Businesses on the Internet do much the same, forming communities with us and around us, and with other businesses. Some, like Web portals, establish dozens of different community structures. These structures cater to particular interests, like a sport such as golf or baseball, a hobby such as fishing, woodworking, or cooking, or a special need such as meeting someone online for dating or romance. These community structures are also embodied in the services that businesses provide on the Internet, such as chat rooms where we can gather with our friends and family, blogging sites where we can share our thoughts, and shareable calendars where we can post our schedules for others to see. All of these facilities are relatively recent, and completely new, creations. Acknowledging that these facilities are responsible for changing the way many of us interact and for creating new forms of community structures may not be necessary to your using these facilities, but it may result in your profiting more from the experience, or perhaps even finding a way to apply the concept to your own personal or business interests.

Other Internet businesses are far more targeted in their interests and intentions, but they are equally focused on the notion of community. Affiliate management organizations are one, perhaps extreme, example. These organizations bring together Web merchants and Web site owners (known as affiliates) in order for them to form relationships and share in the wealth of the Web. Their business is the creation and maintenance of that community of businesses. But nearly every other Internet business, whether geared specifically to the Internet or created as an online corollary to an existing brick-and-mortar store or institution, actively (and sometimes aggressively) courts and pursues us through promotions and promises and all sorts of other solicitations into joining their organization and becoming a legitimate, recognizable member of the community they have created. They will trade us services such as free access to information or tools, offer us lower prices on books, clothing, or other products, tempt us with entry into a sweepstakes or a free gift, all to acquire us as a member. While you may not view your acceptance of membership at an online bookstore or Internet portal as an act of joining a community, many of these businesses will succeed or fail based on the creation and growth of their community of users.

Non-commercial organizations on the Internet, such as non-profit and not-for-profit companies, charitable organizations, and local interest or other group-based organizations, are more explicitly focused on community. They use the Internet exclusively to reach out and widen their own community memberships. The Internet allows them to overcome the constraints of geography. It also enables them to use the two-way communication channel of the Internet to give their community of volunteers and contributing members a voice, whereas before these individuals could only passively listen. Their presence on the Internet is focused on community; they work to build a base of like-minded individuals, to distribute and share information, to incite more involvement from their members, and to create a larger, more powerful, and more effective organization. Whether it's saving an endangered species, protecting the rain forest, or confronting the government on some objectionable economic or foreign policy decision, the larger the community base they can build, the more effective they can be.

Even our government agencies (e.g., local, state, and federal law enforcement, and fire and rescue) can benefit in new and far-reaching ways from the Internet's capacity to create and foster all different types of virtual community structures. Our governments already know a lot about us as individuals. This knowledge includes information about the various communities to which we belong. They know, for example, where we live, which places us in a specific geographic community. They know our race, our financial status, perhaps even our religion and politics, all of which associate us with other types of communities. Now they can also mine the information coursing through the Internet and collected by Internet businesses (e.g., ISPs) to add to their knowledge about us and, more specifically, our associations and memberships.

Government agencies can also use the Internet to develop virtual community structures that will enhance and expand their capabilities to communicate, share information, and interact, much as has already happened with commercial and non-commercial organizations. Government agencies comprise many different sorts of interconnected communities. These community structures can be found in the different levels of government that reach downward from the federal to the state to the local level. They can also be found in many inter-agency organizations that serve to interconnect agencies, such as health, police, and fire departments, to coordinate efforts in situations that require more than one agency to respond. The Internet can serve to unite and interconnect all of these communities, too. For them, however, the process is only just beginning.

The following sections explore the concept of the Internet as community, as seen from the different perspectives of non-commercial organizations, business, the government, and the individual. The future of the Internet may well lie in its innate capacity to build and foster community and in the constructs we append to the Internet, which may one day transform the Internet from a network of machines and data into one of people, their knowledge, and their community interactions.

Organizations That Embody Community

Probably the most easily recognizable Internet community structures are those built by non-commercial entities, such as non-profit, not-for-profit, and charitable organizations. The sole purpose of these organizations is to promote their interests by sharing their philosophy, beliefs, concerns, knowledge, and goals and by attracting like-minded individuals to join them and thereby strengthen and expand their influence. Nearly every large and moderately-sized general interest group (and countless small groups), activist organizations, and associations that were in existence before the commercialization and privatization of the Internet in the early 1990s have built a presence for themselves on the Internet in the form of a Web site. Their Internet presence serves to supplement the community-based meetings, functions, and services that occur off the Internet. Other groups that formed in the mid 1990s and later have been built from the ground up with the Internet in mind, and some of these have been built exclusively on the Internet, as is described below.

Whether they dispense information, provide support or advice, advocate change and activism, promote common interests, or all of the above, non-commercial organizations employ the technology of the Internet to embody a new form of community structure. These community structures strive to be all-inclusive and to meet the needs of both small groups and large; their ability to do so is made possible by the Internet, specifically by its capacity to eliminate traditional constraints on enrollment and participation imposed by geography. Moreover, these organizations want to engage us; they aspire to use the Internet's inherent two-way communication channel to get to know us better and to encourage us to do more than contribute money and passively stay informed.

Examples of these Internet communities are easy to find and are remarkably diverse. There are faith-based organizations, such as Beliefnet, that strive to meet the religious and spiritual needs of individuals by providing a source of information, inspiration, and a place of community where people can come to pray, help one another, and grow. There are political-based organizations, such as Moveon.org, that endeavor to encourage and facilitate greater political activism by offering individuals a new way to participate in grassroots movements. These political-based organizations make up an online community of advocacy groups that attempts to counter the influence of big business and big money with the collective power of individuals. There are also smaller, localized, community-based organizations, such as barharbor.org, that are sprinkled throughout the Internet and throughout the globe. They are often created by a local chamber of commerce or another local civic group, and they function as the virtual counterparts of physical communities, inheriting and building on the efforts of the early electronic bulletin boards to provide information and services geared specifically to the local members of a community and to those interested in visiting or learning about that community.

What these organizations, and thousands of others just like them, have in common is that they have used the fundamental technology of the Internet to build effective and vital virtual communities. Most of the individuals in these communities have never met face-to-face, nor is it likely they ever will. This lack of direct, personal contact, however, has in no way diminished their ability to interact, share and debate ideas and issues, help one another, and create something larger than the sum of their individual participation. There's no rule that requires people to meet under a church roof, in a town hall, or in any other central location in order to come together as a community and function as a community. The Internet has proven this. What remains to be seen is what, if any, limitations may exist with respect to the types of communities that may be created and the extent of their reach.

Consider the following example. Founded in 1990, an organization called the Electronic Frontier Foundation (EFF) is a virtual community of like-minded individuals that was established specifically to illuminate and protect the fundamental rights of individuals on the Internet. The EFF grew out of an incident described and debated in an early online discussion forum called the WELL, which is described later in this chapter. The incident began with the U.S. government's investigation of an illegally obtained document relating to the operation of its emergency 911 system. As part of its investigation, the government confiscated and examined the computers of Steve Jackson, an independent book publisher and electronic bulletin board enthusiast. In the process, they accessed and deleted personal messages related to private users of his company's bulletin board. For many people who participated in the WELL, this incident heightened growing concerns over a lack of fundamental protections for electronically stored information and it exemplified the need for clarity regarding an individual's online or electronic rights to free speech and privacy. They saw the government's actions as a clear violation of these rights and they feared that their own online activities and communications would become subject to the same intrusive and unwarranted scrutiny.

When no civil liberties groups could be found that understood the technology and its issues well enough to represent Jackson's case, news circulated on the WELL. As a direct and immediate consequence, the EFF was formed to represent Jackson as well as the bulletin board users. Since that time the EFF has grown into a membership-driven, grassroots organization determined to protect the basic freedoms and civil liberties of individuals and communities on the Internet. They are at the forefront in analyzing and confronting issues related to the technology of the Internet, its intersection with the legal system, and our fundamental rights. As a community in its own right, the EFF functions to keep us informed, provides a way for us to get help, and gives us a voice through which to be heard.

An organization with ties to the EFF, and with similar beliefs and interests, is the Free Software Foundation (FSF). The FSF, founded by Richard M. Stallman in 1985, espouses a community-based, collective approach to building and distributing software for the betterment of the community at large, a philosophy embedded in the creation and evolution of the Internet itself. You can think of the FSF as the technology implementation side, or corollary, to the EFF's legal and informational awareness efforts. The EFF focuses its efforts on preserving the rights of individuals, as opposed to those of large corporations or the government, with respect to the digital technologies of computers and the Internet.

Their work consists of pursuing greater legal protections for the privacy of our electronic information and establishing a greater awareness of our right to privacy and emerging infringements of that right. The FSF pursues these same protections through its promotion and protection of the software that constitutes these technologies.

The FSF achieves its goals by means of a unique, community-based approach to promoting and protecting the software rights of individuals — the principal consumers and users of software applications. This approach stands in direct opposition to the long-standing copyright and software protections afforded the businesses that manufacture and distribute most commercial software. The FSF is a grassroots organization that comprises a large and widespread community of independent software engineers and developers. Its members and contributors share the same commitment to the free distribution and redistribution of the software they make available through the FSF. This commitment is backed up by the licenses from the FSF that accompany this software: the GNU General Public License and its associated Copyleft license. Unlike standard, commercial software licenses that are designed to prohibit copying and changing software, the FSF licenses guarantee an individual's freedom to share and modify the software. The FSF licenses must remain a part of any modified and shared versions of its software, thereby preserving these freedoms for future users. The protections found in the FSF licenses that empower individuals to freely use, copy, enhance, and distribute these software applications speak to an ideology common to most, if not all, of the non-commercial organizations that provide and promote community building on the Internet. This ideology is based on sharing knowledge and pooling individual resources to empower people and to share the wealth. All of these organizations provide the means to pursue common interests and achieve common goals in new and more powerful, effective ways.

It doesn't take all that much exposure to the Internet to realize that organizations — such as those described above — that cater to and build grassroots communities on the Internet are plentiful, diverse, and frequented daily by many thousands of people. Such organizations are made up of ordinary individuals who share a passion for helping others. In many ways, they embody the true spirit of the Internet and, in ways large and small, they demonstrate how a simple network of computers and shared information can focus the collected power of like-minded individuals to change the world.

Businesses That Build and Depend on Community

Virtual communities are not just for charities, non-profits, and other non-commercial organizations. Opportunities for building (and profiting from) communities on the Internet are also very well represented by commercial business ventures. Many Internet businesses rely on community structures to help fulfill two of their most important objectives: to keep us on their site for as long as possible (how well a site can keep us on its pages before we click away is referred to — and measured as — the site's *stickability*) and to keep us returning to their site again and again. Internet businesses are also responsible for providing the tools and services that enable us to participate in community-based activities on the Internet, such as chat rooms where we can congregate and talk and virtual meeting rooms where we can make presentations and hold discussions. There is also the fast-growing business-to-business (B2B) sector of the Internet, which consists of businesses forming associations and communities with other businesses in ways that were not possible or even conceivable before the advent of the Internet. One simple example of this type of business-based Internet community is the virtual Internet mall.

Consider eBay, the online giant of auctions and merchandise reselling. eBay is first and foremost an Internet community structure. It was built on the premise that individuals and businesses would join its highly contrived (eBay created the rules of conduct, the means for people to interact, and the punishments for people who refuse to follow the rules), but well-defined and well-managed community in order to sell their goods and to form both personal and professional relationships. eBay itself owns the community and profits from its transactions. The larger and more diverse the community, the more transactions will occur and the greater the profit for eBay. There's nothing complicated or revolutionary about that.

The general business model of eBay is simple but effective, and so is the technology. eBay's success, however, doesn't simply derive from it being the first to offer this type of service on the Internet. The creators of eBay recognized from the start that the success or failure of the business would be determined by how people responded to the community structure they built, how easy it was to use, and, not least of all, how quickly it would grow. Accordingly, they didn't just create simple, functional interfaces through which products could be offered for sale, bids could be entered, and transactions could be concluded. They also created an array of associated, community-building tools that members of the community could use in order to share information and interact. For instance, discussion groups and chat boards provided by eBay are open community forums that allow community members to express opinions, form relationships, discuss topics of mutual interest, and provide advice and insights on the process of trading. These tools constitute an essential part of the eBay experience and of the eBay business model, in which maintaining the health and growth of the eBay community is foremost to the success of the company.

On a larger scale, eBay is also a community of businesses. Pawn shops and other small merchandise businesses use the tools provided on eBay to build eBay storefronts, either creating a virtual storefront as part of a new business venture, or extending the reach of their brick-and-mortar establishment through the online eBay community. However, what makes it all work — and what is most responsible for eBay's initial and continued success — is that eBay's community is a product of the people who make up that community and their overall adherence to its rules, which is no different than other successful communities on the Internet or, for that matter, any thriving community in general.

eBay may have created the community structure for its Internet site, but it's the community members who largely ensure that its rules, etiquette, and guidelines are followed. Individuals and *Neighborhood Watch* groups on eBay monitor and openly comment on the behavior of others in the community. The vigilance of its community members and the information they collect and distribute regarding the past behavior and performance of other members is responsible for assuring eBay shoppers an important measure of confidence in making transactions.

Moreover, many people return frequently because eBay is, in its own unique and vibrant way, a thriving community of individuals who actively participate in and are interested in growing and protecting this eclectic community.

Web portals, like Yahoo! and Netscape, regard the community aspect of the Internet from a somewhat different perspective. Like eBay, their success is largely dependent on membership. Our membership in these portal sites means two things to them. First, through membership, they know who we are; we are no longer an anonymous person out there in the Internet mist. Knowing who we are and, through direct or indirect means, knowing something about our interests, our buying habits, and our browsing behavior means they can (or, at least, attempt to) customize their services, products, and advertisements specifically for our tastes. This, in turn, should increase the stickability factor of their site (i.e., keep us on their site for a longer period of time), which means more revenues for them. It should also increase the likelihood of our making a purchase or visiting a sponsored site, which means more revenues for them. Moreover, it should provide us with more motivation to return, which means more revenues for them.

Second, our membership represents one identity in a much larger community; we are part of a larger demographic, and our stated and implied preferences are shared with some number of other community members. This has value and significance all its own. As eBay amply illustrates, it is worth time and money to build large, diverse community structures on the Internet. Moreover, our use of the Internet shows that we are attracted to locations that support community structures, familiar places where we can interact with people we already know and perhaps even start new relationships, whether for personal or for business reasons. Portal sites typically provide a wide assortment of forums to facilitate such interactions; newsgroups, open, moderated discussion groups, message boards, chat rooms, and even dating services are common. They also provide tools that help us organize and develop our own personal, group, and community interactions. Portal-based calendar, address book, and conferencing tools assist us in socializing with our friends, family, and associates. All of these tools and facilities encourage us to extend our use of such sites from an information resource to something more directly connected to our personal and community-based relationships.

A portal site's community of users represents a large and profitable business asset. The free services provided by Internet portals — however valuable or trivial you may consider them — are not entirely free. Advertising revenues from such sites are tied to the demographics created out of our membership in their community. Data mining, too, relies on large, community-based information structures to generate the kind of information needed to build its models and produce reliable reports on our interests, buying trends, and online behavior. When we enter into membership on these sites, therefore, we become part of their particular communities whether or not we recognize our involvement as a member of a community. Even membership on simpler commerce sites, such as online book stores or toy stores, is regarded by such businesses in much the same way as it is by the larger, more diverse portal sites. They actively encourage us to join their community through merchandise discounts or free shipping. They often offer tools for us to write book or product reviews. They seek out this two-way exchange of information in order to build and enrich their user communities. In doing so, they expect to reap the same rewards as those of the portal sites and of the more explicitly recognizable Internet communities, such as the one found on eBay.

Business-based communities on the Internet are not just for big name sites with lots of capital. They can be a significant and valuable asset of Internet sites of any size, and they don't necessarily require a large computer systems infrastructure or a large budget to create and operate. Internet sites solicit our membership for reasons that range from building mailings lists for the promotion of products or services, to mining demographic data for internal use or for resale, to building sophisticated community structures for gaming, socializing, telecommuting, or any number of other uses.

Smaller Internet sites are more effective when they are geared to specific audiences. Common examples of such sites include those devoted to health issues, astrology, diet and fitness, hobbies, and finances. Moreover, members of these sites can be presumed to share some common interest, and this shared interest is the basis for an implied community among members. Whether the business owners of these sites are interested in their site's community or are solely focused on selling products or information is not necessarily relevant to the community itself. The community is there: we visit these sites; we browse through pages of information; we submit questions; we offer advice, sympathy, humor, and sarcasm. Our presence and actions on these sites is recorded and can be measured; we are neither anonymous nor passive. Our visiting these sites — even if it feels otherwise — is an entirely different experience than the passive and anonymous act of collecting information on the same subject through a magazine, radio program, or television show. In the process of joining and visiting these sites, we form a community of individuals interested in astrology or personal fitness or some other subject. It's then up to the site owners whether to recognize this community for what it is, whether to nurture its growth or let it develop or flounder on its own, and how to treat the information collected on the site about its members and the community as a whole.

Some businesses offer free membership and promote products and services along with their free exchange of information. Other businesses choose to offer fee-based membership. These businesses are either more selective about the particular type of community they want to build, or they want to provide a higher (and more costly) level of service, or they are using membership fees, rather than advertising or sponsor-provided funding, to cover the costs of the service. Both types of sites are equally dependent for their survival and success on building thriving community structures. Without our continuing involvement with their site, regardless of the extent of our interaction with other members or whether our participation in the community is overt or implied, they will fail.

Business-based community structures on the Internet are not always directly about us, the consumers. A large number of business enterprises serve the needs of other businesses in the B2B market, and the Internet has created fresh opportunities in this area. Affiliate management organizations, which are described at length in *The Information Revolution*, offer a perfect illustration of building a specialized business community on the Internet by providing an environment in which different types of Internet business entities can communicate, form relationships, and collectively share in the distributed resources and commercial opportunities of the Web. eBay's facility for enabling businesses to set up storefronts on their site is another example of creating B2B community structures.

Virtual Internet malls provide another compelling example of B2B community structures. Small, independent Internet storefronts have a difficult time getting noticed and developing a customer base when they are off on their own. Existing businesses can easily and inexpensively use the Internet to set up a Web site and, in so doing, establish a whole new avenue through which to attract business. But they can only expect so much traffic, and most of that will be from people who already know about their location on the Internet (i.e., their Internet site address), just as is the case for brick-and-mortar stores that are on a side street or off the beaten path.

Place that same storefront within a larger community of stores, and the business dynamics are considerably changed. Virtual Internet malls are a powerful new paradigm for commerce that only the Internet could have created. They use the combined drawing power of several businesses in an effort to attract more customers to each of the individual businesses that make up the community. Suddenly, a small, family-owned fishing equipment supply store located in a tiny town on the coast of Oregon has a chance to divert the virtual foot traffic searching for products at Sears, or Wal-Mart, or a wide variety of other merchants of varying size and status. A virtual mall provides the community to make this happen. Businesses, just like individuals, can in this way be drawn to and profit greatly from such forms of community membership on the Internet.

Governments That Ignore Community

With respect to government agencies, little effort has been made to incorporate the kinds of virtual community structures prevalent on so many commercial and non-commercial Internet sites for purposes that might suit the needs of government and its many different types of organizations. It is not difficult, however, to envision the potential applications for virtual communities to government agencies.

Governments across the globe have been expanding their presence on the Internet each year. Like the U.S. government's official Web portal, Firstgov.gov, these sites provide considerable information resources. They present a wide array of useful data, helpful advice and assistance, and government forms that are directed towards individuals, businesses, and other government agencies. Government Internet sites make it easier for us to cut through the red tape so commonly confronted when we need to interact with government agencies. Even common activities, such as replacing a lost passport or obtaining tax or licensing information, can be completed easier, faster, and at a lower cost with the assistance of a basic Internet site that has been set up to provide needed information, handle questions, and process application forms. It's apparent, however, that the U.S. government, and most other governments for that matter, have not yet realized that the Internet is more than just another medium for broadcasting information.

What are governments if not composites of our communities and communities in their own right? At least three large-scale and distinctly different types of community structure are easily identifiable in any government body. First, governments themselves are community structures with their own special hierarchies, departments, organizations, and associated social interactions. Second, all governments are part of some larger community of governments, such as the United Nations, the European Union, or NATO. Third, each government body has an implied community structure with its specific constituents (e.g., city government agencies and the residents of the city, state or province government agencies and the residents of the state or province, and so on). All of these types of communities, however, remain largely under-represented on the Internet. Our governments remain relatively anonymous, distant, and disconnected entities, even though the technology exists to turn their presence into one that is open, welcoming, and integrated.

Governments are in the data collection and data analysis business, so much so that their needs and wants have driven many of the major advances in the development of computer hardware, software, and, of course, networking. What began with civilian applications of computer systems, such as the recording and analysis of census data, later became military applications, such as the creation of ballistics tables and breaking the codes of encrypted data transmissions, eventually led to the birth of the ARPANET and its evolution into today's Internet. But what is our governments' principal interest in the collection and analysis of data today: mining data about our behavior, interactions, purchases, and communications on the Internet; spying on the citizenry in the name of protecting the citizenry.

A growing number of commercial organizations mine the wealth of data created on the Internet for any number of purposes. Our governments want to do the same, and already are to some degree. Instead of sending us a promotional email for financing a new house (as a commercial data mining business might make possible for a bank), our governments might mine the same raw data in the hopes of exposing the planning of a terrorist act. Putting aside the problem that this sort of collection and mining of personal data — for commercial or government use — is an invasion of privacy, it shows a complete and utter disregard (or ignorance) of the Internet as a community and of the untapped potential of the Internet's community structures. Why should our governments be covertly collecting information about its citizens when instead they could use the Internet's facility for building communities and sharing information to do so much more. It's worth considering what kinds of virtual communities our government organizations could create that might more directly and positively benefit all of us

Consider something like the Amber Alert system, a U.S. state-based program that uses the communication structures of law enforcement agencies, the media, and the public to broadcast and solve cases of child abduction. The system originated in Texas in 1996 after the abduction and murder of Amber Hagerman, who was just nine years old. Since then, other states have created their own Amber Alert programs modeled on the same basic structure, and efforts are under way to create a nationwide program. The Amber Alert system is dependent on community involvement, and the Internet community can help.

The idea behind these Amber Alert programs is to broadcast information about a child's abduction as quickly as possible after the event and to as many organizations and individuals as possible in the hopes that someone who comes into contact with the child, the person who is thought to have performed the abduction, or the vehicle involved will report back to police. Reaching out through the Internet to both the Internet community at large and to local, state, and federal government agencies is a fast and effective way to broadcast this critical information to as many people as possible in the shortest amount of time. It's easy to imagine that many Internet sites, portal sites among them, would offer their services to communicate Amber Alerts directly to their communities using some sort of highly visible Web site alert mechanism (e.g., a breaking news ticker). Since this type of alert would typically be localized to one community or geographic region, Internet sites that participate in some type of Amber Alert program could easily use information from their members' profiles to distinguish who should, and who need not, see such an alert.

It's a short road from the government's broadcast of Amber Alerts to the Internet community to any number of other types of emergency-based broadcasts, such as ones relating to terrorist acts, natural disasters like fires and flooding, prison escapes, and mass transit problems. Depending on the nature of an event, such alerts could be broadcast to the entire Internet community or to localized, geographically-defined communities. The technology is already in place to make this happen. The only thing lacking is our governments' interest in and commitment to this type of public service. First, however, they must recognize the inherent community structure of the Internet and take steps to become members of that community. Only then can our governments use the Internet's remarkable power and reach in the service of their citizens. This should be part of their mandate and it would yield far better results than any type of covert data mining operation could ever hope to produce.

Such alert mechanisms constitute one way in which our governments can use the existing virtual communities of the Internet to exchange information and interact with us in a constructive and mutually beneficial manner. Another way involves our elected representatives and the building of new virtual communities. All elected officials represent some community of constituents, and they are accountable to that community. These officials can use the Internet to engage their constituents in the operation of the government and to inform them of the effects of government rulings and legislation on their community with a level of detail and an immediacy that was never before possible. Should they wish to avail themselves of it, the technology that makes community structures possible on the Internet enables them to keep their constituents fully informed on their activities, voting records, and service to their community. It can also be used by them to interact directly with community members through email exchanges, asynchronous discussions forums (i.e., threaded postings of information exchanges, often the form of questions and answers, arranged by subject), and virtual town meetings.

While some elected officials already use government-sponsored Internet sites to keep their electorate informed, most existing efforts amount to little more than Web site home pages. They provide information and photographs, but they offer nothing new or engaging. Nor do they demonstrate an awareness that the Internet is full of people, and, because of this, it provides them the opportunity to form closer, more intimate ties with their community members. Perhaps one day the Internet and its technology will help hold our representatives to a higher standard of involvement with their constituents and encourage them to use the potential of the Internet to better embrace their communities.

Government also has the opportunity, some would argue the obligation, to use the Internet to establish virtual communities at every level and for every office. But what we see today, in the midst of a revolutionary transformation in how people communicate and interact and how information is shared, is that government agencies are becoming increasingly disassociated from the individuals they are mandated to help, support, and protect. The higher up they are in the government structure, the more removed and isolated these agencies, the people who work in them, and their activities become. Communication technology, with the Internet at its center, has truly made the world smaller, more intimate, and better known to more people. It is not unreasonable to expect the same sort of transformation in our governments and their service to us. All they need to do is build the digital bridges and virtual communities necessary to better interconnect themselves with us and, in the process, better interconnect their own people and organizations.

Individuals, the Internet, and Virtual Communities

Without communities on the Internet, we would all be lost, cast adrift in a sea of endless information sources and services. Who would we interact with? Where would we obtain our news and weather and other information? How we would reach out and get involved? Why would we bother to go online?

You may think this is a bit extreme, but the Internet would be a poorer place without its capacity to establish communities (however loosely or precisely you define the term). We want to belong; and we crave familiarity and consistency. So we join up, become a member, obtain a login and password. We go online, connect to *our* sites, and read the latest football scores or stock quotes or weather report, just like dozens or hundreds or thousands of other individuals. Many of us go a little further and contribute our knowledge, help others in need, share ourselves and our experiences. Some even build their own community structures and hope that others will join them.

Whether we recognize it or not, whether it's personally significant to us or not, we go online and join communities comprised of countless, nameless, faceless others. Some of these communities are explicit and easily identifiable, like a singles Web site where people come to meet others and start new relationships. Others are simply implied and not necessarily significant to us, like joining a Web portal to better manage our information needs or signing up for a weekly newsletter that contains a calendar of events for the city in which we live. We may share nothing with the other, largely anonymous people who have also become members of these virtual communities. Or we may be connected to them in some way due to a common interest or hobby, our profession, or a shared experience or belief. Regardless, we are part of the same online communities. If nothing else, we are at least part of the same, overall Internet community.

Not surprisingly, when you think about it, the same holds true for our lives off the Internet. The location of our homes, for example, places us in a community. We are a member of that community whether or not we interact with our neighbors (or even know their names), whether or not we've visited the elementary school gymnasium, the town hall, or the local fire station to cast a vote, and whether or not we've bought a box of cookies from the local girl scout troop. We are a de facto member of the community due simply to the location of our chosen residence.

Other choices we have made in our lives are responsible for making us members of various other types of communities, associations, and groups. We form our individual communities, or cliques, from the people with whom we choose to socialize and from the groups we choose to join. At work, we become part of one or more groups, both as a function of our jobs and by choice. We donate our money and our time to charities and to other organizations, such as our alma mater, thereby establishing and/or continuing our connection to these communities. We join a place of worship. We become part of professional associations related to our vocations or avocations. We also make conscious decisions, based on any number of factors, regarding the newspapers we read to stay informed about current events and the television shows or movies we select to watch for our entertainment. All of these choices shape who we are and, ultimately, how and where we belong in the community at large.

One consequence of all these different choices and decisions, however subtle or abstract they may seem, is how these shared experiences and this shared information invariably establishes that we are part of a wide range of different and disparate types of communities. We belong to these communities because of the interests, characteristics, goals, knowledge, and experiences we have in common with other people. For instance, we are part of, or not part of, a community of people who read the New York Times, or a community of people who watch CNN. We are part of, or not part of, a community of people who contribute to Greenpeace, or who volunteer for Habitat for Humanity, or who attend and vote at our town's yearly meeting. We are part of, or not part of, the baby boomer generation or the population of individuals who have retired from their jobs. There are communities to which we belong, such as those formed by our local church, synagogue, or mosque, in which we may know every other member. But there are myriad other communities we belong to in which our membership is more implied than stated; it occurs at a more abstract, impersonal level.

We may not know another soul in the community, or even know that the community exists, but that doesn't necessarily make our membership any less real or significant.

So, what does any of this mean with respect to the Internet? Why is this in the least bit interesting or important? The answer starts with the inspiration and motivation behind the creation of the Internet; the fact that the Internet is not simply a network of connected computers, but a network of connected people and their ideas, ideals, knowledge, and interests. The Internet is in many respects the ultimate realization of free expression; it is a communication medium that allows us to gather and publish information on equal terms with everyone else, and it is a meeting place where we can interact with others in real time or when convenient, whether with individuals or with groups across the street, across town, across the country, or across the globe. Viewed in this way, the Internet can be understood as a builder of communities. It provides the tools and materials to build an endless number and variety of virtual locations where people can gather regardless of where they reside, effectively allowing the creation of countless virtual communities. If nothing else, the Internet is changing our definition of community.

Before the advent of computer networks, virtual communities were restricted to the realm of fiction. With the arrival of networking, but long before the commercialization and widespread acceptance of the Internet, this newfound facility for communicating and sharing information first and foremost functioned to bring people together, to establish new communities in the digital ether of the network. For instance, before the Internet was accessible outside of government and academic environments, highly localized virtual communities manifested themselves as electronic bulletin board services that peopled dialed into with their modems to post and read messages, exchange software, and engage in other activities consisting of simple personal communication and information sharing. These early meeting places on the network established the importance of constructed virtual spaces where people could go to escape the constraints or isolation of their physical location and freely interact with others. Later, after the commercialization of the Internet and the exponential growth of the Internet population in the late 1990s, the number and variety of virtual communities on the Internet exploded, and the type of virtual community one could create was limited only by one's imagination.

An early, and still thriving, example of virtual community on the Internet can be found in online discussion forums called newsgroups. One of the oldest newsgroup services is called Usenet. It was started in 1979 and comprises hundreds of millions of postings from contributors across the globe. Usenet contains (among countless other pieces of information) the earliest announcements of many small and seemingly inconsequential computer projects that would later change the landscape of the Internet. These announcements include Tim Berner-Lee's posting about his information management system called the World Wide Web, Richard Stallman's posting of a Unix-compatible software system called GNU (for Gnu's Not Unix), and Linus Torvald's posting about a new operating system that would come to be known as Linux.

Newsgroups promote the free exchange of ideas on just about any subject imaginable, from humor, to employment, to health, to literature, to current events, to social issues, and so on. They function as subject-specific message boards, and each message board consists of individual topics for discussion called threads. People come and go from the discussion forums, reading through threads of ideas and the associated comments, criticisms, humor, and sometimes even accusations and insults that become part of the postings in each thread. Some people start and moderate the discussions, contributing their thoughts when so inclined and maintaining order. Others choose to remain passive and silent, reading along and following the discussions. Still others contribute a little, or a lot, depending on their level of interest and their individual personalities. Such different levels of participation and interest are typical of all basic community structures.

Recognizable in these newsgroups — and made possible by the Internet — is an endless variety of virtual communities where people with similar interests come together to discuss and debate ideas and viewpoints. Where else, through what other means, could someone with an interest in a particular subject, like starting a horse farm, breeding cats, or becoming better acquainted with the stars in the night sky, expect to find and interact with a group of people who share that interest and who can possibly answer questions, provide guidance, and even supply humor or compassion? To some people the discussion forums of newsgroups are simply another information resource; the information they contain is a huge and diverse store of information that offers solutions and advice about both common and esoteric problems. The existence of these discussion forums, however, is first and foremost about community. Individuals create newsgroups and begin threads because they want to become involved and interact with others; they want to share what they have learned as well as learn from others. In the process, it's not uncommon for friendships to form, too. It's the Internet that enables these newsgroup communities to form and flourish, by removing the geographic and the time constraints that would otherwise prohibit these same people from coming together, interacting, and conducting their discussion.

Another example of a virtual community on the Internet based on subject-matter discussions is the Whole Earth 'Lectronic Link (WELL). The WELL was founded in 1985 by Stewart Brand and Larry Brilliant and offers a more focused, more controlled, and less anonymous type of discussion forum. Organizers of the WELL describe their services as "a cluster of electronic villages on the Net, inhabited by people from all over the world." The description applies equally well to countless other online forums where people congregate to establish virtual communities. The WELL's longevity and continued popularity stems largely from the literate quality of the discussions. The requirement that WELL members identify themselves, as opposed to the more common approach of letting individuals remain hidden behind some largely anonymous Internet pseudonym, also contributes to controlling the tone of and the behavior of the participants in the discussions.

Online collaborations are another common and easily recognizable form of virtual Internet communities. Here, again, the elimination of geographic and time constraints allows individuals to meet and work together in a virtual location in order to collectively build any number of different creations. These collaborations are often artistic in nature, as evidenced by the number of sites built by writing groups and authors in order to pursue the relatively new concept of collective fiction writing. Scientific collaborations are also common; they allow researchers from different parts of the country or world to effortlessly exchange and combine data, observations, and theories in a collective effort to reach some goal or advance a shared interest.

These types of explicit, recognizable virtual Internet communities consist of online social spaces. The gaming world of MUDs (Multi-User Dimensions) expands the same basic concept of virtual social interaction and applies it at the level of virtual world building and role playing. It seems inevitable that these two environments will eventually merge to form new ways for people to interact in virtual settings. Such efforts will no doubt use the advanced graphics and the location construction tools for creating buildings, objects, and settings found in MUDs and apply them to the needs of building complex, highly detailed virtual communities. They will facilitate the construction of three-dimensional representations of space, as well as virtual embodiments of our own identities, to augment existing communication and collaboration tools. To what end? To facilitate and enhance the interaction between members of the community in the online ether of cyberspace.

For instance, complete virtual office buildings can be constructed in cyberspace, allowing individuals to interact in the virtual world over the course of the day much as they already do in the physical world: working alone in a private office, attending various meetings, going to the cafeteria with a group of friends, having a one-on-one conversation with the boss. Think of how empowering such a virtual representation could be for someone who has disabilities that limit his or her movements, or for someone who can greatly contribute to the effectiveness of the business but for any number of reasons cannot reside locally. The possibilities, and the potential, are limitless with respect to both business applications and all sorts of other virtual communities.

More and more people are turning to their computers and to the Internet as part of their daily routine. We boot up and log in. We sit quietly at a desk all by ourselves, or perhaps at the dining room table, as our spouse or children or siblings go about their lives. We open a browser window, check for new mail messages, reply to some, ignore others, send out some new mail. We start up a chat session and see who else is online. The message windows flash on and off and the computer starts dinging as friends or family or business associates start to engage us in conversation. Meanwhile, we log onto a portal Web site to see the latest headlines, check the stock market, or update our calendar with the latest meetings for next week and a long overdue dental appointment. A new mail message arrives and grabs our attention, while two more friends enter the chat room and start to talk about their day.

An hour of all this frenetic activity goes by quickly, and then we log off. Where were we? We were deep in the Internet's virtual community. What were we doing? We were socializing, gathering and updating information, exchanging ideas. We were participating in a new type of social structure. Whether this new type of socializing, interaction, and community becomes something good, bad, or indifferent, is entirely up to us and what we make of it. But it is here now; and many of us are an active part of it each and every day.

Virtual communities are ones in which people share interests rather than location. This was observed several decades ago by the ARPANET pioneers, J. C. R. Licklider and Robert Taylor. Virtual communities have brought us the acronym IRL (in real life) to help clarify the boundary between our movements in the physical world and those in the ether of the Internet's cyberspace. Virtual communities, many believe, are only going to become more common and, as they do, they will become more relevant in our busy and our more computer-connected, networked lives.

But how do we define these virtual community constructs? Will we regulate or legislate our behavior in them? Will we begin to replace some aspects of our IRL communities with virtual counterparts? Many types of virtual communities give birth to, and serve to evolve, long-lasting and multifaceted relationships. Are these relationships necessarily any less nurturing or compelling than their IRL counterparts? Do the artificial constructs of these virtual communities make them any less genuine or lasting? It will be up to us to decide.

Synergies: A Whole That's Greater Than the Sum of Its Parts

7

Synergies

The Internet is a global computer network, interconnecting smaller, independent networks located throughout the world, the computers that compose those networks, and the people who own, operate, and use those computers. The Internet houses a vast quantity of information that is both broadly diverse in content and widely distributed in location. It carries countless messages every minute of every day, ranging from mundane dispatches in the form of appointment reminders, newsletters, horoscopes, and weather forecasts to personal correspondence filled with words of love, hate, joy, sorrow, humor, satire, and sarcasm to business mail consisting of brochures, bills, legal documents, advertisements, and tax forms. It brings together and engages people in such virtual constructs as interactive gaming environments and cyberspace recreations of meeting rooms, office buildings, and entire cityscapes. It provides equally well for the commercial needs of corporations, the infrastructure needs of governments, the community needs of non-profit organizations, and the personal needs of individuals. It functions as a new realm for commerce, creating whole new business enterprises, changing the supply and distribution of commodities and services, and radically altering how many jobs are performed. It challenges our long-standing definitions of community and social interaction. It attracts and commands the attention of the young, the not-so-young, and people of every age in between.

Attempting to define or describe the Internet is a challenge in and of itself. The task, whether you limit yourself to a few sentences, a few pages, or several hundred pages, is fraught with difficulties. You can, for instance, list and describe all the discrete components that make up the technology, but the technology continues to evolve, and an explanation of the Internet's technology only tells part of the story. You can list and describe all the various types of information sources, commodities, tools, games, services, and so on, that one can find on the Internet, but no list can be exhaustive, and people are inventing new Internet-based products, services, and features all the time. Even if you could create some definitive and exhaustive description of the Internet, you would still fail to capture one of the Internet's most critical and compelling characteristics: its limitless capacity for creating synergies. Synergy is defined as the fortuitous, typically unanticipated, and complex mixing and melding of discrete elements that produces a combined effect greater than the sum of their individual effects. Synergy is responsible for a whole being greater than the simple sum of its parts. The Internet is rich with synergies.

The sum of the Internet's technology, resources, and services cannot account for the number and quality of changes it has made in our lives or for the pervasiveness of its impact. This explains, at least in part, why many individuals on the far side of the digital divide, who regard the Internet from a distance, frequently feel no compulsion to, or even interest in, going online and bringing the Internet into their lives. They may be aware of the abundance of information available through the Web, for instance, and of the speed with which people communicate using email and chat; and they may — correctly or not — argue that much of the same information is available elsewhere, through radio, television, newspapers, and libraries, and that the telephone and the postal service can continue to meet their communication needs, just as they always have. What they cannot understand or appreciate, however, is the diversity and, more importantly, the combined effect of all the discrete elements that compose the Internet. That's because the Internet is something far grander and more meaningful than a cleverly engineered, global network of interconnected computers, and its environment is as dynamic as it is diverse. Our presence on the Internet is partly responsible for its significance, its diversity, and its highly dynamic environment. The Internet's ever-changing composition of information, services, and resources is also responsible.

The Internet is full of synergies, both in terms of how its technology works and in the types of facilities its technology makes possible. For example, the Web, email, and Internet gaming, like MUDs, are all responsible for social, economic, and political changes that transcend their intended purpose, design, and engineering. The Internet as a whole is also a perfect embodiment of synergy. Consider its role as an open, cooperative environment where individuals from all over the world can meet, interact, share information, and form communities. Consider also its potential to help build a more peaceful, better interconnected world, with far fewer inequities. These synergies and others like them are what incited and are what help to sustain the Internet Revolution.

Since revolutions begin and end with their effect on the individual, the best way to characterize the revolution incited and fed by the Internet is its empowering of the individual. This empowerment is apparent in the services (e.g., email and the Web) made available to us through the Internet that were, before the Internet's arrival, not simply absent from our lives, but were never anticipated. These services empower us through the wealth and variety of information that they make easily and freely accessible and through the array of communication channels that enable us to express ourselves and share information with remarkable ease and immediacy. This empowerment is also apparent in the tasks the Internet allows us to accomplish that just a few short years ago were beyond our capabilities. These tasks include working and interacting with co-workers from our home or from some other location distant from the office, participating in an organization, such as a grassroots political movement, that has no presence in our local community, or starting a new business and selling one's goods or services without geographic constraints. This new and provocative empowerment of the individual may be the ultimate legacy of the Internet and its most far-reaching form of synergy.

Recognizing this synergistic quality of the Internet is first and foremost a matter of perspective. It requires viewing the Internet, and our interaction with it, from different points of view. We need to examine the Internet up close in order to see, acknowledge, and understand the various components that constitute its basic mechanics and unique, empowering technology. Only then can we comprehend the immediate and dramatic impact of the Internet and its technology on our daily lives. But we must also step back and take in the long, broad view, the big picture, in order to grasp the Internet's importance and relevance as a swift, sweeping, and ubiquitous force of change. Only then can we see revealed the revolution that is the Internet.

The following sections explore the Internet's synergies as viewed from the different perspectives of its technology, its role as a communication structure, its formation as an information space, and, not least of all, its environment as a place where we reside, interact, and build communities.

Technology: It's the Journey, Not the Destination

Consider the Internet's fundamental, or core, technology. One component takes the form of the Internet's data highways, the network's data transportation infrastructure. These highways comprise countless miles of copper, coaxial, and fiber optic cable strung between tall, wooden poles and buried inside conduits by the sides of roadways and along ocean floors. They also comprise an increasingly popular wireless counterpart, a skyway of satellite dishes, orbiting satellites, and other wireless transmission and reception devices that is redefining the reach, relevance, and influence of the Internet. This data transportation infrastructure is capable of carrying information to and from just about any location on the planet.

Another of the Internet's core technology components directs traffic and operates the safeguards of the network's infrastructure. This component takes the form of the data highways' traffic lights, road signs, laws, and codes of conduct. Making up this component are the Internet's packet switches, gateways, routers, firewalls, and other associated network devices. Together, these devices serve to handle the flow and direction of traffic, promote order, and keep data moving along safely, quickly, and efficiently towards its destination. The protocols residing in these devices, and in the host computers, are also an integral part of this component of the Internet. They define and enforce the rules and regulations that enable all of these individual and disparate devices to coexist on the network, handle their assigned tasks, and interact in a prescribed, reliable, and efficient manner. The protocols and these network devices together define and manage the interoperability of the Internet, which is the hallmark of the Internet.

Another component of the Internet's technology packages the data for safe transit across the network's infrastructure. This component takes the form of the data vehicles that contain and transport the network's traffic. These vehicles are the Internet's data packets; they travel the network, holding all of our love letters and overdue payment notices, our local weather information and book orders, our dating profiles from our personals ads, and our latest bank statements. The packets make their way along the data highways, traveling at varying speeds, alone or in groups, unlocked and open to inspection or encrypted into some indecipherable format and safe from prying eyes. Internet packets and the network technology of packet switching are responsible for the Internet's overall efficiency and evenhandedness in the transmission of information.

The final core component of the Internet's technology stores the data that makes up the network's resources. This component takes the form of the data residences. These residences are the computing devices attached to the Internet: the laptops and desktop personal computers, the Web servers and data warehouses, the mainframes and supercomputers. These residences dot the landscape alongside the data highways. They are located in city centers, suburbs, rural communities, distant, isolated settings, and everywhere in between. The networking infrastructure of wires and wireless devices interconnects them. The routers, other network devices, and protocols ensure the safe and efficient transit of data between them. The Internet packets package and transport the data. The computers themselves provide the means for us to travel the Internet and constitute the destinations we visit.

That's the focused, narrow view; it is the small picture of the component parts that together make up the Internet's core technology. When we stand back from the specifics of the technology and take in the big picture, however, we see something entirely different. We see a Web page describing the day's top news stories, which is full of photos, text, and animated graphics, that loads onto our computer instantaneously, or at least within a few seconds. We see that we have new mail and read that our daughter's cat, Dexter, just destroyed one lamp, two crystal vases that were wedding presents, and knocked over a full glass of red wine onto an expensive, white wool rug, all in the happy, compelling pursuit of a common house fly. We see a chat window flashing with a question from one of the junior executives who reports to us. We see an accounting application showing us real-time order information for a cookbook of lobster recipes that was published two weeks earlier. In effect, we don't see the technology at all. The technology remains hidden, its individual components working together quietly, seamlessly, and effortlessly behind the scenes. What remains, the product of their synergy, is the Internet we encounter through our computer: windows onto the digital realm of cyberspace, which we can open and close at will, through which we can escape and interact with others, or through which we can simply and passively watch the information world go by.

You might think, as many people undoubtedly do, that it is its seemingly complex, esoteric, interdependent technology that defines the Internet. To some, this technology is magical; it enables them to do so much even though they know little to nothing about how it works. To others, it is hateful, frustrating, and potentially dangerous; it doesn't work the way they want it to or expect it should, and it has introduced problems and dangers that they fear will never be remedied or removed, such as children's exposure to pornography and the erosion of our privacy. Still others find inspiration in the technology; it enables them to bring their ideas to life, and some adopt it to pursue their livelihood. But, surprisingly, the Internet's technology may be its least significant and even least defining feature, unless, of course, you happen to be an engineer. After all, an examination of the technology can only reveal so much; it manifests the small view, the short and narrow perspective that delights and fascinates some, but does little to explain the context and impact of its use. To reach some understanding of the Internet's value, we must look past how the Internet's technology works and focus instead on its impact on us as individuals, its transforming effect on our communities and societies, and its contributions to our ever-widening and even global interactions and information exchanges.

Consider the history of the automobile and the relevance of its technology with respect to the use of the automobile and its impact. The technology of the automobile has changed considerably since it was first introduced over one hundred years ago. These changes comprise small, incremental enhancements that were made every few years and large, engineering, mechanical, or material improvements that occurred every decade or so. What matters to most of us, however, is that the automobile's technology takes us from place to place, safely, reliably, economically (for some), and in high style (for others). But if you were to compare an automobile built in the early 20th century to one built today (or in the past several decades), you would discover that how they were manufactured, the parts that they contain, and the mechanics that make them function are more different than alike. The purpose and general operation of automobiles, as well as our daily interaction with them, has remained strikingly consistent. The technology that makes an automobile function, however, has over time been adapted, been made obsolete, and been reinvented. What this shows us is that the technology and its corresponding mechanics and engineering is only marginally responsible for how we use technology and its impact on how we live.

Technology is always a product of the tools and materials and the engineering and manufacturing capabilities of the day. Technology is always changing, as new ideas emerge and as we endeavor to build products that are better, smaller, and less expensive to manufacture. Technology is a study in contrivance; it is composed of layer upon layer of abstractions (artificial, man-made creations) that function together to perform some predefined task. Ironically, technology often functions to mimic or recreate some naturally occurring event or capability. Studying the flight of birds, for example, contributed to the design and engineering of airplanes; technology was used to direct the flow of air around aircraft wings in a manner similar to how birds used their wings to control their flight. Technology is rarely, if ever, intuitive. We study and learn about technology the old fashioned way, from the ground up, one piece at a time.

Because technology is always changing, every particular technology represents one stage in some larger context of development or evolution. Computers and the Internet are hardly the exception, and most would argue that their development is still at a very early stage. It wasn't all that long ago that the term computer applied equally well to human beings who performed scientific calculations and analysis and to a generation of finicky, electro-mechanical computers that filled large rooms. There is good reason for this earlier, dual definition. It has to do with how computer designers have sought, through technology, to mimic our innate communication, information storage, and computational abilities. Considered from this perspective, therefore, the technology of computers, and by inference that of the Internet, can be regarded as perhaps the ultimate journey of contrivance. This technology aims to mimic us. The ultimate goal of this pursuit — on the far end of this journey — is the creation of some sort of artificial intelligence. Artificial intelligence is an abstraction of how we store and process information, how we analyze that information and make deductions, and how we communicate and interact with others. Meanwhile, what we see and use today are precisely what today's technology can successfully implement. For instance, the computational speed and information storage capacity of our computers — the simpler elements to engineer and implement — continue to multiply by leaps and bounds. The deductive reasoning and higher language skills of these computers, on the other hand, continue to progress at a far more modest pace.

Looking backward in time along the journey's path we see Babbage's efforts to produce his Analytical Engine in 19th century England. His technology was mechanical in form and a far cry from today's silicon-based microprocessor chips. But it was as cutting edge for his time as today's experiments with nanotechnology and circuits reduced to the size of single molecules. More importantly, Babbage's interests, as well as his goals, were not far removed from those of today's engineers. It's really only the technology that has changed. The endeavor, the encompassing journey, remains as exciting and as challenging as ever.

Computers once had mechanical relays to process information; they functioned well with this technology for several decades. Mechanical relays were eventually replaced by vacuum tubes, making the relay obsolete, and computational speed and the types of problems that could be programmed (and solved) both changed as a consequence. Not many years later, transistors replaced vacuum tubes, making the vacuum tube obsolete, and the size of computers greatly diminished, while their reliability and their capabilities increased dramatically. Then microprocessor technology arrived, and just as radios evolved from furniture-size family entertainment centers to pocket-size personal conveniences, computers evolved from rooms filled with boxes the size of refrigerators to desktop, laptop, and handheld personal conveniences. These, and other equally important advances in the technology of computers, have brought us the technology that surrounds us today.

What we can see in the history and development of this technology and what we can see in the dreams of the many visionary individuals who were responsible for its major advances, such as Vannevar Bush and his inspired memex device, is the culmination of this work — and the achievement — in the significance of its application in our lives. Our embracing the technology of computers and the Internet is unique to our lifetimes. We have brought this technology into our homes, schools, libraries, government agencies, hospitals, community centers, and businesses. Some of us even carry the technology with us, attached to a belt or tossed into a handbag or knapsack. We use it every day, and we rely on it more and more. We build our lives around it — and into it — as we use it as a tool to assist us with both the complexities and drudgeries of our daily lives. We use it personally and professionally, for fun and for our work-related pursuits. This technology has fundamentally altered the way we live our lives, largely by becoming part and parcel of how we live our lives. We made this happen, by choice.

But, again, it is not the specific technology that's important. A short ten or twenty years from now the technology we rely on today may be something we read about on the Internet or visit in a museum. Our homes may have a single Internet appliance installed in the basement next to the circuit breaker panel, thermostat, or telephone junction box, while touch-screens distributed throughout the house interconnect this Internet appliance with other appliances, entertainment devices, communication modules, and a security system. We may carry a small handheld device that connects us to the Internet and plug it in at work, on the train, in the car, or back at home. Such changes are easy enough to imagine. They wouldn't even be all that difficult to implement with what we know and can manufacture today. What's important is we recognize that the technology will continue to adapt and develop. It's changing right now. It will continue to evolve.

Meanwhile, what will remain the same, more or less, is us. What will be important tomorrow, and what is important right now, is how we employ the technology in our lives: what we do with it, how we rely on it, what we demand of it, what dreams and aspirations we attach to it. In our future, there will exist some manifestation of the Internet; and we will have devices through which to access and interact with it. We will undoubtedly continue to use it to communicate with our family, friends, business associates, and others. We will rely on it for access to a world of information far richer than the vast resources we can already access today. We will continue to extend ourselves out through the Internet, learn and teach, share our joys and sorrows with those who don't reside with us, conduct business matters as well as affairs of the heart, and entertain ourselves, too.

As the following sections discuss, this new and radically different technology of the Internet serves to fulfill some of our oldest and most basic needs, namely interacting with others, sharing information, educating and entertaining ourselves. What's new, aside from the technology itself, is the effect that our use of this technology is having on the way we live, the communities to which we belong, the way in which we interact with others, and the interactions of a networked, interconnected world of other individuals equally empowered.

Communication: Convergence and Individualization

Consider the communication component of the Internet. Let's start by examining email. Email, which is one of many popular communication services available on the Internet, is the most widely used Internet service. Email is in our homes, at the office, and available through public library computer terminals and other types of shared Internet access terminals. Additionally, email can be sent and received on mobile devices we carry along with us. Email's exceptionally fast transformation from a simple and informal messaging tool used by a small number of academics and researchers into a multifaceted, indispensable business application used by everyone from secretaries and administrative assistants to CEOs clearly conveys email's importance as a fundamental and essential productivity tool. Perhaps more importantly, underlying this use of email is its wholesale integration into the communication infrastructures of large and small, commercial and non-commercial, organizations. Email is as embedded as the telephone in the operation of most organizations. Meanwhile, email's swift rise to prominence as a commonplace, and sometimes preferred, form of communication for teenagers, octogenarians, and all ages in between, makes clear email's importance to us as individuals.

What impact has the Internet in general, and email in particular, had on the way we communicate with our friends, family, and business associates and on how we share information in our personal lives and in our work lives? Conversely, how has the way we communicate affected the Internet? The creation of networked email is the earliest and clearest example of a transforming Internet synergy. Email altered the very dynamics of networking, not in terms of how computer networks functioned, but with respect to what networks, and the Internet in particular, would be used for, what networking would come to mean to us as individuals, and what networking would mean to the design, engineering, and manufacturing of computers. In other words, more than any other single Internet feature, tool, or facility, email is responsible for bringing computer networking and the Internet into our lives. Conversely, and equally important, we have eagerly and wholeheartedly adopted email as a principal way to communicate with others. We have used email to take our lives onto the Internet.

Email, moreover, was just the beginning of taking our lives onto the Internet. To understand the full impact and synergies of the Internet and its communication facilities we must examine our use of email alongside our use of chat rooms, message boards and newsgroups, MUDs and other virtual reality environments, and telephone calls placed over the Internet (commonly referred to as voice over IP, or VOIP). Much as the telephone resulted in innumerable changes to many different facets of our lives, email, instant messaging, video conferencing, and even MUDs, are altering where and how we live and work, the relationships that we enter into, and many of the routine ways in which we interact with others and conduct our lives. In simple terms, the effect of our using the communication services of the Internet can be seen in how we choose to exchange information, with whom, and how frequently. But, ultimately, how we exchange information and communicate relates to how we choose to interact with others and what this means, in a larger social context, about the communities to which we belong.

Before we can appreciate the synergies of the Internet's communication facilities or recognize how utterly new, different, and empowering their impact is, we must first place them into the larger context of the history of human communication. By considering how these facilities relate to our earlier, far more restricted modes of communication, we may arrive at a clearer understanding of what they signify for our present and what they suggest about our future.

A Brief History of Human Communication

There was a time, before the rise of the nation-state and when technology was more art than science, when our communication was tied directly to, and limited to, our immediate, physical, local community. The words themselves, communication and community, were more closely interconnected, and their definitions still resonated with the characteristics of sharing and commonality. We spoke and interacted solely with the other members of our village or town. We knew everyone and everyone knew us, for better and for worse, from birth and throughout our life. The known world was a relatively small place and we stayed within its boundaries. The community kept us safe, secure, and protected. That was all that mattered.

Slowly, our individual worlds started to expand as our communities grew larger, as we as individuals started to interact directly with members of neighboring communities, and as news began to travel more frequently and more consistently into and out of our local communities. As early as the second century CE, Roman couriers carried government mail all over the empire, establishing what was possibly the first communication network to span several continents. In the thirteenth century, monasteries in

Europe created their own letter carrying system to share information about events transpiring in each of their communities. Shortly afterwards, the first private postal businesses emerged in Europe, among them one provided by the Turn and Taxis family. These private postal services catered to the special needs of the wealthiest families, aiding them in their business ventures and in their pursuit of power. Meanwhile, more importantly, the communication capabilities of the vast majority of the population remained unchanged. Most people were limited to word of mouth communication within our local community.

Over the course of the next few centuries, national postal systems, generally functioning as governmental monopolies, were created in Europe, the Americas, and elsewhere throughout the world. These systems grew quickly and flourished, and as they grew they became capable of delivery an ever increasing volume of communication with greater efficiency, increased speed, and reduced costs. Their development paralleled that of the technology and transportation systems of the times. There was also a direct correlation between increased use of the postal system and both improved methods for manufacturing paper and the growing rate of literacy. Depending on the era and the distance, communication could take days, weeks, or months. Regardless, these postal systems handled the tasks at hand; they kept lines of communication open during times of peace and times of war, made sure governments remained informed about what was transpiring within and outside their lands, assisted in the transactions of businesses, and carried the family correspondence, love letters, and junk mail of their times.

These national and private postal systems wielded total control over the exchange of personal, professional, business, and government-based communication. This meant, in general, that the choices for communicating over any sort of distance were few, limited to written messages, expensive, and serviced only a small minority of the population. Additionally, the delivery of information from one location to another was tied to and limited by the existing modes of transportation: by foot, on horseback, by ship, or by train. Then two inventions in the nineteenth century — first the telegraph and later the telephone — abruptly and radically changed how, when, and where information could be sent and received. For the first time in our history, communication could take place in an interactive form over any distance and information could travel faster than any man (or woman) and any mode of transportation.

The telegraph was invented in 1837 by Samuel F. B. Morse in the United States and Sir William Cook and Sir Charles Wheatstone in Great Britain. It's an historical curiosity that such an innovative and revolutionary creation should be arrived at through independent efforts at roughly the same time. The far-reaching implications of the collective achievement of Morse, Cook, and Wheatstone were abundantly and immediately clear to the scientific community and to the inventors' respective governments. Just as steam engines were powering ships and railroad locomotives to bridge the great distances between communities, regions, and countries, the telegraph could now accomplish precisely the same end for the purpose of communication. Suddenly, the technology existed to provide near instantaneous communication over potentially any distance. All that was lacking to make such communication possible was the existence of a network and its infrastructure of wires and relay posts. Not surprisingly, this network went up alongside the railroads, which were doing their own part to make the world a smaller, better connected, more intimate place.

The telegraph introduced into the world the capability of sending and receiving real-time information, thereby allowing information about events to be communicated only moments after they occurred. This immediate, two-way communication changed the face of the world, not for most individuals, but certainly for governments, businesses, and the wealthy. It was a later invention that would introduce the same basic capability into the lives of most individuals. The invention of the telephone by Alexander Graham Bell in 1877, a short forty years after the invention of the telegraph, brought real-time, two-way communication into the lives of millions, and eventually billions, of people across the globe. The telephone quickly found its way into every aspect of people's lives. It was readily and generally accepted, welcomed into homes, and recognized as part of the essential apparatus for conducting business. Here, at last, was a technology everyone could understand, operate, and appreciate. It extended one's natural ability to communicate effortlessly and with considerable reliability, and it functioned equally well for local or long-distance communications.

The telephone is now so thoroughly entrenched in our lives that it's not easy for us to appreciate how this deceptively simple communication device has had an impact on everything from the makeup of our households to the building of cities to the pursuit of war and peace. The telephone allowed families to retain their closeness despite the breakup of traditional, multi-generational extended families into the more compact nuclear family. It installed itself in the very heart of our homes, bringing the outside world in through its sudden, intrusive, disruptive ringing. It provided us with incomparable convenience, a heightened sense of community, and endless hours of entertainment. It also instilled in us a greatly increased sense of personal security and safety by allowing us to effortlessly reach out beyond our four walls and to be reached, should some trouble or danger come our way. Ironically, it also contributed to distancing us from our immediate neighbors and other members of our local community, whom we had been accustomed to relying on and interacting with in our daily lives before we came to rely on the telephone.

The telephone changed our social behavior and etiquette, too, as we learned to give its loud and intrusive ringing priority over our face-to-face interactions. It added to and changed our use of language, as we adapted our speech and our social skills (or lack thereof) to the more impersonal, detached, and distant nature of telephone-based conversations. It also resulted in most of us writing fewer personal letters, and some of us stopped writing letters altogether. In large and small ways, the telephone altered our behavior as individuals, the structure and dynamics of our family life, our opportunities in the business world and the performance of our jobs, the connectedness of our community structures, and even the relationships between nations. For better and for worse, the telephone was the first technology to interconnect us, our residences, our places of business, our governments, and our public locations on a global communications network. Strikingly similar in some ways to the Internet today, this communications network was designed to be readily accepted and easily usable by nearly all individuals, to be accessible from nearly any location, to allow for local, regional, or long distance service, and even to be affordable for the majority of the population.

It didn't take long for the telephone to change our lives forever. Even today, its technology continues to become ever more intimately attached to us and we seem as eager as ever to let it change our behavior, as is evidenced by the millions of people across the globe who have embraced the relatively recent advances in portable cellular telephone technology. Despite unresolved problems related to quality of service and even commonplace interruptions in service, many people consider cellular telephones essential to their personal safety, or an all-important lifestyle choice, or a necessary tool for the performance of their jobs. Such individuals keep themselves constantly connected to the global communications network while they go about their active, increasingly mobile lives. Whereas the introduction of the telephone quickly succeeded in eliminating distance as an obstacle to communication, the widespread proliferation of the wireless technology of cellular telephones has gone one step further and succeeded in eliminating all barriers to being reached or reaching out regardless of where we may be or what me may be doing.

Our use of cellular telephones is already producing its own particular and peculiar social changes. People walk the streets with tiny earpieces, carrying on conversations with distant friends and associates, while to those of us in their immediate vicinity they seem to be (and might as well be) talking to themselves. Elevator rides that used to be filled with the crushing, uncomfortable silence of strangers packed together into a small space now often include one or more people holding animated conversations with remote individuals about their sex lives, a business deal, or a basketball game. The immediate, surrounding environment and the people it contains are ignored, while these mobile conversations with remote individuals take precedence. In little more than a century, the telephone and its technology have taken us from living in largely isolated communities with strong, life-long ties built from intimate, face-to-face communication to living lives isolated and detached from our immediate communities, but more intimately integrated with a larger, but dispersed, global community.

The Arrival of the Internet

Now consider the Internet and its communication tools. Keep in mind that the Internet is still in its infancy, despite all the media coverage and the Internet's phenomenal growth in the past few years. As was true of the impact of the telephone during its first years of widespread use, the impact of the Internet on our behavior and on our social structures has only just begun to be felt and measured.

The Internet's global communication network was engineered and built for machine-to-machine, computer-to-computer communication. Its quick adaptation into a person-to-person communication network was purely incidental to its purpose as an experimental network for sharing information and sharing access to expensive computer resources. This was the situation when email was unexpectedly introduced to the early users of the fledgling Internet. It was not long, however, before Internet-based communication evolved into a driving force behind the continued growth and evolution of the network. The development and use of email applications and other types of personal communication tools became the passionate pursuit of individuals and corporations alike. As a result of this development work the Internet's communication environment began to provide wholesale replacements for or enhanced alternatives to existing and commonly used communication systems: the courier services and postal networks, the telephone network and its associated messaging systems (for faxes, telexes, and the like), the early, dial-up bulletin boards and newsgroups, and even specialized services like video conferencing.

As the Internet continued to evolve, most, if not all, of these services became faster, cheaper, more efficient, easier to operate, and far more adaptable to the needs of the individual and to those of an organization. But the communication capabilities of the Internet were not limited to providing alternatives to familiar forms of communication, such as the sending and receiving of personal letters and business documents. Entirely new forms of communication services began to appear on the Internet that were unique to the Internet's technology and that took full advantage of the capabilities of the Internet's distributed and interconnected environment, such as MUDs and instant messaging. A birthday card or a tax bill, a phone call to your daughter at college or a fax to your lawyer, a reminder to your business partner to join a meeting that started ten minutes earlier, a discussion by the virtual water cooler about your boss's latest dictate or tie selection, all of these communication activities are now commonplace on the Internet; they take place through email, voice over IP (telephone calls placed through the Internet), and instant messaging or chatting and in gaming and virtual reality environments like MUDs.

What accounts for our widespread adoption of the Internet's communication facilities? More specifically, what accounts for the fast and remarkably thorough integration of these communication facilities into our personal and professional lives and into the way in which business is transacted? Their novelty has certainly contributed to many people going online and starting to use them, but little about the facilities themselves or our use of them suggests that they constitute a fad. The improved speed and efficiency and reduced operating cost provided by these facilities has contributed to their continued and growing use, but these features can at best only partly explain their success.

One key factor contributing directly to the widespread and growing use of the Internet's communication facilities can be explained by convergence. These facilities function together to create one place, one medium, through which we can fulfill all of our growing and various communication needs. This convergence, like so many others on the Internet, is one type of synergy that contributes to both the influence of the Internet over our lives and to its immense popularity. Another key contributing factor can be explained by customization or individualization. Our use of the communication facilities of the Internet can be tailored to our specific needs. Our use of the telephone network and the postal system, on the other hand, must conform to the limited and necessarily generalized services they offer, services designed to best meet the needs of the general population. We send and receive letters and bills, for instance, based on the limited days and hours during which the postal service operates. Similarly, we often make telephone calls based on when our service costs are lowest, rather than when we might prefer to call. With the Internet, all the choices related to when and how we communicate, as well as how much or little we want to make ourselves reachable, are entirely our own.

It's easy to appreciate the ease, efficiency, and even affordability with which the Internet provides for all of our communication needs. Have you sent off an email when before you might have posted a letter? Have you opted to receive one or more of your bills online instead of or in addition to receiving paper statements through the postal system? Do you pay any bills online to save the time and cost of mailing a check? Have you signed up for any daily, weekly, or monthly emailed newsletters? Have you discovered chat and, as a consequence, noticed that you are making fewer telephone calls? Do you set aside any time to spend interacting with others in online forums, such as those provided by newsgroups, auction sites, or community action organizations? A single connection to the Internet from your home, your office, a library, or even from the fresh, open air of a park or the closed, cramped quarters of a train or plane, enables you to pursue all of these common communication activities.

Adding to this convergence of communication options, or channels, are the factors of time and immediacy. Not only can we pursue these activities from virtually any location, but we can do so at any hour and for any length of time (and, typically, cost does not factor into when or how long we communicate online). The effects, furthermore, are immediate. Real-time, two-way communication channels are plentiful on the Internet, as represented by chat, MUDs, video conferencing, and voice over IP. We can easily check to see if someone is online and then reach out to connect directly to him or her. Even an asynchronous mode of communication such as email, in which we dispatch a message not knowing when it will be read, has its own measure of immediacy and instant gratification. While we can't be sure our message will be read right away, we fully expect that it was delivered only moments after we sent it. Over time we can even develop a sense of how those with whom we frequently communicate spend their time online, based in part on when and how quickly we receive emails in reply to our own, for instance.

This issue of convergence, however, is more subtle and profound than revealed at first glance by its consolidation of communication channels on the Internet. We still need our postal systems, and not just for the large percentage of individuals who remain on the far side of the digital divide. They are responsible for carrying hundreds of millions of letters, periodicals, and packages each year. But the number of items they carry has been declining each year over the past several years. What will happen to these postal networks, with their huge infrastructures and their many thousands of employees, as we rely on them less and less, as undoubtedly we will? Their services simply cannot compete with the speed and efficiencies of email. Will it come to a crisis of adapt or perish? If so, how will they transform themselves?

What about the huge infrastructure of the circuit-switched telephone networks and their many thousands of employees? The Internet's packet-switched network can supply all the functionality and features of the telephone network, while the telephone network is limited to voice transmissions or to data that's been converted into a form it can handle and transmit reliably. (The tones produced by a modem or fax machine are the product of such a conversion, as digital information is changed into an analogous audio waveform.) Many individuals who currently have broadband Internet connections via cable, DSL, or satellite also have the option to purchase unlimited local and long distance telephone service through their ISP. This doesn't mean they need their computer to make phone calls, although they certainly have that option. A specialized network device interconnects their phones with the network, hiding the differences in how their calls are being transmitted (e.g., digitally instead of analog) and simplifying the transition from the old technology to the new. This new type of telephone service isn't a fad or an aberration. It's the future, a future in which one service provider may be responsible for our connection to the Internet and for all of our broadcast and on-demand information, entertainment, and communication services.

This same convergence of communication services on the Internet is also apparent in many of today's most popular electronic devices. Just as your computer and Internet connection can be used to place phone calls, many cellular phones are now including basic features for simple Internet connectivity, such as receiving and sending email through the cellular service's wireless network. Cellular phones, as well as beepers, also include the capability of sending and receiving text messages, supplying a scaled-down alternative to Internet chatting that is appropriate for the scaled-down devices involved. At the same time, handheld devices like personal digital assistants (PDAs) are packaging in wireless networking capabilities that allow these devices to be used as both telephones and scaled-down Internet devices for Web browsing, email, chatting, and other activities, thereby driving our desire to be connected and reachable at all times and in all places further towards convergence.

Today's desktop and laptop computers manifest a strikingly similar evolution towards convergence. Their convergence, too, is centered on communication and, accordingly, is tied directly to the growth of the Internet. Before the Internet, personal computers were task-oriented, productivity-based devices that had been engineered to replace typewriters, calculators, and accounting ledgers through software applications that functioned as word processors, spreadsheets, statistical programs, and electronic checkbooks. They achieved with a keyboard, a monitor, and digitally encoded files what the earlier technology had achieved with paper and ink. Personal computers sold today, while they still perform these same, basic functions, are multitasking devices that have been engineered to satisfy many of our information, communication, and entertainment needs. Most importantly, networking is built into the core components and many of the software applications that come as part of the standard equipment on these computers. Networking is part of the fundamental design and manufacture of these computers because, like that of the Internet, their fundamental purpose is now to share and interconnect information, resources, and us. Today's personal computers, therefore, demonstrate a parallel convergence to that of the Internet, one centered on information sharing between applications, computers, other networked devices, and people, and the underlying communication capabilities that enable this to happen.

As with the technology of the telephone, the converging technologies of the Internet and computers are not only catering to our communication needs, they are also feeding, and in some instances wholly creating, our hunger for more persistent and more multifaceted forms of communication. We don't just want to talk on the telephone any more. We want to be reachable, on the network, at all times. Moreover, talking alone is no longer sufficient. We also want to be able to send text messages and photos back and forth, or meet in a chat room, or forward a recipe or a poem, as we're talking or otherwise communicating with someone else. Often we also want to follow up our various conversations with email. Some even prefer to venture a little further, perhaps into the virtual constructs of MUDs or some other type of virtual spatial environment. The Internet and the devices that connect into it are enabling and fueling the convergence of all this popular and disparate communication activity.

While convergence is a large factor in fostering our avid acceptance and enjoyment of the Internet's communication facilities, it may be individualization that proves to be the most significant factor. The individualization, or customization, of our use of the Internet begins with email. Why is email so popular across all the types and ages of people online? Why is it that the first thing most of us do when we connect to the Internet is check for new mail? It's because email is in many respects our most fundamental presence on the Internet. It is predominantly through the communication channel of email that we extend ourselves onto the Internet's vast expanse and, in turn, make ourselves known and reachable.

It is not coincidental to the popularity of email, or to that of many of the Internet's other communication facilities, that their form and function can be so well tailored to our individual needs. Our online identities require a large measure of individualization for them to function, and we use the features provided by these communication facilities to customize our presence on the Internet. For example, an email address — our principal identity on the Internet — is necessarily unique. So are our identities in the environments of chat and MUDs. Unlike a postal address or phone number, which are also necessarily unique, an email address and our other Internet identities are something we create for ourselves. Consequently, what these identities by themselves may mean or convey (if anything) is for us to decide. Some simply create an identity that contains their full name. But others create an identity that identifies them in a more descriptive manner, such as one that indicates they are a fancier of cats or a dancer, by selecting a nickname from their childhood or by making some reference to their business or profession. What's significant is that we make this choice, and this decision has an impact on how we are known and reached on the Internet.

This factor of individualization carries through to how, when, where, and even what we communicate over the Internet. Internet chat provides some good examples of this. Most chat environments, for instance, allow us to select an icon or other graphical object to accompany our screen name as part of our identity. We can also create a profile for others to view (or, equally significant, decide not to create a profile). Creating a profile helps to confirm our identity, making it easier for people who know us to locate us on the Internet. A profile that contains information about our profession, interests, and hobbies might also help us to meet new people. Conversely, the less information we choose to provide, the more our privacy remains protected. Most chat environments also allow us to create our own away message (i.e., text that is displayed when someone tries to connect with us in a chat environment when we are not online or we don't want to be interrupted) to let people know that we're off on a blind date or out to lunch. This type of customization of information enhances our ability to communicate information even when we are not currently online. Or we can choose not to use an away message or to use one of the standardized messages, which will help to protect our privacy. We can also control what our messages look like by choosing typographical elements, such as fonts and point sizes, and by inserting graphical objects, such as emoticons (e.g., a smiling, frowning, or kissing face), to help convey the tone or sentiment behind our words. How much or how little we choose to customize our identify, how much or how little we reveal about ourselves and our activities, how much or how little we extend our presence onto the Internet — using chat or any of the Internet's other communication facilities — is entirely under our control.

This sort of communication and identity customization contributes a great deal to the empowering effect of the Internet's communication facilities. What also makes these facilities empowering is how they accommodate the increasing mobility of our lives. Our lives are becoming more and more mobile with respect to our daily personal and professional activities and with respect to our more frequent moves from house to house, city to city, state to state, and even country to country. The growing popularity of wireless communication and cellular technology manifest our desire to regain some control over our lives and to maintain our interconnectedness with others as we travel from place to place, run errands, attend meetings, or are otherwise engaged.

The Internet allows our online identities to remain constant, regardless of our location. Email will find its way to us despite our increasingly mobile lives. Other communication facilities, like chat and MUDs, can be used to track our accessibility alongside our movements by signaling that we are in transit from home to office, in a private meeting, or at the airport waiting to board a plane. Consequently, we remain better connected and more reachable and we can, if we so desire, let others know where we are and what we are doing even when we cannot be reached. What began with the telephone in eliminating distance and location as obstacles to basic communication, the Internet has enlarged to an extent that no one anticipated.

Because of the Internet, communication itself has become a new focal point in our lives. We communicate more frequently with more people and through a wider variety of channels than ever before. The Internet's communication facilities made this possible, and nothing states the importance and effectiveness of these facilities better than their widespread use. For most of us, however, it was not a simple matter of using email or chat as an additional means of communication in our lives. Instead, we adapted our life in some way, shape, or form to their use. We made time each day to log on to the Internet and check for new mail. We connected to our chat service when we arrived at work or returned home from work (or both) to look for someone online and start up a conversation or to let others know that we were available. In many different ways, we have incorporated the use of these new communication facilities into the routines of our daily lives.

For some of us, particularly those who connect to the Internet every day for hours at a time, Internet communication in all its various forms represents a new mode of human interaction and a new type of community building and social involvement. Such individuals might be physically isolated, off in their own room at home or perhaps living alone in a remote community, but their feeling of isolation and their opportunities for interacting with others and contributing to a community have been dramatically and permanently altered by the Internet. Other individuals might be connecting to the Internet from any and every possible location as their day progresses: a home office, a train station, a moving train, a taxi, a business office, a restaurant. Such individuals often choose to ignore one communication environment in favor of the other, or they become adept at integrating the two and they succeed at operating simultaneously in both worlds.

For those of us who have incorporated the Internet into our daily lives, whether we live quiet, isolated lives, coexist in two busy worlds, or anything in between, we share many of the same objectives in our use of the Internet: to form and pursue relationships, to extend our involvement with others, to follow our areas of interest, to take part in communities that we identify with and that we may want to contribute to, to listen and to be heard. We do not, however, need to alter our lifestyle to reap the benefits of this new, influential, and empowering mode of communication. It's entirely up to us how much, or how little, we get ourselves involved.

What can be seen occurring on the Internet is the continuing evolution of earlier modes of communication and their associated technologies in conjunction with the invention and widespread adoption of many new, provocative, and empowering forms of communication. What may be less apparent is the profound revolution in our behavior and expectations with respect to the ways in which we communicate and interact with others as we shift our preferred methods of communicating from the older technologies and their associated infrastructures to the communication facilities of the Internet. We are simultaneously reaching out to more people and more places and, conversely, being reached by more people with little or no restrictions on time or geography. This is occurring just as we appear to be increasingly distancing ourselves from the people and places in our immediate vicinity, thereby enlarging the effect introduced by the telephone.

The services of email, chat, bulletin boards, newsgroups, and MUDs transformed a network of computers into a network of people. What began as a means to exchange data, work remotely, and better share access to and uses for expensive computing equipment, evolved into a powerful and popular new way for people to share thoughts, ideas, knowledge, experiences, and feelings. One long-term consequence, for better or worse, is that our use of the Internet's communication technology is redefining our notion of community. Hopefully, this effect will one day come full circle and help to reestablish and reinvigorate our ties with our local communities as well.

Information: The Point-and-Click Sum of Human Knowledge (and More)

Consider the Internet from the perspective of its information sources and services. From its inception, the networking of computers was inspired by the vision of sharing information and sharing computer resources. By anyone's measure, the Internet has far exceeded the scope of this vision. Information abounds on the Internet, as do information-related synergies, and the abundance and diversity of this information is a direct consequence of the Internet's ability to interconnect computers and their resources, regardless of their location, hardware, operating system, and other factors.

Through the Internet we can visit a store, browse its merchandise, find detailed product information, check a product's inventory, place items into a shopping cart, and make a purchase. Alternatively, we can employ a personal online shopping bot (i.e., a programmable agent, or robot, for conducting Internet searches) to seek out items that interest us and return information to us on prices and availability. We can visit a museum, tour an exhibit, linger at one or two paintings and glance at a few dozen others; and we can extend and enhance our experience by accessing online facts and stories associated with each work or with the artist's life. We can visit a library, browse its book collections, and examine one-of-a-kind manuscripts that would otherwise be inaccessible. We can listen to broadcast radio, or select a program from a station's recorded archives and enjoy it at our convenience. We can customize an Internet page to display all the types of information we routinely consult for business, our family, or simply for entertainment. We can open a virtual storefront for our business on the Internet, or create a site on which to publish our personal observations and insights, share family photos, promote our art, and so on. The list is endless.

What do all of these activities have in common? They are all driven by information content. These activities illustrate how we routinely use the Internet's information space. They are, for the most part, online corollaries to activities we pursued before the Internet came into our lives. How do they compare? Are we better off for having access to the Internet and these new capabilities? Or are the Internet's information services negatively impacting our more traditional information sources, like newspapers and libraries, and such fundamental activities as reading a book or flipping through an encyclopedia?

Your answer will likely be influenced by which side of the digital divide you stand on and how you feel about technology in general, whether you reside in a big city or a rural community, whether you are physically fit or physically challenged, a teenager or a grandparent, or any number of other factors. What is certain is that the Internet and its information sources and services are here now, they are new and different, and they are changing how we seek out and purchase merchandise, how we ask and answer questions, how we locate information and stay informed, and, more importantly, how we live our lives.

Even when regarded simply as a purveyor of information, the Internet stands in a class by itself; there is nothing even remotely comparable. But it's not just the quantity and diversity of its content that sets the Internet and its information apart and contributes to the Internet's synergies. Just as significant, if not more so, is the form, function, accessibility, and interconnectedness of that information. The Internet has turned information into a new type of commodity, enabling it to be bought and sold, searched through and analyzed, retrieved on demand or delivered according to a schedule, combined and interconnected, individually configured and customized according to any number or type of criteria — all this in ways that were never before possible. The Internet is bringing the information of the information age to (potentially) everyone. The result: a newfound empowerment of the individual.

References to the Internet's information space — in the form of Internet site names and Web page addresses — are all around us. They appear everywhere in the print media; they are on the pages of pamphlets, magazines, journals, and newspapers. They are used commonly in the broadcast media; they are read out, and often spelled out, on the airwaves of radio and television. They are printed on the products we purchase; they can be found on the cellophane wrappers enclosing heads of lettuce, the care labels on clothing, and the covers of books. They adorn billboards, dominate the advertising at sports stadiums, and often appear on the sides of trains, cars, trucks, and planes. These references imply (albeit wrongly) that most if not all of us know of the Internet's existence and have acquired some sort of access to it.

References to the growing relevance of the Internet's information content and services and its ever advancing integration into our daily lives are also all around us in the form of the devices used to connect to the Internet. These devices can be commonly found everywhere we work, play, and live; they are in business offices and college dorm rooms, libraries and coffee shops, hotel lobbies and community lounges, trains and planes, home offices, living rooms, and bedrooms. The spaces taken up by all of these references to the Internet imply the omnipresent nature of the Internet. The extent and commonplace nature of these outward signs of the Internet's existence and relevance are surprising in and of themselves. When you consider, however, that most people had never heard of the Internet as recently as the late 1990s and that the Internet was privatized and opened to commercial traffic only a few years before that, these references are that much more remarkable and revealing. They manifest how pervasively the Internet has integrated itself into our lives, and how readily we have accepted its integration. What does this type of wholesale integration signify, if not a revolution?

The best way to recognize the revolutionary and uniquely empowering effects of the Internet's information synergies is to put them into a general historical context. Computers alone transformed the information landscape and our use and reuse of information. But, as the following section, with its overview of our history of recording, distributing, and accessing information, will help to clarify, the Internet remade the information age into an information revolution by transforming the information processing and storage capabilities of computers into a global, egalitarian, unifying information network that has the potential to touch and affect everyone.

A Brief History of Information Storage and Access

Long before any type of writing system was developed, we recorded events and information within ourselves and passed on that knowledge through millennia of oral traditions. These oral traditions persisted long after the invention of alphabets and the creation of manuscripts and bound books, and they survive in various forms today. The creation, protection, and propagation of oral literature and folklore and, more generally, the passing on of knowledge relied on immediate and intimate community structures and on the face-to-face, individual-to-individual, or individual-to-group dynamics of sharing information. Someone spoke, and everyone else listened and learned. The acquisition and sharing of information was directly and completely tied to and dependent upon the people around us.

But even when oral tradition was the principal means for recording and sharing information, it was common for some knowledge to be held back and shared with only a few, select individuals (just as is still done today). Apparently, it was understood very early on that knowledge was power. Controlling information meant retaining and building on that power, whether you were a shaman, a priest, a king, or some other person of power, position, or privilege. This early interconnection of information, knowledge, and power continued to grow over time, which meant that individuals were largely limited to and dependent on local information sources that maintained control over the information that was released to the general public. It was only recently, as is explained below, that access to and the control of information began to shift in favor of the individual, and the Internet is in many ways responsible for this shift.

(Today, unfortunately, many of the stories regarding our ancient oral traditions are about the loss of those traditions. More and more languages are disappearing, as the few remaining individuals who still speak these imperiled languages are dying off. A common result of the disappearance of these languages is that the stories and the knowledge that are part of the culture and history of these languages are also being lost. It's sadly ironic that even in the midst of today's information age we seem unable to put a stop to such tragic and irrevocable information loss.)

The first system of writing, called cuneiform, dates back to 2600 BCE Mesopotamia. A reed stylus was used on wet clay to draw abstract pictures, and these pictures served to record business transactions and laws. A less abstract type of writing called hieroglyphics developed later in Egypt. It used pictograms to form a more direct correlation between a picture and its corresponding object or concept. For a writing surface, the Egyptians created papyrus, which was the first paper-like material used in writing. Papyrus was derived from a reed — the papyrus plant — that was pounded, polished, cut, and overlapped until sheets could be formed. These earliest forms of writing changed their respective civilizations, empowering those who could use and understand them to record and control history for their own benefit and communicate more securely with people outside the local community.

With the development of the first alphabets, such as the alphabets of the Hebrew, Greek, and Roman languages, came the development of books. At first, recorded information was contained in parchment scrolls. But by around the 4th century, scrolls were replaced by the codex, and the first books to resemble our own, with folded leaves made from parchment and book covers made from wood, started to be produced. The transition from scrolls to the codex brought with it a fundamental shift in how information could be accessed. For the first time, the reader could move quickly back and forth through the whole body of a text and more easily compare different parts of the text as he or she saw fit, which was quite a contrast to the predominantly sequential reading demanded by scrolls. This simple change had profound effects on the reading process and the interaction between an individual and a book; this was especially true for larger books, such as the bible. New discoveries and new knowledge could be gained by more readily reading from any number of different sections in a text. These early books, however, just like the scrolls that preceded them, could only be read by a small percentage of the population. Literacy in the general population was still severely limited, which restricted access to knowledge and helped to protect all recorded information.

Up until the fifteenth century, access to information and knowledge remained highly controlled. The production of books changed little and literacy had not yet started to spread to the general population. Manuscripts were created by hand, often by monks or other members of religious orders, and later by guild-based scribes. The process was slow and costly. Books were, for the most part, the property of the very wealthy and of the elite who ruled the kingdoms, as well as of the religious scholars and leaders. By the thirteenth century, however, paper arrived in Europe by way of Northern Africa. With it came a new form of book production that relied on wooden blocks. Text and pictures were carved onto blocks, ink was applied, and the blocks were pressed onto the paper. This new process greatly reduced the time and cost associated with producing books. Moreover, it led to the introduction of picture books, which were the first books that could be distributed to the vast majority of the (as yet illiterate) population. Printing with wooden blocks was the first, basic technological advancement responsible for the mass production of book-bound information. More books that more people could understand and access was critical to moving towards a broader, more egalitarian sharing of information and knowledge.

Then, in 1450, came the second, basic technological advancement directly related to the mass production of books. This was Johannes Gutenberg's invention of moveable type and the printing press, which brought about a revolution in book printing that would forever change the control and access to information and knowledge. The Protestant Reformation in Germany is regarded as one of the first radical effects of the introduction of the printing press due to its ability to produce large quantities of books, such as the bible, that could, for the first time, reach the masses. Literacy started to spread, which meant that religious and scientific information could be distributed to more individuals and not just those individuals who were members of religious orders, governing bodies, or the ruling elite. Gutenberg's new technology didn't just produce books. It made knowledge more accessible and it allowed ideas to travel farther, faster, and to more people than ever before. Its greatest effect was to change the very fabric of society in ways both subtle and profound. Just as important, the effect was permanent; there was no going back.

In the seventeenth century, Holland was regarded as the book publishing capital of Europe. Unlike other European countries where the Catholic Church managed to control information access by restricting publication of material to that which met its narrow criteria of information acceptable for the masses, Holland was free of this censorship. The publication of scientific information in particular, which was of critical importance during this age of discovery, was largely dependent on Holland and its printing presses. The advancement of learning was considered a pursuit of science. But some of the scientific discoveries of the time contradicted the teachings of the church, which resulted in a struggle over how to control the publication and distribution of this potentially dangerous and damaging information. Nothing illustrated this struggle better than the writings of Galileo — considered by many to be the father of modern science — and his trial for heresy by the Pope's Inquisition.

Book production that is strikingly similar to what we find today was introduced during the eighteenth century. It was also during the eighteenth century that publishing became established as a trade; prior to this, patronage publishing was the predominant way of doing business. Book composition became standardized on the type and order of information that is familiar to us today: a title page, a printing date, an index, pagination, and so on. Literacy continued to increase in the general population, as more and more people yearned for knowledge and advancement. But books were still expensive to own. Greater publication runs, however, led to the creation of circulating libraries. These establishments were not free, but they provided far greater access to books to many more people than ever before. Due to economic constraints and widespread illiteracy, the majority of the population was still limited in their access to information to what they heard through other individuals or through the reading of proclamations. But even their circumstances were on the verge of changing.

Publishing took on new forms and new meaning as information became a basic commodity in the eighteenth century. Pamphlets were published for the first time, which introduced the notion of mass media information. Similarly, a new way to distribute news and entertainment to a large audience appeared in the form of periodical publications. The first encyclopedia was published in France. It represented the earliest effort to provide an all-inclusive compendium of knowledge. More importantly, however, the alphabetically organized encyclopedia dramatically changed how information could be accessed and it introduced a way for questions to be quickly answered and, more generally, for knowledge to be quickly gained. Its effects were as transforming and far-reaching as those brought about by the transition from scrolls to paged books that took place centuries earlier.

The Industrial Revolution of the nineteenth century brought widespread mechanization to the business of publishing. Mechanization substantially reduced the cost of producing books and other printed material. The invention of the steam press meant higher production runs in far less time. Cloth bindings, as opposed to leather, also contributed to lowered production costs, as did machine-produced wood pulp for the production of paper. Alongside these cost reductions came a sizable increase in both the volume and diversity of information being printed. Mass production printing in the nineteenth century meant that distributing information to the masses was, for the first time in history, a bigger business, with greater potential for financial gain, than producing books for the wealthy.

New technology, due in large part to the Industrial Revolution, had effectively reversed the economics of printing. This change in the driving force behind publishing and distributing information from catering to the wealthy to printing for the masses is something that carries through to the present day (and to the Internet). Consequently, newspapers and magazines grew quickly in number and in circulation. The publishing process changed, as the publication and printing businesses separated and each set off to pursue a different segment of the emerging market. The distribution of printed information also changed, as bookstores and public libraries became commonplace and as mail order businesses emerged with their printed catalogs of merchandise. Additionally, delivered periodicals became popular, as magazines, newspapers, and other types of printed material started to be shipped within nations and between nations. This dramatic change in information distribution and access brought about equally dramatic changes in education and literacy. Information was again altering the fabric of society in strikingly new and far-reaching ways. The inventions of the telegraph in 1837 and the telephone in 1870 compounded these changes to information distribution and access by impacting the speed and distance of transmitting information.

The changes and trends that began in the nineteenth century developed more rapidly and become more widespread during the twentieth century. Printing technology improved as chemical-based photographic typography was introduced, and it improved again in the latter half of the century as computer-driven digital typography further reduced printing costs and supplied greater printing efficiencies. Printing businesses grew in number and expanded their influence, producing an ever greater diversity of publications and targeting the information needs of ever smaller and more highly specific audiences. Scholarly journals, trade publications, textbooks, reference books, and product catalogs quickly became commonplace, as all types of information became a commodity of one sort or another.

The post-World War II mass market paperback industry, the ever-increasing demand for newspapers, magazines, and other periodicals, and the widespread popularity of the broadcast media of radio and television made it clear that the information age had arrived and that our consumption of information was without bounds. The number of different information sources and the sheer quantity of information that most individuals now had access to gave substance to the information age. An indication of just how much things had changed with respect to an individual's access and exposure to information is expressed by the fact that the amount of information a typical eighteenth-century Englishman was exposed to over the course of his entire life was exceeded, just two centuries later, by the information contained in a single edition of the Sunday New York Times.

The twentieth century also brought us computers, which in turn brought us a revolution in how information could be stored, accessed, and shared. Computers added yet another dimension to the burgeoning information age. Their broadest contribution was in bringing about a digital revolution, which centered on recording and representing all types of information (e.g., text, images, music, films) in a binary digital format (i.e., a sequence of zeroes and ones that is read and interpreted by a computer). Before the advent of the personal computer and its proliferation for business and individual use, computers produced a fundamental, but significant change with respect to the representation of information and our interaction with information. Computers eliminated the need for paper documents. The digital representation of information that made this possible also made it possible to store information indefinitely and to make copies of information that were identical to the original. Some viewed computers and the recording of information in a digital format as little more than a convenience. For them, it was simply another way to read and page through a document. Others, however, saw that when information was made accessible through a computer, its transformation went beyond a change in format from paper to a digitally encoded file. Once information was available on a computer, all sorts of new and engaging uses became possible.

Digital information, unlike its printed corollary, could be electronically searched, analyzed, indexed and categorized, reused endlessly, and experimented with in any number of ways. These new facilities allowed (among other things) new meaning and knowledge to be extracted from the same information, which was reminiscent of the consequences of the information format transformation from scrolls to paged books. Digital information empowered the reader with more options in his or her examination and exploration of any text than its printed version could provide, as was true of paged books in comparison to scrolls. At the same time, and also thanks to this digital revolution, information became easier to copy, share, and transport. Vast amounts of information could now be loaded onto some form of magnetic medium, like a reel or cassette tape, and carried effortlessly and quickly from place to place.

The invention of computer networking revolutionized the portability of information, just as the telegraph and telephone had revolutionized the communication of information a century earlier. Networking enabled information to be transmitted quickly, efficiently, and effortlessly between computers sitting adjacent to each other in the same room or between computers separated by a continent or half the world. This new capability had different implications for different types of information. For instance, a breaking news story or details regarding a scientific discovery could reach more people in less time than ever before, while large volumes of data, like that produced by a census or meteorological information collected for weather forecasting, could receive more timely processing, analysis, and distribution of its information.

Computer networking brought about a dramatic and permanent change in how information could be transmitted. One measurement of this change could be found in the increased quantity of information being transmitted, which has contributed to increases in basic literacy, general improvements in education, and greater employment opportunities. Another measurement could be found in the increased speed at which information was moving from place to place, from community to community, and from person to person, which was making the world seem a smaller, more intimate place, just as it was filling our world with an ever-increasing quantity and diversity of information.

Computers also changed the whole framework of information storage and access, which had ramifications for individuals, businesses, academia, and government. Prior to computers, our most common information resources were dictionaries, encyclopedias, other reference books, and library card catalogs. With computers, especially after the introduction of workstations and the personal computer, our access to information resources increased significantly with respect to both the breadth of those resources and their number. Our physical ties to books and local libraries, and to printed information in general, were severed. We could get access to substantially more information resources. We could interact with information contained in these resources faster and with greater ease. We could also pursue information in a more refined, targeted way, and collect, store, and manipulate information in ways that were never before possible. Well before the arrival of the Internet into most of our lives, computers had opened the floodgates of information, fundamentally and permanently changing how we acquire information and what we can do with it.

Not long after the introduction of personal computers and workstations in the 1980s, desktop publishing applications were introduced. These applications promised to transform the traditional publishing paradigm, in which publishers, the government, and corporations wielded near total control over the printing and distribution of information. Now, for the first time, information could be both owned and controlled by individuals or small, independent organizations. Here, again, the change seemed simple and inconsequential. Desktop publishing applications provided another new capability made possible by the evolving computer technology. They were fun and exciting to use, and they were full of potential. Moreover, these applications promised to reduce publishing and printing costs by approximating through relatively inexpensive and simple-to-use software what had long been produced by expensive, complex, and difficult-to-operate equipment.

The ramifications of this new technology of computers, computer networking, and desktop publishing were part and parcel of the shifting forces at play with respect to information in general, and to its creation, distribution, and access in particular. Not only was the volume and the diversity of information sources we could access growing in leaps and bounds and not only were our options for becoming better educated and better informed growing as a consequence of our new, faster, improved access to these information resource, but now we had the power to become publishers, too, as members of a small group or organization, and even as individuals. Finally, we gained direct control over the type, quality, and composition of the information itself.

The Arrival of the Internet

Computers transformed the composition of information by enabling information to be captured and stored in a digital representation of zeroes and ones. This transformation gave form to an information revolution that radically changed how information could be accessed, shared, used, reused, combined, and manipulated and how knowledge could be gained. The Internet adopted, enlarged upon, and, in many respects, remade this information revolution in its own image by providing the means to establish a global, shared information space. Computers made all of this possible. But the infrastructure of the Internet, which interconnected our computers and, in the process, interconnected us, brought all the elements of the evolving information age together and added several completely new features to the mix. The hallmark of these new features, like the synergies they helped to create, is their empowerment of the individual. This empowerment can be seen in how the Internet turned each of us into information operators, able to obtain and customize information according to our needs and tastes, and how it enabled anyone, anywhere, to produce and publish his or her own information.

Information synergies are everywhere one looks on the Internet. The World Wide Web is the simplest and most obvious example. Through the Web, any combination of text, graphics, audio, and video information content can be quickly, easily, and seamlessly integrated. The result of this seemingly simple, but powerful content integration is a highly dynamic information environment that's just as capable of meeting the diverse needs of a large, multinational corporation as those of a one-man furniture shop, a charitable organization, or an inquisitive and enterprising boy scout.

The Web brought a much needed measure of uniformity and interoperability to the distributed and diverse information content that the Internet comprised. This uniformity, best represented by HTML — the Web's file coding language for describing and marking up information content — provided an all-important framework that could be used to make any type of information immediately and easily accessible to virtually anyone on the Internet. The result was instantaneous, paperless publishing for an audience far greater than any printed information could ever hope to reach.

The simplicity and efficiency of the Web's core components — HTML, the URL (the Web's standard for referencing the location of information objects, such as the location of an HTML file or an image file), and HTTP (the Web's protocol for exchanging information and files between computers) — were responsible for the Web's fast and widespread growth and for it quickly becoming the Internet's predominant information management system. Use of the Web by individuals and organizations brought new types of information and ever-increasing quantities of information onto the Internet. Some of this new information was stored on older, legacy systems that, before the introduction of the Web, could only be accessed through specialized equipment or through proprietary software. The Web made it possible to greatly broaden access to these systems and the information they contained by providing a generic gateway through which to access this information, thereby eliminating the need to use specialized equipment or software. Also new, and equally powerful, was the Web's capacity to interconnect information by linking one reference to another within a document and between documents, without making any demands on the location of the documents or the types of information. This capability was the information equivalent of the Internet's communication facilities, which allowed individuals to easily exchange messages, chat, and interact in virtual environments regardless of their location.

The success of the Web can be attributed in large part to its treatment of information as objects and the provisions it made for collecting, combining, and interconnecting those objects. The Web's treatment of information as objects paralleled the Internet's treatment of computers (and computer resources) as objects and the provisions it made for collecting, combining, and interconnecting those objects in order to form its network and provide the network's services. The information objects of the Web — files of drawings, animations, photos, film clips, plain text, other documents, and so on — exist independently of the Web, just as the computers of the Internet exist independently of the encompassing network. But the value and reach of the information contained in these objects became immeasurably enhanced when they became part of the Web. This is the same sort of large-scale synergy evidenced by the Internet itself through its internetworking of the world's computers.

The Web made accessing, presenting, and publishing information so fast, easy, and popular that many people either confuse the Web with the Internet or they are confused about how the Web and the Internet relate to each other. Graphical, simple-to-operate Web browsers are perhaps most responsible for this all-too-common confusion, since they are the primary interface through which most people interact with the Internet. What this confusion reveals about a large number of people who use the Internet is that what first comes to mind when these people think about, talk about, or interact with the Internet is information access. The Web happens to be today's best known and most easily recognizable information space on the Internet. But it represents only one dimension of the Internet's information resources; it comprises a single system for information management on an Internet than can accommodate any number and type of information management systems. Moreover, most of the objects that constitute the Web are neither specific to the Web (e.g., image files of photographs or drawings and document files from desktop publishing applications) nor confined to the Web (e.g., HTML files can be viewed by any number of applications or easily converted into other file formats for viewing). Nevertheless, the Web turned information into a commodity on the Internet, jump-starting the commercial invasion of the newly privatized Internet of the early and mid-1990s and turning many individuals into publishers and avid information consumers.

Surfing the Internet is another form of Internet synergy. The popularity of surfing the Internet, like the expression itself, suggests that information access has taken on a freer, more energized and recreational character. Surfing is characterized by information exposure. Sometimes this exposure takes the form of an information thread, such as a search for a specific product or an answer to a question that takes us from page to page. At other times this exposure is similar to flipping through a compendium of information, like an encyclopedia or dictionary, and allowing the journey through the information to build a path for us as new and unexpected associations form among the information encountered.

Surfing the Internet is an entirely new way to locate information and acquire knowledge. The Web's use of hypertext enabled information providers to interconnect the distributed information content of the Internet that made surfing possible. The accumulation of information content on the Internet, however, is what made surfing popular and powerful. Like the digital revolution made possible by computers and the far earlier transformation of information access made possible by the production of paged books (as opposed to scrolls), surfing the information content of the Internet will have far-reaching consequences for how we locate, use, and share information and for how we learn. Moreover, the act of surfing adds another dimension to the Internet's rich collection of newly accessible information. It empowers the individual to find information and create new information interconnections with few if any constraints.

The individualization that characterizes and enlivens the communication facilities of the Internet is also a quintessential element of the Internet's information synergies. The Internet turned upside-down the existing information distribution paradigm, which consisted of information being broadcast to us. No longer are we simply members of a passive audience, waiting for information to be delivered to us on a schedule not of our choosing. Through the Internet, we have become independent information operators. We can pull down the information we want when we want it. Moreover, we are no longer limited to the local, narrow, and sometimes biased information sources that feed our particular geographic community, such as those supplied by our town or city's newspapers and nearby radio and television stations. An entire world of information sources is now ready, waiting, and available, providing us with a volume and diversity of information that the Internet alone was capable of making accessible. Control over our information sources is finally ours. We can control when we get our information and what source is providing that information, and we can control how that information reaches us by opting to have certain types of information delivered in email or collected onto a waiting Web page.

Like the factor of individualization, the factor of convergence is as significant to the Internet's information component as it is to its communication facilities. Much as the Internet has established itself as a point of convergence of both pre-Internet and emerging communication technologies and affected how we communicate with others, so too has the Internet established itself as a point of convergence of a wide variety of information technologies and information sources and affected how we acquire information. Consider the types of information typically pulled from the Internet: weather forecasts, stock prices, sporting event scores, comics, job listings, news stories, television and movie listings, magazine and journal articles, and so on. We rely on this information, make decisions based on it, incorporate it into our work, and amuse ourselves with it. What's more, as described above, we can arrange to have many of these information sources customized, by arranging for information to be delivered to us according to a schedule or in response to some change (e.g., the cost for a plane fare dropping below a set value or the selling price for a stock exceeding a set value) and by configuring preferences at a Web portal site to collect different types of information onto a single Web page, making access to all this information much easier, faster, and more efficient. Consider the information you routinely access on the Internet. Now think back to where this information came from and how you accessed it before you started to use the Internet. The differences are striking.

Throughout our history, controlling information distribution and access has been a paramount concern of governments, religious orders, and others. These practices are no less common today, but the existence and composition of the Internet makes such efforts more difficult to sustain. We've seen that, once information is made available on the Internet, it is impossible to reestablish control over access to that information. Since the Internet is distributed as well as global, the information it carries is also distributed and global. Information accessible over the Internet can reside on any computer, within the borders of any country, and in virtually any location. In effect, this means that the technology of the Internet now has the ultimate control in the publication and distribution of information, as opposed to the government, the publishing industry, or some other controlling organization. This technology empowers the individual to make information available for others to easily find, copy, read, and distribute. Controlling information in the Internet age, therefore, is a highly challenging prospect.

The same Internet technology that empowers individuals to find and share information can, unfortunately, also be used to monitor, restrict, and control information access and the exchange of information. Some governments routinely mine the Internet's information traffic for various purposes, and some attempt to disable access to specific information sources — both within and outside their borders — that they deem inappropriate or harmful. Such efforts, however, are not likely to succeed for very long. As methods of information encryption become more widespread and easier to use, the information traffic of the Internet will become more difficult to monitor, copy, and mine. Moreover, as individuals become more savvy about the Internet and its technology and more aware of the volume of information it carries from us, to us, and about us, more legislation will be written to safeguard our information on the Internet and assert our control over that information. The technology of the Internet and the information revolution it made possible are first and foremost about the empowerment of the individual and the shift in information control and access from *them* to *us*. The transformation that started during the industrial revolution with its shifting the focus of information sources and the business of publishing towards the individual, the Internet completed with its information revolution and its delivering of equal and unrestricted information access to individuals.

It's not difficult to conceive that the future will bring more information synergies to the Internet, which will further expand the Internet's reach, increase its popularity, and make its presence that much more integral to our lives. As more people switch from the slower, more limiting Internet access provided by a dialup service (i.e., telephone line and modem) to the higher bandwidth access provided by cable, satellite, and DSL services, use of the Internet will undoubtedly change. New services will become available to take advantage of the increasing number of users who are connecting over these faster, broadband connections, and use of these new services will in turn alter the composition and information content of the Internet. The broadcasting of television and video on demand services across the Internet is already available. Can animated information kiosks, in the form of computer-generated characters that can understand plain language statements, typed or spoken, and respond in kind, be far behind? This type of service seems a likely extension of today's live text-based chat forums that are provided on many sites to answer questions about the site's products or services.

Will the Internet continue to complement and coexist with other sources and channels of information and entertainment, such as books, newspapers, libraries, radio, and television? Or will it, as some fear (and warn against), eventually subsume these more traditional ways of acquiring information and lead to their transformation or perhaps even to their demise? There are plenty of reasons to believe that all of these different information sources will remain separate and distinct. But the Internet will continue to have an impact on what they consist of, who uses them, and how they are used. Ideally, each of these information sources will find a way to benefit from the presence of the Internet and use the Internet's growing popularity to enhance its value and extend its reach. Radio stations provide an example of how one traditional information and entertainment resource has adapted and enhanced itself to coexist with and operate on the Internet. Many radio stations broadcast their content over the Internet in addition to broadcasting over the airwaves, which allows them to reach a far larger number of listeners than ever before possible. Moreover, some radio stations also archive their programs online and allow listeners to retrieve previously broadcast programs on demand, which also has the benefit of allowing them to reach more listeners.

Libraries provide another example of a traditional information resource that has succeeded in enhancing its facilities and services by welcoming and integrating the Internet into its operation. It is now common for most libraries to provide Internet terminals for use by the general public. Libraries were built on the belief that open and free information access benefited the public good. Free, public Internet terminals are clearly an extension of this belief. Libraries and librarians are considered an important, if not essential, resource in most communities, and integrating the Internet into the basic operation of a library and training librarians to help their patrons use the Internet to locate information can only serve to enhance a library's value to its community.

Even the publication and distribution of books have been improved and enlarged as a result of the Internet's growing popularity. This effect can be seen in the number and variety of places on the Internet that sell new and used books and, accordingly, the improved facilities for locating books, the lower prices for buying books, and the ability to easily sell one's books. This effect can also be seen in the Internet's creation of a new book publishing paradigm that enables individuals and small publishing companies (and other small groups and organizations) to print, publish, market, and distribute books without the assistance (and controlling influence) of one of the few remaining major publishers or book distributors. The creation of online bookstores and on-demand printing (a process of printing books in response to incoming orders, rather than the traditional method of printing, stocking, and distributing books in advance of any purchases) are two factors that have helped this paradigm succeed. One result of this new paradigm is that more new books are reaching the marketplace than ever before. Another result is that authors have a greater opportunity to retain their publication rights and receive a greater percentage of royalties from the sales of their books.

The Internet will also continue to influence how we work with information at our computers, and the form and functionality of the computers themselves. One recent effect can be found in the networking components embedded into the computer products we buy. Whether or not we intend to connect a new computer to the

Internet, it will come with all the hardware and software necessary for it to connect to a network and function on the Internet. This was not the case only a few years ago, when networking components were treated as accessories that could be added to a computer's configuration at additional cost. Another effect is manifested in the technology and mindset behind mobile computing and telecommuting, which owe their existence and popularity to the Internet. As limitations with connection speeds and bandwidth diminish over time, what our computers look like and how we use them will continue to evolve. In a not too distant future, for instance, we may find far simpler and friendlier devices on our desks, as difficult-to-manage operating systems, frustrating, poorly engineered applications, and devices that are prone to failure or susceptible to attack and corruption, like local disk drives, become a thing of the past. The Internet may instead provide for all of our needs. Just as today you can easily and quickly call up a weather forecast, tomorrow you may be able to start up a word processor, a drawing program, or a spreadsheet application from the Internet site of your choice and archive your files there, too, safely and securely. The network, as embodied by the Internet, will provide for many of our information needs, while making it simpler, safer, more efficient, and less expensive to create, work with, and store our own information.

As we have seen in the previous section, the Internet forms a communication network that allows us to interact with one another with greater immediacy and flexibility and in ways highly customizable to our individual needs and likes. As explained in the section that follows, the Internet also enables us to build a presence and take up residence on its network; and in so doing, we are able to make ourselves better known and accessible to others and to pursue our interests in ways never before possible. But the element that constitutes the bulk of the Internet's substance and makes tangible the empowering influence of the Internet is the information it carries and makes accessible. Unlike any other information source or paradigm for representing and accessing information, the Internet's ability to store, organize, and publish information is without bounds. But the Internet's information content, information resources, and information tools are not simply bringing more raw data and information sources into our lives. The Internet has transformed the way we locate, interact with, and employ information in nearly every aspect of our personal and professional lives. The Internet is changing our behavior and expectations with regard to information and the pursuit of knowledge at a fundamental level.

Information is power, which means that the Internet has the potential to empower us all equally through the open and unlimited information access it provides. The Internet also offers to give each of us a voice. These capabilities of the Internet are what constitute the Internet revolution. This revolution may be the first with the potential to liberate us all equally and individually, from the oppression and misinformation frequently produced by our government leaders, the tyranny of monopolistic corporations, and the often baseless fear of our neighbors, neighboring nations, or remote and unfamiliar nations.

People: Taking Up Residence in a Brave, New World

The Internet's infrastructure of computers, wires, cables, satellites, databases, and protocols and its communication facilities, information sources, and services only account for part of the Internet's composition. The people who use the Internet account for the rest of its composition, and they make up its most significant part. The people who use the Internet are (among other things) engineers and accountants, CEOs and secretaries, doctors and dog groomers, mothers, fathers, grandparents, and great-grandparents, teenagers and octogenarians. They are also the most easily overlooked and underestimated part of the Internet, and they are the greatest source of the Internet's synergy.

Few people would consider themselves part of the Internet. How many of us have even thought about what our use of the Internet means to the Internet? But we all bring something unique to the Internet, and every time we use the Internet we contribute something to its composition. We make different demands, express different likes and dislikes, use the vast resources of the Internet for different purposes, and rely on the Internet to fulfill different needs. In the process, we introduce all sorts of information onto the Internet and, in doing so, we are continuously changing its essential composition. The information we contribute to the Internet can be found in the messages we exchange in email and chat, the questions we post and the answers we supply in newsgroups and other online community forums, the pages we customize to hold our frequently accessed information sources, and in the sites we create for our personal and professional pursuits. What you discover when you consider all of the activities we pursue on the Internet and all of the information we contribute to the Internet in pursuing these activities is that we have, in effect, personally and permanently taken up residence on the Internet. We, as individuals, have become part of its network. What this may ultimately mean to us, or to the Internet, no one can presume to know. But we can explore how we take up residence, examine the immediate consequences of doing so, and speculate a little on what this might mean for the Internet's future in our lives.

To begin, we must recognize that the Internet is an entirely new and unique creation. Like other new and innovative technologies that we eagerly adopted and quickly became dependent on, such as the telephone, radio, and television, the Internet began its existence as more a novelty and curiosity than a revolutionary invention that would transform everything it touched. Little about the Internet's early history or its creators' original objectives reveal any expectation that the Internet would evolve into the communication-driven, information-rich, commercial, and international Internet of today. But its history to date makes clear the breadth and depth of the changes it has brought, and these changes can be attributed to the Internet's new, unique, and empowering technology. The Internet has changed the products we purchase, the jobs we perform, and the services we use for communication, education, and entertainment. More importantly, the Internet has changed our expectations, behavior, needs, and wants. The Internet created the opportunities and conditions that made these changes possible and, like the ripples that emanate in all directions after tossing a stone into a lake, these changes will continue to effect more changes as time goes on.

More than any other single factor, our presence on the network is responsible for setting the Internet apart. We are operators of the technology, not simple subscribers, and we ourselves define many of the characteristics that constitute our Internet presence. We travel the Internet, as we communicate with others, locate and exchange information, and play games. The identities we create to acquire a presence on the Internet (e.g., email addresses, online accounts, and gaming world avatars) are part of its composition, just as the computers we sit in front of are part of its network. Moreover, the more we use the Internet, the more we become part of it. This capacity to define our own identities and to communicate and interact with others across a vast network of interconnected computers is (as simple as it might sound) something utterly new to us and to our times. But in welcoming the Internet into our lives, we have taken some measure of ourselves and our lives onto the Internet, which has turned us into inhabitants of the Internet's vast, nebulous, global network, for better or for worse.

Have you ever thought about what it means to cross the digital divide? There is no fanfare to mark the event. We get our first username and password when we sign up with an ISP from home or when we are given an account at work. We sit down in front of our computer, click on the icon for a Web browser or email application, and we join millions of other people across the globe in the cyberspace of the Internet. But maybe there should be something to mark the occasion. It's not that farfetched to think of crossing the digital divide as a technological rite of passage. Nor is it unreasonable to consider our presence on the Internet a privilege.

The act of crossing the divide implies a certain measure of awareness and understanding of the environment and community that we have joined. Or does it? Most of us, adults and children alike, start using the Internet without first pausing to consider the consequences of our crossing the divide, and once we become familiar with browsing the Web and sending email we don't take the time to reflect on what our use may mean or what hazards may await us. We may behave a bit cautiously as we first explore the Internet and learn about how to use it. But the Internet continuously beckons us to explore further and do more, and we respond, for the most part, by visiting more sites and slowly but surely discovering more and more of its territory, services, exhibits, and curiosities. The process seems, at least at first, not all that different from clicking a television remote and surfing through a seemingly endless number of channels. Any and all such similarities (between surfing the Internet and channel surfing television stations), however, are purely superficial.

Our arrival on the Internet and our use of its technology is neither passive nor anonymous. Through our unique email address, and through the numerous other means the Internet puts at our disposal to explicitly or indirectly advertise our presence, like creating a Web page or joining Internet sites, we suddenly and inextricably become part of the world's first global communication and information network. It's not like joining an alumni association, acquiring a gym membership, choosing an automobile club, or getting a library card. It's also unlike signing up for phone or television service. We have personally entered into the frontier of cyberspace by crossing the digital divide, and cyberspace consists of a two-way, give-and-take communication environment that can identify who we are and where we and our computer are located, silently track our behavior as we browse the Web, chat with friends, and make purchases, and learn about our likes and dislikes. Moreover, it can do all this without our consent and even without our knowledge.

On the surface, signing up for Internet access means acquiring an email address and surfing the Web and discovering the staggering number of communication tools, information sources, and entertainment channels that the Internet makes available. In the process, however, and like it or not, we also join a community, just as we did when we took up residence in our current home. This community just happens to span the globe rather than several city blocks or a few square miles.

Consider email, and more specifically an email address, as the simplest and most common type of Internet presence. Our email account is more than a gateway that enables us to exchange messages. It is a unique Internet destination, and it is an integral and formal representation of who we are on the Internet. You may not have given it much thought, but having access to email can have some unanticipated consequences. In general, for instance, do you think you started communicating more or less once you acquired an email account? How much time on average do you spend each day sending and reading email? Have you restarted relationships through email that long distance phone calls or longer work hours caused to wither away or die? Have you begun and pursued new relationships due entirely to email as a consequence of joining an online dating service, posting information on a newsgroup or some other type of discussion forum, buying or selling a product on an Internet auction site, or joining an Internet-based community group? Are you more reachable now? Does email help you stay in closer touch with the members of your busy, dispersed, extended family, with friends, and with colleagues at work? Do you feel a little freer to express yourself through email than you might in person or over the phone? Do you stay in touch with more people? Do you think you are now considered more approachable and accessible by others? Have you ever asked yourself if your email presence on the Internet has changed the way you interact with others? For instance, do you now give out your email address when before you would have given that same person your phone number or street address?

Whether or not you acknowledge the change, or appreciate the subtle, and sometimes not so subtle, differences in your behavior and expectations, your life nevertheless did change as soon as you crossed the divide. You became reachable through your email address any hour of the day or night and every day of the year. It's also likely that you changed how you communicate with others, increased how often you communicate, increased the number of people with whom you routinely communicate, and perhaps expanded how much of your life you choose to share with others. These changes may be subtle or overt, but they exist. Over time these changes typically become more difficult to ignore. You may find, for instance, that you are buying fewer stamps and envelopes, that your phone bill has finally started going down, or that you are more engaged in the daily lives of more friends and family members. There's no reason to believe these changes can't all be positive in their effect. But use of the Internet, not unlike most other things in life, has its share of hazards, too. Needing to contend with spam, email-borne viruses, and identity thieves are commonplace problems that all Internet users must face. These problems, however, can be turned into minor annoyances when you are properly equipped to deal with them.

If you acknowledge, at least for the sake of argument, that your email address conveys more information about you than your phone number or postal address, consider what your email address may mean to others. Think about spam, for instance.

Every piece of unsolicited email you receive represents another instance of your identity — your Internet presence — reaching further out across the Internet. Your identity is being captured, copied, sold and resold, in order to become the target, for example, of some marketing campaign for a new wonder drug or investment scheme. More importantly, think about the email address on your business card or the one you scribble onto a scrap of paper at a holiday party. That address is both advertisement and invitation. It says, simply and clearly, you reside on the Internet and that is where you may be found.

While everyone on the Internet has an email address, not everyone uses chat and has a chat-based identity (i.e., a unique identifier, not unlike an email address or a login name for an online account). For those who do, however, chat provides a more immediate, reachable, and customizable type of presence on the Internet. Since chat is a synchronous activity that involves two or more people exchanging information in real time, chat applications provide features that allow one to monitor the comings, goings, and activity (or idleness) of someone else. For instance, you can set alerts to notify you when one of your buddies, such as your favorite sibling, comes online in the morning or when he or she returns from lunch and becomes active again in a chat room. Other features are designed to let you customize your chat presence. You may be able to choose an icon as a graphical representation of your identity (e.g., a cartoon character, a tree, or a cat dressed in a three-piece suit) or set up a personalized away message to let everyone know that you're out on a blind date and that when you'll be back online will be determined by how well, or badly, things go.

Chat provides a far more explicit way than email for us to take up residence on the Internet. It allows us to be more readily located, seen and contacted, and it also allows us to refine our presence and control how much (or little) we reveal about ourselves and our activities. Moreover, chat is specifically designed to help us manage and pursue personal relationships across the Internet. It enables us, for example, to construct lists of the friends, family, co-workers, and others with whom we routinely interact. These *buddy lists* represent our own, personal community structures, which form, in essence, a type of customized, Internet neighborhood. We fashion this neighborhood out of the people we know who also reside on the Internet and in so doing we reduce the vast, remote, and distributed environment of the Internet to one that is intimate, manageable, and built exclusively for our wants and needs.

Our presence on the Internet, however, is not simply a factor of which communication tools we choose to use and how much we choose to communicate across the Internet. Information access is also a significant part of our Internet experience and a factor in our taking up residence on the Internet. We make our presence felt every time we load a page from the Web, click on an advertisement, fill out a form, or start up an application that relies on information being broadcast across the Internet, like an applet that shows our stock portfolio or a financial program that reconciles our online bank account with the data stored on our personal computer. Just as our computer is considered a client on the network as we make requests and submit and receive information, we and our Internet presence are considered information clients from the perspective of the Internet's information service providers. They cater to and serve our information needs, and they view us as a source of income. The more they know about us, the better they can profile us; and the larger and more complete their profile, the better they can target their services and advertisements and generate more revenue.

Therefore, both our presence and our information needs are valuable commodities on the Internet. Our presence is significant in two distinct ways. First, our collected information wants and needs are unique: we are an audience of one. Second, these same individual wants and needs are shared by others: we are part of any number of demographic groupings (e.g., we read mysteries, we follow the stock market, we summer in Maine, we buy cat food). As we go about surfing the Internet, bits and pieces of information about our presence and activities are being recorded all the time. Depending on the sites we visit, this information may be ignored, used only on the local site, sold to others, combined with other data for the collection of aggregate rather than individual profiles, or it may be used for any number of other purposes.

You may or may not care that your presence on the Internet is considered a commercial target or that you and your interests, preferences, and habits, represent a resource for others to exploit. You should, however, at least be aware of such pursuits, remain alert to their impact on your use of the Internet, and maintain a special vigilance with respect to any child's presence on the Internet. A little knowledge and a few precautions in this area will help to ensure that your use of the Internet is a safer, more rewarding experience. The first step involves realizing that when you connect to the Internet you are taking yourself onto the Internet. Taking up residence on the Internet has clear and certain ramifications for every adult, and the significance for children is greater still.

Spending more time on the Internet typically leads to a greater involvement with its resources and facilities, which in turns leads to a larger and better defined Internet presence. More specifically, our presence as part of the general Internet community develops into a presence in any number of more specific Internet communities and organizations. We join a portal site to consolidate our daily information needs and interests. We get an account at an online bookstore in order to receive discounts or free shipping. We sign up to receive a weekly newsletter on yoga, astrology, or poetry. In the process, we become a true Internet denizen; we use the Internet to locate the particular resources and join the particular communities that match our individual set of interests. We discover, like so many others, the powerful and empowering effect of customizing our access to the limitless resources of the Internet for our individual use. In the end, our connection to the Internet has evolved into our own, unique online presence.

What may be less apparent — and is certainly more unnerving — is that acquiring a presence on the Internet does not require that we personally connect to the Internet. As ever more information makes its way onto the Internet, more personal information about all of us is suddenly becoming openly accessible to anyone with Internet access, and it seems that little or no consideration is being given to what this easier, faster access to information might mean to us as individuals. Routine records of court appearances and encounters with the police, state licensing requests, denials, and appeals, photographs and presented papers from conferences, local newspaper reports and editorials, or any other type of document that someone, somewhere, has published on a Web server, may include our name and thereby establish our presence on the Internet. Visit a search engine site and enter your name or the name of a friend. You may be surprised by the number and type of results returned. These searches clearly reveal that it may be impossible *not* to have some sort of presence on the Internet. Moreover, they raise the question of what — if any — control we can exert over the information that exists and continues to accumulate about us.

In taking up residence on the Internet, we all bring something unique and tangible to its composition. Our presence was the catalyst behind the Internet's transformation and remains today its most essential and dynamic element. We transformed the Internet from an academic experiment and proof-of-concept into a rich and revolutionary environment for communication and commerce, intellectual pursuits and entertainment. Without the endless stream of information emanating from us and our activities on the Internet, without our capacity to take up residence and develop a unique and dynamic online presence, even in the simplest form of an email address, the Internet would never have left the confines of university computer centers and research institutions.

Computers make the Internet work and provide us access, but we supply the Internet with its substance, interest, and purpose. The Internet consists of a network of networks, but every one of those networks is full of people. We are, moreover, more than the sum of our email correspondence, instant messages, published Web information, tracked behavior, and aggregate usage statistics. Our knowledge, interactions, interests, and demands, and all of the associated events and information about us, make the Internet what it is today and what it will be tomorrow. The synergy that results from each of us joining the Internet is multiplied millions of times over each and every day, as we connect to the network and go about our business. Even today, with the Internet still in its infancy and with only a fraction of the world's population having crossed the digital divide, the Internet embodies the richest, most diverse environment of people and information that has ever existed. What will it be like when everyone has access, and a voice, and their own, online presence?

The Working Internet: Something For Everyone

So, how do you name, describe, or characterize something that includes the potential to interconnect everyone on the planet? How do you evaluate or speculate on the significance of a system that can provide access to any and all types of information, particularly when that information can be located anywhere and stored in any number of different ways? Where do you start in studying the effects of a technology that gave form and meaning to the existence of virtual communities and instituted entirely new ways for people to communicate with one another and to share their ideas, feelings, and, ultimately, themselves?

The answers all begin and end with the individual. No matter how you look at it, all of these questions, and many others just like them, lead back to you and me. They speak to the role the Internet has to play in relation to the daily life of the individual and, conversely, to the role the individual has to play in the daily workings of the Internet. TCP/IP brought the Internet onto our computers. But we brought the Internet into our lives and, in doing so, we shaped the Internet into what we see today.

Step back and take a long and broad view of the Internet. Consider the Internet as the ultimate equalizer: a technological construct that gives substance to the pursuit of basic equality among individuals and an environment that gives form to a type of egalitarianism. The term egalitarianism is defined as: "a belief in human equality especially with respect to social, political, and economic rights and privileges" and "a social philosophy advocating the removal of inequalities among people".[1] The Internet's potential to become this sort of equalizing force for individuals derives from its engineering and construction as an equalizing technology to interconnect computers irrespective of their size, location, manufacture, hardware, software, and operating system. We sit behind all of those computers. Therefore, this equalizing force carries through to us and to our use of the Internet.

Prior to the arrival of the Internet, nothing allowed for the uncensored, free exchange of information or the open, immediate, unrestricted communication between individuals, or groups of individuals, across the globe. Then, seemingly overnight, the

Internet established a basic framework through which we could interact with strangers as easily as with family or friends, and through which we could exchange information as cheaply, easily, and efficiently with individuals thousands of miles away as we could with our neighbors. By virtue of its elegant and unassailable simplicity, the resulting system affords all of us an equal voice amongst an entire world of individual voices, and equal access to an entire world of uncensored, unfiltered information.

The communication and information-sharing framework established by the Internet provides the potential to transcend the long-standing barriers, prejudices, misinformation, and fears that we have known and contended with, in one form or another, all of our lives, and that are responsible for establishing and fostering the basic inequalities between people. Such potential is tied directly to the Internet's empowerment of the individual. The Internet turns upside-down and inside-out the existing control mechanisms that have kept the individual predominantly powerless and passive, at the mercy of the local government and other local institutions that distribute information and control public opinion. How? By allowing each of us to publish information, without an intermediary and without being edited. By allowing each of us to pull information down from anywhere and at any time, rather than being limited to the local news sources and other sanctioned, often sanitized or skewed information sources that get pushed down to us. By allowing each of us to interact freely, directly, and with some measure of privacy, without a government minder, a translator, some sort of conduct or language police, or anyone else to get in the way.

The Internet is not confined by geographic or national borders. Even though its technology includes the capacity to be controlled and monitored — locally, nationally, or anywhere in between — its design and grassroots influence compete directly with such efforts. To date, these influences have succeeded in keeping the Internet more like a frontier than a heavily controlled, legislated, and policed environment. The Internet is largely unconstrained and monitored and policed by individuals for individuals rather than by nations for their citizens. The Internet is also colorblind and, more generally, unconcerned with and unaffected by our other individual, personal characteristics, such as gender, age, race, faith, and political affiliation. Each connected device is effectively unique and equal from the perspective of the Internet's technology and its administration and management. This is precisely what grants each of us sitting behind these devices an equal voice and equal access to the rich information resources and communication services of the Internet.

What you make of this fundamental, equal-opportunity environment is entirely up to you, which in itself is part of the point. But if you take into account all the factors through history that have prevented such equality, such as limitations and restrictions in communication, the control and manipulation of information, and huge variations in socio-economic conditions, you may start to see and appreciate the kind of equalizing and empowering force that the Internet offers to individuals everywhere.

In terms of its technology, the Internet represents the first creation capable of realizing a global and unifying egalitarianism. Unfortunately, this doesn't mean that the Internet will deliver on this potential. If anything, the Internet's history makes clear that no one cannot predict or plan its future. But the potential for such a future is there, embedded in both its fundamental technology and, to a larger degree, in the people who make up the Internet's constituency, the people who reside on the Internet and support its many grassroots organizations. If you recognize the all inclusive potential of the Internet's environment (and, for the moment, put aside the large number of individuals still on the far side of the digital divide), what else can you think of that even comes close to the Internet's global, unfiltered, and equal access to information? What else exists that gives everyone a voice through which to express themselves and be heard?

But what precisely does it mean to have access to a system, any sort of system, that offers something for everyone? What happens when people from all over the globe can (relatively speaking) effortlessly and inexpensively, even freely, connect to a common and distributed information space and interact one-to-one or as part of a group? What changes when you as an individual can both express yourself in the privacy and seclusion of your own home *and* be heard by countless others; and, in being heard, also evoke a response? Who retains power and control and how do they exercise that power when information becomes freely accessible to all of us?

The Internet is removing more walls between people, peoples, and nations than most of us ever noticed or, in noticing, ever felt constricted or alarmed by. It's happening whether you are personally a part of it or not. But this empowerment of the individual and the consequential erosion of barriers is less desirable to some, particularly to those in positions of power. Does any current government, the great western democracies included, believe their political systems can withstand an environment in which every individual can speak their mind and more easily connect with like-minded individuals, to share ideas, effect change, or simply voice their concern or displeasure? Some of us are fortunate enough to live in countries where such rights as free speech and the ability to gather and demonstrate are considered integral parts of our nations' founding mandates or constitutions. But few people today believe these rights are protected to the extent that their authors intended or even to the degree asserted by our educational systems or the media.

How will these existing power structures change as more people express themselves, both as individuals and as part of bigger, better organized, more vocal groups? Will such efforts lead to better, more equal representation and clearer, more demonstrable accountability from our civic leaders? The ultimate question in this area may be: can a world of individuals interconnected through the Internet lead us one day to a world of fewer or no national borders? No one expects our nations' power structures or borders to change overnight. But small changes are already occurring as greater access to information, new capabilities to publish and share information, and new capabilities to create groups and form communities — all of which were made possible by the Internet — are enabling more voices to be heard and for those voices to reach more people. If you are not sure that individuals and the Internet are capable of effecting change, visit a site like Moveon.org or do a search and see just how many sites already exist that are watching and waiting for and advocating such change.

As you may now better appreciate, it's the distributed and open technology of the Internet that is most directly responsible for the Internet's impact on our lives and, perhaps even more importantly, for its future, all-empowering egalitarian potential. The Internet was built, continues to operate and thrive, and is controlled by the collective efforts of individuals — despite frequent and considerable efforts by organizations to exert their influence and control — rather than the narrow, typically self-serving interests of big business or government agencies. Moreover, the Internet represents the hard work, patronage, and kindness of individuals. Through our computers we embody its vast network. Our voices constitute its global chorus. Our histories, individually and collectively, and our insights, opinions, and stories, along with the products and services we make and sell, make up its enormous warehouse of information. For each of us the Internet offers something different and distinct. The fact that it offers something for everyone is tied directly to the fact that it is we who compose it.

If we turn away from the big picture view of egalitarianism, we see that it's really the small picture view of the Internet, the one that focuses on the individual, that best captures what the Internet means today and its greatest, immediate impact for tomorrow, too. As individuals, most of us fall into one of the following, general categories. A small, but vocal percentage of us eagerly pursue large parts of our lives on the Internet, as we endeavor to remain connected and reachable at all hours of the day and night, and as we socialize on the Internet, conduct business or pursue other interests, hobbies, education, or entertainment. A great many of us depend heavily on the Internet but take it for granted and don't bother to consider how it has changed our lives, as we log on daily from home and work, continuously exchange email with friends, family, and business associates, buy products from stores we may or may not be able to locate on a map, pay bills, schedule meetings, read about the latest current events, and so on. Others of us dismiss the Internet as the latest technology toy or fad, as we use it on occasion, when we must, to take care of some business that won't tolerate the relative slowness of the postal system or to search for the answer to a question when we don't have the necessary book at hand and we don't feel like a trek to the library or calling someone who might know. Others remain on the other side of the digital divide, either by choice or circumstance.

Which category do you fall into? More importantly, has your perspective on the Internet changed now that you know something of its history and how it functions? Do you now pause before you go online and consider, even if only for a instant, that you're participating in something larger in scope and significance than you previously acknowledged? Do you feel that through the Internet you now have more options to locate information that's relevant to you, and that you enjoy a greater ability to interact with others on your terms, within your particular schedule and lifestyle constraints? Has the Internet enriched your life? Or do you feel, as many do, that the openness and information resources of the Internet are instead eroding the privacy of your personal information and eliminating the necessary information barriers and safety measures for children. Do you worry that the immediacy of personal interaction is being replaced by the remoteness of online interaction and virtual communities? Do you regard the technology as intrusive and see a future in which more and more people are spending more and more hours in front of their computer displays and keyboards, at the expense of reading a book, walking along a beach or trail, playing a sport, meeting a friend for coffee, or even brainstorming as part of group packed into a small, poorly ventilated conference room?

The Internet is not going away. It's growing in size and evolving in form and function each and every day. A considerable percentage of school age children are growing up with the Internet; and it's not difficult to believe that one day this may be true for all children. They use the Internet as part of their education no less commonly than previous generations visited the local library and spent hours thumbing through card catalogs and perusing shelves of books in pursuit of information resources. The Internet routinely acts as their private communication network, too, and as a frequent source of entertainment. They take the Internet for granted and extend their lives through it, seamlessly and without pause; and they will take this attitude with them as get older, find jobs, and have their own children.

It didn't take long for the Internet to become part of most business operations, from multinational corporations to mom and pop rural storefronts. More and more jobs don't just use the Internet to help conduct business, they rely on it. So, if you're employed and the Internet hasn't yet arrived at your desk, there's an ever growing probability that the Internet will be coming your way shortly. Even the world's governments are finally incorporating the Internet into their operations in order to reduce expenditures and increase efficiencies, to say nothing of their interest in mining the Internet for policing and political operations.

It's a little surprising how late they are in welcoming the Internet, given that it all began as a government project in response to growing geo-political tensions. But from now on their involvement is only going to increase, whatever that may mean for the rest of us.

It may only be a matter of time before the Internet becomes as commonplace and ubiquitous as the telephone. It's not because we can't live without it. In a way, it may have more to do with the reverse. As the Internet entwines itself with more and more people, business functions, government institutions, and educational bodies, and embeds itself further into our communities and daily lives, it will make greater demands on all of us having access to it and on access points being made available everywhere we go, just as occurred with the telephone. It's already happening. How pervasive, and even invasive, the Internet will become over the next decade or two is anyone's guess. Would you consider living today without a phone in your home? It may only be a few years before the same question will be asked of the Internet.

In the end, the choice of whether or not to take up residence on the Internet, or even to welcome it into your life in some very limited or marginal way, is entirely up to you. It's easy to find fault with the Internet and dismiss it on the grounds that it's too difficult to use, too costly, or simply unnecessary. It's also perfectly reasonable to keep your distance because of the ever-increasing number and seriousness of complaints about privacy and security, pornographic and other objectionable content, and outright fraud and other types of malicious behavior.

But with a helping hand, the technology hurdle can be quickly overcome; and more locations with free access are becoming available all the time (e.g., local libraries and community centers) Awareness of the dangers on the Internet along with a little common sense when it comes to things you should and should not do, will go a long way to ensuring your interaction with the Internet remains safe and secure. What then awaits you is the fun and adventure, the exploration of a vast environment that will dazzle you, entertain you, educate you, beckon you to become more involved and better connected with a whole world of people who want much the same thing. You can't (yet) bring your cat along, but he or she can be happily snoozing in your lap as you connect and check the latest news, reply to some email, locate a star chart for the night sky, or read today's Garfield cartoon strip.

Milestones, Netiquette, and Jargon

Privacy Issue Milestones

The following milestone information highlights some of the key privacy issues and related legislation in the U.S. during the 20th century.

1927   Federal Radio Act proclaims radio airwaves to be public property, requiring broadcasters to obtain a license.

1928   U.S. Supreme Court rules search warrants unnecessary for wiretapping telephone conversations given that citizens do not have a reasonable expectation of privacy when talking on the phone.

1934   Federal Communications Act makes it illegal to intercept telephone or any other communications without a court order, reversing the 1928 Supreme Court ruling.

1942   U.S. Supreme Court determines that "fighting words," meaning words likely to incite a fight, are not protected by the First Amendment.

1957   U.S. Supreme Court rules that obscenity, which it defines as sexual explicit material without social value, is not free speech and therefore not protected under the First Amendment.

1970   Fair Credit Reporting Act gives consumers the ability to access, correct, and limit external access to their credit reports.

1973   U.S. Supreme Court clarifies definition of "obscene" speech as violating contemporary cultural standards, as a patently offensive depiction or description of a sexual act, and as lacking serious literary, artistic, political or scientific value.

1974   Congress passes the Privacy Act of 1974, preventing the disclosure of government records without consent from the individuals involved.

1976   A market research company named Claritas uses census data to build the first national database, called PRIZM, to target specific audiences.

1978   U.S. Supreme Court upholds the government's right to regulate indecent speech broadcast over public airwaves, explaining that the broadcast media is "uniquely pervasive" and easily accessible to children.

1986   The Electronic Communications Privacy Act prohibits wiretapping computer activities and Internet subscriber data without a court order.

1988   The Computer Matching and Privacy Protection Act restricts the ability of federal agencies to match and merge the records of citizens.

        The Video Privacy Protection Act protects the confidentiality of video rental records.

1995   SurfWatch develops the first computer software program that helps parents control and oversee access to information available over the Internet for their children.

1996   Congress passes the Communications Decency Act, making it illegal to make indecent material available to minors via the Internet. The U.S. Supreme Court strikes down the indecency sections of the act in 1997, explaining they are unconstitutionally vague and overly restrictive of the free speech rights of adults.

        The Child Pornography Prevention Act bans computer generated images that present "the appearance of minors engaging in sex." But the law was overturned in 2002 by the U.S. Supreme Court when it ruled the measure too broadly written, which meant it could suppress legitimate artistic expression.

1997   Lexis-Nexis and 13 other information brokers agree voluntarily to restrict public access to some personal information and allow consumers the option to correct their records and to limit the sale of personal information.

1998   The Child Online Protection Act requires operators of commercial Internet sites to institute some form of adults-only screening system, such as requiring a credit card, to protect children from accessing information deemed harmful to them.

Richard Machado, a former University of California student, is the first person convicted of a hate crime on the Internet for sending derogatory email to roughly 60 university students, most of whom were Asian-American.

The FBI introduces Carnivore, an email surveillance tool. The Internet wiretapping devices is met with resistance from civil libertarians and privacy advocates who argue it could pick up email unrelated to any criminal investigation.

Congress passes the Digital Millennium Copyright Act of 1998, applying copyright laws to books, movies, and music offered online.

1999   The Financial Services Modernization Act of 1999, also known as the Gramm-Leach-Bliley Act, requires financial institutions to notify consumers that they can "opt-out" of allowing their personal information to be shared with third parties.

Security Issue Milestones

The following milestone information highlights some of the key security issues since the creation of the first modern computer.

1945 The term *bug* is first used in relation to a computer when Rear Admiral Grace Murray Hopper identifies the root cause of a computer problem as a moth trapped between relays in one of the Navy's computers. The term had been used previously to describe any number of general problems that were common with electrical devices. She coined the term *debugging*, using it to describe the activities related to finding and fixing computer problems.

1949 The theory of self-replicating programs, a tactic commonly used in today's computer attacks, is constructed by mathematician John von Neumann. His work forms the foundation for how memory is employed in modern computers.

1964 In an attempt to locate individuals using illegal *blue boxes*, devices that mimic the tones used by the phone system in order to make free calls, AT&T starts monitoring phone calls. Over the next 10 years, 33 million toll calls will have been monitored in their campaign to find the *phone freaks* or *phreakers*.

1972 Later known as Captain Crunch, John Draper determines that a plastic whistle packaged in a breakfast cereal produces a 2600-hertz tone that, when used with a blue box, acts as a key to AT&T's phone network, enabling free toll calls and other illegal changes to the network.

1978 John Shoch, an engineer at Xerox Palo Alto Research Center, creates a new type of semi-autonomous program called a computer *worm*, a beneficial program designed to increase the operating efficiency of a computer and to help automate certain functions. Unfortunately, the program develops some unanticipated behavior at night and ends up spreading like a virus on their internal network, crashing most of the machines.

1983   A group of young crackers known as the *414s* are located and arrested by the FBI after breaking into a several U.S. government networks, at times using only an Apple II+ computer and a simple modem.

Fred Cohen, a doctoral candidate at the University of California, coins the term *computer virus*. He uses it to describe a computer program that can adversely modify another computer program in such a way as to include an exact or enhanced copy of its own program. His research is later used by others to develop techniques to defend against computer virus attacks.

1986   The Brain, one of the earliest PC-specific computer viruses, is created and released by programmers in Pakistan.

1988   Robert Morris, Jr., a graduate student studying Computer Science at Cornell University, creates a worm and unleashes it on the Internet. Within hours the worm infects thousands of computers across the U.S. and chokes the transmission of data across the Internet. The following morning, November 3, 1988, becomes known as Black Thursday for many system administrators who have to confront and clean up the mess.

1991   Philip Zimmerman creates a data encryption tool called Pretty Good Privacy (PGP) and releases it on the Internet for free. The U.S. government opens an investigation, alleging Zimmerman broke U.S. data encryption laws in releasing the technology, but the charges are later dropped.

The Norton Anti-Virus software package is released by Symantec.

1994   A popular virus hoax is forwarded by countless people in email, warning individuals not to open an email that includes the phrase "Good Times" in the subject. It demonstrates the ease and speed at which hoaxes, and potentially viruses, can be willingly spread across the Internet.

1998   A series of computer system intrusions occur in which
       outsiders take control of more than 500 military,
       government, and private sector computer systems. The
       incidents become collectively known as Solar Sunrise in
       reference to vulnerabilities in the Sun Solaris operating
       system found on the affected computers. While it was
       thought the attack originated in Iraq, it was instead
       perpetrated by two California teenagers.

       Yahoo! notifies users that anyone recently visiting its site
       might have downloaded a logic bomb and worm which
       was planted by crackers protesting the jailing of Kevin
       Mitnick.

       Using a single, customized PC, the Electronic Frontier
       Foundation and "Cypherpunk" John Gilmore break a 40-
       bit DES key in 56 hours.

1999   The Melissa virus spreads through vulnerabilities in
       Microsoft Word and Microsoft Outlook, sending copies of
       itself and copies of Word documents to the first 50 names
       listed in the user's address book stored under Outlook.
       More than $80 million in damage is reported. Sales of
       anti-virus software surge in response. Later in the year,
       David L. Smith pleads guilty to creating and releasing the
       Melissa virus in one of the first such prosecutions related
       to a computer virus.

       American Express introduces the "Blue" smart card, the
       first chip-based credit card in the industry.

2000   A virus similar to the Melissa virus, the I Love You virus,
       infects millions of computers nearly overnight. It also
       sends usernames and passwords from infected computers
       back to the virus's originator, enabling his identification
       and arrest. The Filipino computer student responsible,
       however, goes free since the Philippines have no laws
       against such activities, prompting the European Union's
       creation of it global Cybercrime Treaty.

       A large-scale, distributed Denial of Service (DoS) attack
       causes many prominent Web sites, including Yahoo!,

Ebay, Amazon, and Datek to be unreachable or effectively unusable for several hours. Investigators later discover that the attack was originated by crackers who had broken into and taken over computers located at the University of California at Santa Barbara.

President Clinton signs the "Electronic Signatures in Global and National Commerce" (E-Sign) into law, making digital signatures legally binding.

2001   The Anna Kournikova virus, a relatively benign virus that includes mention of pictures of the tennis star, begins to spread via a vulnerability in Microsoft Outlook.

The Code Red worm targets computers running Microsoft NT and Windows 2000, resulting in more than $2 billion in damages. Part of the worm's programming involves using infected computers to attack the White House's Web site on a specific date. Collected efforts thwart the attack just as it begins.

Coming days after the September 11th terrorist attacks, a sophisticated program incorporating five separate methods to infect systems and reproduce itself called the Nimda virus infects tens of thousands of computers across the globe.

Heightened Sino-American diplomatic tensions result in U.S. and Chinese crackers producing Web page defacements that many dub "The Sixth Cyberwar."

Dmitry Sklyarov, a Russian programmer, is arrested at the annual Def Con hacker convention and becomes the first person criminally charged with violating the Digital Millennium Copyright Act (DMCA).

2002   The creator of the Melissa virus, David L. Smith, receives a sentence of 20 months in a Federal U.S. prison.

The Klez worm exploits Microsoft Outlook to send copies of itself to all email addresses in an infected machine's address book. It also causes local file damage and disables some anti-virus software products.

A DoS attack on all 13 DNS root servers, the computers at the top of the hierarchy which controls network and computer names and IP addresses, does no harm but raises concerns over the vulnerabilities in the security of this core element in the Internet's infrastructure.

The Bush administration files a bill to create the Department of Homeland Security, which will be charged with protecting the nation's critical IT infrastructure.

2003   A very fast spreading worm called the Slammer infects hundreds of thousands of computers worldwide in the course of a few hours, taking cash machines offline, delaying airline flights, and harming other businesses.

Netiquette

Communicating over the Internet, whether by email, chat, or some other means, is not likely to be well regarded by people who have high standards when it comes to spelling and grammar, or by those who fondly recall learning in school all about salutations and the various and sundry parts that compose a well formed paragraph. You can blame the keyboard or bad typing skills, or both. Or you can blame the innate sense of informality in the medium. Or you can attribute it to the immediacy of the environment and that feeling of urgency to send out a quick email or to keep pace in a fast moving, chat room conversation.

Netiquette, short for network etiquette, is a loose collection of rules and conventions applied to online behavior, particularly to communicating over the Internet. Most of what is commonly understood as netiquette — specific perspectives and formal descriptions vary considerably — represents common sense behavioral considerations, things we try to apply in our general interactions with others but adapted to the new and unique communication environment of the Internet. In general, these conventions focus on respecting other people's time and privacy, sharing knowledge rather than withholding it or lauding it above others, not abusing one's power (e.g., when acting as moderator in a chat room or newsgroup), and forgiving mistakes, especially with respect to new Internet denizens, also known as newbies.

Netiquette also tries to cover some operational basics, like knowing when and how to ask for help, understanding that all uppercase letters make you appear as if you are shouting, thinking twice before responding emotionally (also known as flaming someone), not forwarding unsolicited mail to your friends, and so on.

The simplest and most fundamental netiquette rule is not letting the remoteness imposed by the technology allow you to forget that you are interacting with other people. Typing in your thoughts at a computer keyboard, in the isolation of your room or in the public space of an office or library, makes it easy to forget that someone else will eventually be reading those words; and they won't necessarily know what you were feeling when you wrote them, or precisely what you intended. You can't accompany your words with your facial expressions (well, see below, you can try). You can't easily or exactly communicate your tone of voice. You can't clearly identify when you're being serious, and when sarcastic. So, don't be surprised when you are misunderstood, and try to use whatever conventions you can, including those in the tables below, to assist you in communicating both your thoughts *and* the sentiments behind them. Equally important, apply the same conventions when reading what others have written. Do not presume you know exactly what your friend, business associate, or even your favorite in-law meant to convey when reading his or her words in an email message or in a chat window. Give them the benefit of the doubt, because the technology only goes so far.

If you want to communicate over the Internet using some of the language constructs that the Internet has inspired and propagated, or if you just want to better understand the common acronyms and expressions that commonly punctuate much of the Internet's communication traffic, you'll find the following tables of assistance.

Internet Shorthand Acronyms	
Acronym	Meaning
AFAIK	As Far As I Know
AFK	Away From Keyboard
AOLer	America OnLine Member
A/S/L	Age/Sex/Location
BAK	Back At Keyboard

Internet Shorthand Acronyms	
Acronym	Meaning
BBIAF	Be Back In A Flash
BBL	Be Back Later
BD	Big Deal
BFD	Big Friggin' Deal
BFN	Bye For Now
BRB	Be Right Back
BTW	By The Way
CUL8R	See You Later
CYA	See Ya
FB	Furrowed Brow
FWIW	For What It's Worth
GDM8	G'day Mate
GMTA	Great Minds Think Alike
GRD	Grinning, Running, Ducking
GR8	Great
HTH	Hope This Helps
IAE	In Any Event
IANAL	I Am Not A Lawyer
IM	Instant Message
IMHO	In My Humble Opinion
IMNSHO	In My Not So Humble Opinion
IOW	In Other Words
IYSWIM	If You See What I Mean
J/K	Just Kidding
LMAO	Laughing My A-- Off
LOL	Laughing Out Loud
LTNS	Long Time No See
M4M	Men seeking Men
NFW	No Friggin' Way
NP	No Problem
NRN	No Reply Necessary
NW	No Way
OIC	Oh, I See
OTOH	On The Other Hand
PBT	Pay Back Time

Internet Shorthand Acronyms	
Acronym	Meaning
ROTFL/ROFL	Rolling On The Floor Laughing
RTFM	Read The Friggin' Manual
SOL	Sooner Or Later
TOS	Terms Of Service
TTFN	Ta-Ta For Now
TTYL	Talk To You Soon
WB	Welcome Back
WTG	Way To Go
YL/YM	Young Lady/Young Man
YMMV	Your Mileage May Vary

Internet Shorthand Expressions	
Expression	Meaning
O:-)	Angel
*^_^*	Big Grin
T_T	Big Tears
@^_^@	Blushing
:'-(	Crying
}:>;	Devil
:-e	Disappointed
:-L~~	Drooling
X=	Fingers Crossed
:-(	Frowning
$-)	Greedy
8:)3)=	Happy Girl
{{{{Whomever}}}}	Hug for Whomever
{}	Hugs
X-)	I See Nothing
:-X	I'll Say Nothing
******	Kisses
:*	Kissing
:=)	Little Hitler
:-D	Laughing
@]'-,-----	Rose
:-@	Screaming

Internet Shorthand Expressions	
Expression	Meaning
:-O	Shock
:-)	Smiling
:-P	Sticking Out Tongue
^_^;	Sweating
(hmm)Ooo..:-)	Thinking Happy Thoughts
(hmm)Ooo..:-(	Thinking Sad Thoughts
;-)	Winking
\\//	Vulcan Salute

Common Internet Age Jargon

The following list contains a sampling of the jargon inspired by the Web, the Internet, and the ever growing pervasiveness of computers in our lives.

404

Someone who's clueless. From the Web error message "404, URL Not Found," meaning that the document you've tried to access can't be located. "Don't bother asking him...he's 404, man."

Adminisphere

The rarefied organizational layers beginning just above the rank and file. Decisions that fall from the adminisphere are often profoundly inappropriate or irrelevant to the problems they were designed to solve.

Alpha Geek

The most knowledgeable, technically proficient person in an office or work group. "Ask Larry, he's the alpha geek around here."

Assmosis

The process by which some people seem to absorb success and advancement by kissing up to the boss rather than working hard.

Beepilepsy   The brief seizure people sometimes suffer when their beepers go off, especially in vibrator mode. Characterized by physical spasms, goofy facial expressions, and stopping speech in mid-sentence.

Blamestorming   Sitting around in a group discussing why a deadline was missed or a project failed, and who was responsible.

Bookmark   To take note of a person for future reference (a metaphor borrowed from web browsers). "I bookmarked him after seeing his cool demo at Siggraph."

Blowing Your Buffer   Losing one's train of thought. Occurs when the person you are speaking with won't let you get a word in edgewise or has just said something so astonishing that your train gets derailed. "Damn, I just blew my buffer!"

Career-Limiting Move (CLM)

Used among microserfs to describe an ill-advised activity. Trashing your boss while he or she is within earshot is a serious CLM.

CGI Joe   A hard-core CGI script programmer with all the social skills and charisma of a plastic action figure.

Chainsaw Consultant

An outside expert brought in to reduce the employee headcount, leaving the top brass with clean hands.

Chips and Salsa   Chips hardware, salsa software. "Well, first we gotta figure out if the problem's in your chips or your salsa."

Chip Jewelry	A euphemism for old computers destined to be scrapped or turned into decorative ornaments. "I paid three grand for that Mac SE, and now it's nothing but chip jewelry."
Circling The Drain	Used to describe projects that have no more life in them but refuse to die. "That disk conversion project has been circling the drain for years."
Cobweb Site	A Web site that hasn't been updated for a long time. A dead web page.
Crapplet	A badly written or profoundly useless Java applet. "I just wasted 30 minutes downloading this stinkin' crapplet!"
Crash Test Dummies	Those of us who pay for unstable, not-yet-ready-for-prime-time software foisted on us by computer companies.
Critical Mess	An unstable stage in a software project's life in which any single change or bug fix can result in the creation of two or more new bugs. Continued development at this stage can lead to an exponential increase in the number of bugs.
Cube Farm	An office filled with cubicles.
Dancing Baloney	Little animated GIFs and other Web F/X that arc useless and serve simply to impress clients. "This page is kinda dull. Maybe a little dancing baloney will help."
Dawn Patrol	Programmers who are still at their terminals when the day shift returns to work the next morning. Usually found in Trog Mode (see below).
Dead Tree Edition	The paper version of a publication available in both paper and electronic forms, as in: "The dead tree edition of the San Francisco Chronicle..."

Depotphobia	Fear associated with entering a Home Depot because of how much money one might spend. Electronics geeks experience Shackophobia.
Dilberted	To be exploited and oppressed by your boss. Derived from the experiences of Dilbert, the geek-in-hell comic strip character. "I've been dilberted again. The old man revised the specs for the fourth time this week."
Domain Dipping	Typing in random words between www. and .com just to see what's out there.
Dorito Syndrome	Feelings of emptiness and dissatisfaction triggered by addictive substances that lack nutritional content. "I just spent six hours surfing the Web, and now I've got a bad case of Dorito Syndrome."
Dustbuster	A phone call or email message sent to someone after a long while just to "shake the dust off" and see if the connection still works.
Egosurfing	Scanning the net, databases, print media, or research papers looking for the mention of your name.
Elvis Year	The peak year of something's popularity. "Barney the dinosaur's Elvis year was 1993."
Email Tennis	When you email someone who responds while you are still answering mail. You respond again, and so forth, as if you were carrying on a chat via email messages. "Ok, enough of this email tennis, why don't I call you?"

Flight Risk	Planning to leave a company or department soon.
Generica	Features of the American landscape that are exactly the same no matter where one is. "We were so lost in generica, I actually forgot what city we were in."
Future-Proof	Term used to describe a technology that supposedly won't become technologically outdated (at least anytime soon).
Glazing	Corporate-speak for sleeping with your eyes open. A popular pastime at conferences and early-morning meetings. "Didn't he notice that half the room was glazing by the second session?"
Going Cyrillic	When a graphical display (LED or LCD screen, monitor, etc.) starts to display garbage. "The thing just went cyrillic on me."
GOOD Job	A "Get-Out-Of-Debt" job. A well paying job people take in order to pay off their debts, one that they will quit as soon as they are solvent again.
Gray Matter	Older, experienced business people hired by young entrepreneurial firms looking to appear more reputable and established.
Graybar Land	The place you go while you're staring at a computer that's processing something very slowly (while you watch the gray bar creep across the screen). "I was in graybar land for what seemed like hours, thanks to that CAD rendering."
Hourglass Mode	Waiting in limbo for some expected action to take place. "I was held up at the post office because the clerk was in hourglass mode."

Idea Hamsters	People who always seem to have their idea generators running. "That guy's a real idea hamster. Give him a concept and he'll turn it over 'til he comes up with something useful."
IQueue	The line of interesting email messages waiting to be read after one has deleted all of the junk mail.
Irritainment	Entertainment and media spectacles that are annoying, but you find yourself unable to stop watching them. The O.J. trials were a prime example.
It's a Feature	From the adage "It's not a bug, it's a feature." Used sarcastically to describe an unpleasant experience that you wish to gloss over.
Keyboard Plaque	The disgusting buildup of dirt and crud found on computer keyboards. "Are there any other terminals I can use? This one has a bad case of keyboard plaque."
Link Rot	The process by which links on a web page became as obsolete as the sites they're connected to change location or die.
Martian Mail	An email that arrives months after it was sent (as if it has been routed via Mars).
Meatspace	The physical world (as opposed to the virtual) also carbon community, facetime, F2F, RL.
Midair Passenger Exchange	Grim air-traffic controller-speak for a head-on collision. Midair passenger exchanges are quickly followed by "aluminum rain."

Monkey Bath	A bath so hot that, when lowering yourself in, you go "Oo! Oo! Oo! Ah! Ah! Ah!."
Mouse Potato	The online, wired generation's answer to the couch potato.
Notwork	A network in its non-working state.
Nyetscape	Nickname for AOL's less-than-full-featured Web browser.
Ohnosecond	That miniscule fraction of time in which you realize that you've just made a BIG mistake. Seen in Elizabeth P. Crowe's book, "The Electronic Traveller."
Open-Collar Workers	People who work at home or telecommute.
PEBCAK	Tech support shorthand for "Problem Exists Between Chair and Keyboard." Another variation on the above is ID10T: "This guy has an ID-Ten-T on his system."
Percussive Maintenance	The fine art of whacking the crap out of an electronic device to get it to work again.
Plug-and-Play	A new hire who doesn't need any training. "The new guy, John, is great. He's totally plug-and-play."
Prairie Dogging	When someone yells or drops something loudly in a "cubc farm" (an office full of cubicles) and everyone's heads pop up over the walls to see what's going on.
Print Mile	The distance covered between a desk and a printer shared by a group of users in an office. "I think I've traveled enough print miles on this job to qualify for a vacation."
Salmon Day	The experience of spending an entire day swimming upstream only to get screwed in the end.

Seagull Manager	A manager who flies in, makes a lot of noise, craps over everything and then leaves.
Shovelware	A Web document that was shoveled from paper onto the Web, help system, or whatever without much effort to adapt it to the new medium. Betrayed by, among other things, papercentric phrases like "See page so-and-so," "later in this booklet," and so forth.
SITCOMs	What yuppies turn into when they have children and one of them stops working to stay home with the kids. Stands for Single Income, Two Children, Oppressive Mortgage.
Square-headed Girlfriend	Another word for a computer. The victim of a square-headed girlfriend is a "computer widow."
Squirt The Bird	To transmit a signal up to a satellite. "Crew and talent are ready...what time do we squirt the bird?"
Starter Marriage	A short-lived first marriage that ends in a divorce with no kids, no property and no regrets.
Stress Puppy	A person who seems to thrive on being stressed out and whiny.
Swiped Out	An ATM or credit card that has been rendered useless because the magnetic strip is worn away from extensive use.
Telephone Number Salary	A salary (or project budget) that has seven digits.

Thrashing	Clicking helter-skelter around an interactive computer screen or Web site in search of hidden buttons or links that might trigger actions.
Tourists	People who are taking training classes just to get a vacation from their jobs. "We had about three serious students in the class; the rest were tourists."
Treeware	Hacker slang for documentation or other printed material.
Triple-dub	An abbreviated way of saying www when speaking about a URL. "Check out this cool web site at triple-dub dot enlightenment dot co dot uk."
Trog Mode	A round-the-clock computer session in which your eyes get so tired you have to turn off the lights and toggle the monitor into reverse — white letters on a black screen. Often used at Dawn Patrol period (see above).
Umfriend	A sexual relation of dubious standing. "This is Dale, my...um...friend..."
Under Mouse Arrest	Getting busted for violating an online service's rule of conduct. "Sorry I couldn't get back to you. AOL put me under mouse arrest."
Uninstalled	Euphemism for being fired. Heard on the voicemail of a vice president at a downsizing computer firm: "You have reached the number of an uninstalled vice president. Please dial our main number and ask the operator for assistance." Also known as Decruitment.

Voice Jail System	A poorly designed voicemail system that has so many submenus that one gets lost and has to hang up and call back.
Vulcan Nerve Pinch	The taxing hand position required to reach all of the appropriate keys for certain commands. For instance, the warm boot for a Mac II involves simultaneously pressing the Control key, the Command key, the Return key and the Power On key.
World Wide Wait	The real meaning of WWW.
Yuppie Food Stamps	The ubiquitous $20 bills spewed out of ATMs everywhere. Often used when trying to split the bill after a meal: "We all owe $8 each, but all anybody's got is yuppie food stamps."

Notes

Notes

1. Internet Access: The Digital Divide and Beyond

1   U.S. Department of Commerce, "A Nation Online: How Americans are Expanding Their Use of the Internet," http://www.ntia.doc.gov/ntiahome/dn/html/anationonline2.htm, February 2002.

U.S. Department of Commerce, "A Nation Online: Entering the Broadband Age," http://www.ntia.doc.gov/reports/anol/NationOnlineBroadband04.htm, September 2004.

2   Eurostat, "Internet Usage by Individuals and Enterprises 2004," February 2005.

General References
All table data derives from "A Nation Online."

2. Java: Connecting All the Dots

1   Robert H. Reed, "Architects of the Web," John Wiley and Sons, Inc., 1997, 113.

2   Louis V. Gerstner, Jr., "Speech at Annual Meeting of IBM Stockholders," 2000.

3. The Dot Com Bubble, and Life (So to Speak) at a Dot Com

1   Miller, T., "Top Ten Lessons from the Internet Shakeout," http://www.webmergers.com/editorial/article.php?id=48, Webmergers, Inc., 2002.

4. Internet Privacy: Protected or Abandoned?

1   Electronic Privacy Information Center (EPIC), "Total Information Awareness (TIA)," http://www.epic.org/privacy/profiling/tia/, March 2003.

2   Nadia Poulo, "European Parliament Cross-Party Initiative Against EU Electronic Surveillance," Europemedia.net, http://www.europemedia.net/shownews.asp?ArticleID=14726, February 2003.

3   Will Knight, "Europe Orders Microsoft to Keep Passports Private," http://newscientist.com/news/news.jsp?id=ns99993336, New Scientist, February 2003.

4   "Hard Drive with Gov't Data, Personal Info Missing," The Canadian Press, January 2003.

5   "Internet Company Fights Order to Reveal Customer's Name," http://www.cbc.ca/stories/2003/02/04/Consumers/Internet_030204, CBC News, February 2003.

7. Synergies: A Whole That's Greater Than the Sum of Its Parts

1   Merriam-Webster Dictionary, http://www.m-w.com/cgi-bin/dictionary, 2003.

A. Milestones, Netiquette, and Jargon

General References
    Milestone information for the Internet and the Web adapted from the following sources: Robert H. Zakon, "Hobbes' Internet Timeline," http://www.zakon.org/robert/internet/timeline/, 2003; and Lawrence Roberts, "Internet Chronology," 22 March 1997.

Milestone information for privacy issues adapted from: "Timeline of Privacy and Free Speech Developments, 1927-1999," http://www.publicagenda.org/issues/factfiles_ detail.cfm, Public Agenda Online, March 2003.

Milestone information for security issues adapted from: Brian Krebs, "A Short History of Computer Viruses and Attacks," http://www.washingtonpost.com/ac2/wp-dyn/A50636-2002Jun26, February 2003; and "Infosec Timeline, Information Security," http://www.infosecuritymag.com/2002/nov/timeline.shtml, 2002.

Index

L

Y

Yahoo!
    email filtering, 22

Z

Zimmerman, Philip, 67, 255

Ironbound Press
Winter Harbor, Maine

To order copies of this book:

Visit us on the Internet at:
http://www.IronboundPress.com

Or photocopy the order form on the opposite side of this page and send to:

Book Orders
Ironbound Press
P.O. Box 250
Winter Harbor, ME 04693-0250

Or inquire at your local bookstore.

Ironbound Press Book Order Form

Send completed form to:
Book Orders
Ironbound Press, P.O. Box 250, Winter Harbor, ME 04693-0250

Bill To:	Ship To (if different than Bill To):
Name:	Name:
Address:	Address:
City:	City:
State/Zip:	State/Zip:
Phone:	Phone:
Email:	Email:

Qty.	Item	Description	Item Price	Total
	0-9763857-5-9	The Internet Revolution (paperback)	$22.95	
	0-9763857-6-7	The Internet Revolution (hardback)	$26.95	
	0-9763857-3-2	The Information Revolution (paperback)	$22.95	
	0-9763857-4-0	The Information Revolution (hardback)	$26.95	
	0-9763857-1-6	The Technology Revolution (paperback)	$22.95	
	0-9763857-2-4	The Technology Revolution (hardback)	$26.95	
			Sub-total:	
			*Shipping and Handling:	
			**Sales Tax:	
			TOTAL:	

* $4.00 for the first book; $2.00 for each additional book.
** Please add 5%, if shipping to a Maine address.

Payment Method:
□ Visa □ Mastercard □ AMEX □ Discover □ Check
Signature:
Name on card (printed):
Card number (and 3 digit code):
Card Expiration date (MM/YYYY):